Understanding the Financial System

Social Credit Re-discovered

Frances Hutchinson

JON CARPENTER

Our books may be ordered from bookshops or (post free) from
Jon Carpenter Publishing at the address below
Credit card orders should be phoned to 01689 870437 or 01608 819117

First published in 2010 by
Jon Carpenter Publishing
Alder House, Market Street, Charlbury OX7 3PH
Tel 01608 819117

ISBN 978 1 906067 09 0

Printed in England by Antony Rowe (CPI), Chippenham SN14 6LH

Understanding the Financial System

'To despair because one cannot think that enough people will be found, even in the turmoil of today, capable of receiving such ideas, provided only sufficient energy be supplied to spreading them, this would be to believe human nature hopelessly insensible to healthy and reasonable influences.

'Is it hopeless? This is not a question that ought to be asked at all. One should only ask what we ought to do, in order to make the exposition of these ideas as forcible as possible, so that they may awake confidence.'

Rudolf Steiner

Contents

Acknowledgements

Without the work of countless thousands of authors whose writings were published throughout the twentieth century and during the first decade of the twenty-first century, Understanding Finance could never have been written. In particular, I owe a great debt of gratitude to all the authors referenced in the Bibliography, whether I agree with them or not. Each and every one has raised fascinating questions which demand answers if, in the twenty-first century, humanity is not to continue to pursue twentieth century policies leading to wars, poverty and social disintegration. I acknowledge even those who have, for whatever reasons, sought to sustain the sabotage attacks on Social Credit into the present century. Without their work I would never have discovered why the books and articles I was writing on the subject of Clifford Hugh Douglas and Social Credit were studiously, rigorously and unanimously ignored by career academics and career politicians.

I started work on the present book during 2002. Over the intervening years many individuals have offered advice, encouragement or practical help on a personal level along the way. These include: David Adams, David Adshead, Lorna Arblaster, Alan and Cindy Armstrong, Sr. Margaret Atkins, Terry Boardman, Vic Bridger, Brian Burkitt, Molly Scott Cato, Tony Clay, Erlend Clouston, Rosamund Cunningham, Bill Daly

Ian Dewhirst, Kevin Donnelly, Sr. Anne Donnockley, Wain Farrants, Jackie Fearnley, Jack and Barbara Foster, Anita Gregory, Bob Harvey and the late Bet Harvey, Oliver Heydorn, Tony and Judith Hodgson, Jack Hornsby, Arthur Howie, Jesse Howie, Andrew Huddleston, Betty Hutchinson, Alan Ingham, Helen John, Margaret Jonas, Robert Klinck, Dennis Klinck, Bill Krehm, Betty Luks, Brian Leslie, Michael Luxford, Murray McGrath, Mary Mellor, Ken Palmerton, Barbara Panvel, Gerald and Bryony Partridge, Roxana Preda, Tim Rickaby, James Robertson and Alison Prichard, Clive and the late Maggie Rosher, Michael Rowbotham, Anneruth Strauss, the late Janet Swannack, Roger van Zwanenberg.

I am most grateful to Hazel Henderson for her kind permission to reprint her 'Total Productive System of an Industrial Society' (Three-Layer Cake with Icing) Diagram, and for her reading and helpful comments upon two draft chapters. Many thanks also to James Mitchell and all at the National Library of Scotland for their most obliging assistance. Hannah Messer's reproduction of diagrams is much appreciated, as is Richard Haselgrove's steadying support through technological crises. Wallace Klinck's constant supply of material and information across the wires from Alberta has been invaluable. My thanks to Jon Carpenter for his patient co-operation in the publishing process. Last, but most appreciated of all has been the day-to-day support and assistance from Anne Goss and Keith Hutchinson, without which this book would never have reached the publishing stage.

Introduction

By the twenty-first century ordinary people of all walks of life in the developed world find themselves having to relate to each other through massive anonymous institutions. A network of clinics, hospitals and offices supervise birth, death and sickness. The child is propelled through an educational system moderated by centralised authorities. Employment is offered by massive chain stores, restaurant chains, banks, building societies, benefit offices, prisons and the military. Attempts to communicate as a customer or citizen with the providers of services invariably ends in frustration, a frustration shared on a daily basis by the professionals within those institutions. In and amongst this mess young parents seek to make sense of their role. Reared to expect to follow the orders of an employer within an established institutional workplace, they struggle to understand the responsibilities of family life. The results are thoroughly predictable. For at least two decades, and with increasing frequency, children as young as five years old have been excluded from school for disruptive behaviour. Their frustration at having their emotional needs met by little more than a TV screen render them beyond control. Professionals of all walks of life could take us by the hand and show us the results of policies which have ensured that the rich resources of this planet are being sacrificed on the altar of the mindless self-interest of financial considerations. However, few could today help us to understand how institutional policies are formulated within the centralised bureaucracies of private and state corporations.

In an attempt to understand the present-day institutions we need to scroll back in time. The two decades immediately following the First World War (1914-18) saw a remarkable challenge to the growth of corporate culture, politics and economics. Foreshadowing the environmental, peace, and anti-corporate pressure groups of the late twentieth century, the world-wide Social Credit movement posed a serious threat to the hegemony of corporate international financial interests. Despite the determined opposition of salaried economists, party politicians and the national and international presses, Social Credit publications were studied and debated by ordinary men and women seeking economic democracy in their respective localities. Throughout the U.K., in the Dominions, in the U.S.A. and elsewhere in the world, the attempt by the democratically elected Social Credit government of Alberta (1935+) to implement change in the social order was observed with the closest of interest. The very possibility of success posed a challenge to the corporate *status quo*, to such an extent that, in the post Second World War era, as the following chapters indicate, the episode was airbrushed out of history. Throughout the later decades of the twentieth century the corporate world actively discouraged study in the academy of the Social Credit texts written by the founder of the movement, Clifford Hugh Douglas (1879 – 1952), by the Guild Socialist editor of *The New Age*, Alfred Richard Orage (1873 – 1934), and by the many other contributors to the rich literature of the movement.

The economics of happiness

So successful has the silencing of Social Credit been, that the quest for answers to fundamental questions relating to the theory and practice of finance in economic systems across the world, is conducted without any reference whatsoever to Social Credit publications. In *The Economics of Happiness*, Mark Anielski poses several key questions:

- Why do economists, financial analysts, politicians and media fixate on growth measures (such as the GDP or gross domestic product) as the key indicator of human progress?

- Why do economy and stock market indices have to keep growing if a community has achieved levels of material self-sufficiency and quality of life?

- What is money and where does it come from?

- Why is money always scarce?

- What's wrong with a steady-state, subsistence economy which has achieved sufficiency and homeostasis?

- Why does free market capitalist economics look more like a cancer cell than the self-renewing life cycle of an ancient forest?

- What is driving our more-growth, more-consumption obsession?

- Why aren't economists and our leaders asking hard questions: more growth of what? For whom?[1]

Anielski faces these questions as an economist working in the Canadian province of Alberta, as senior advisor on green issues to the Government of China, and as practitioner and teacher of sustainable business practices. *The Economics of Happiness* goes a long way towards providing answers to the questions posed above, and is set to be a major text of the future. However, one can trace the identical questions back through each of the decades of the twentieth century, to the immediate aftermath of the First World War.

Writing when the Bolsheviks had but recently seized power in Russia, when the phenomenon of Hitler's Nazism had yet to be conjured into existence, and when Roosevelt's New Deal was still a decade into the future,[2] Clifford Hugh Douglas observed:

> There are only two Great Policies in the world today – Domination and Freedom. Any policy which aims at the establishment of a complete sovereignty, whether it be of a Kaiser, a League, a State, a Trust, or a Trade Union, is a policy of Domination, irrespective of the fine words with which it may be accompanied; and any policy which makes it easier for the individual to benefit by association, without being constrained beyond the inherent necessities of the function involved in the association, is a policy of Freedom. ... The fanatical Labour theorist, who would deny the right to live to any person not engaged in orthodox toil, quite irrespective of the facts of wealth production; the Trust magnate who corners an essential article under the pretext of efficient production, are, no less than the mediaeval ecclesiastics who burned men's bodies that their souls might live, practical exponents of salvation by compulsion.[3]

When those words were written, Douglas' work had already made his name known throughout the U.K. and across the world. His two books published to date, *Economic Democracy* and *Credit-Power and Democracy*, were being used as university texts and were being studied by leading economic thinkers like John Maynard Keynes. In those, and in subsequent books, articles and speeches by Douglas, every one of Anielski's questions is fully and comprehensively answered. During the 1930s in Alberta, a democratically elected government sought to put Social Credit into practice. Moreover, Douglas' contemporary observations on the Russian economy under Communism, the financing of Hitler, and the New Deal anticipated the later writings of authors like Anthony Sutton. By the outbreak of the Second World War, Douglas and other prominent social crediters were household names. During the subsequent decades of the twentieth century, all knowledge of Douglas' work faded from the academy.

The era of *Silent Spring*

By 1959 C.P. Snow's *The Two Cultures and the Scientific Revolution* was raising the key topic of the failure of communications between the sciences and the humanities. Rachel Carson's *Silent Spring* was published in 1962. The

Cuban Crisis of the same year had alerted the world for a brief period to the fact that nuclear arsenals could indeed result in Mutually Assured Destruction. Students rebelled in 1968. Thoughtful tutors pointed students towards Steinbeck's *The Grapes of Wrath*, Veblen's *The Theory of the Leisure Class*, Tressell's *The Ragged Trousered Philanthropists*, and Tolkien's *The Lord of the Rings*. Yet nothing changed. The Vietnam War continued unabated until 1975. The so-called 'Green Revolution', the introduction of 'improved' seed to Third World countries, had its predictable and predicted effect of further driving small subsistence farmers off their land to swell the shanty towns surrounding the cities. As poverty and oppression increased, discussion of the causes of war, poverty and oppression was noticeable by its absence. 'The Economy' was deemed to exist to create employment, so that people could go to work to earn the money to pay for all the good things in life.

In the 1970s and 1980s another scenario emerged on the fringes of the mainstream. Perhaps small might be beautiful.[4] Perhaps there was no call for endless growth, with its inevitable destruction of the natural resource base of the soils. Maybe it was possible to think differently about the need to earn more and more money. Living without a car, growing one's own vegetables and cutting down on consumer items as a whole could be less stressful not only on oneself, but on the environment and society in general. The idea of a 'Basic Income' as an inalienable right for all citizens was floated. It joined up with the work of the 'Citizens' Income Study Group' who, in seeking an end to means tested benefits, undertook statistical research into the feasibility of a transfer income from taxation under the auspices of the London School of Economics. The U.K. Green Party adopted the policy of a Guaranteed Basic Income for all as a necessary prior condition of a free, democratic society. A nice thought, said the economists and the politicians in chorus: but economically it could not be done. Where, after all, would the money come from?

The 'ecosocialism of fools'?

In the early 1990s, as my children left home, I registered for post-graduate research in economics in an attempt to understand what exactly the economists were teaching as the twentieth century was drawing towards its end.

To my astonishment, I discovered that a body of economic analysis and theory had existed since the early 1920s, capable of explaining the relationship between the real material economy of the production and distribution of goods and services, and finance which moderates economic activity. In all my general reading on the history of economic thought, politics and history, no mention of Social Credit had ever arisen. Yet there it was: a body of economic thought capable of envisioning a Basic Income, or National Dividend *without* increasing the frustrations of the transfer-tax system; an approach to economics which was anti-war, anti-growth and anti-wasteful consumerism. It was at least worth investigating, if only to dismiss it as impractical and intellectually untenable. I completed my research, attending conferences of heterodox economists, having papers and books published and even teaching Social Credit economics to undergraduates under the title 'An Institutional Analysis of Money'. It was suggested that the lectures could be formed into a further book, and in due course *The Politics of Money*, co-authored with two feminist academics Mary Mellor and Wendy Olsen, was almost ready to go into print. At that point a curious event occurred. Derek Wall, a fellow Green party member who was known to Mary Mellor and myself through the meetings of a national body known as the 'Red-Green Network', circulated a draft copy of his article entitled 'Social Credit: The Ecosocialism of Fools'. The title indicates the quality of the paper itself.

Ostensibly circulated 'for comment', the purpose of the paper was evident from the outset. It was written as a warning to named individuals that they were in danger of being fooled into advocating far-right fascism and anti-Semitism if they in any way promoted the study of Social Credit. David Korten and Herman Daly were cited as having unwisely endorsed Michael Rowbotham's *The Grip of Death* 'advocating social credit ideas, and Daly has provided articles for *The Social Crediter* journal'. Leading members of the U.K. Green Party were named, alongside all who had taken up the theme of Social Credit in the U.K. or collaborated in any way with those named individuals. Some eighteen months later the article was published in *Capitalism, Nature, Socialism* (*CNS*) Vol.14, No.3, September 2003, pp99-122) in a slightly altered form which gives the misleading impression of the paper being endorsed by several individuals including Mary Mellor and myself.

As a result of the circulation of Wall's draft article, my collaboration with Mary Mellor ceased. Her immediate reaction was to withdraw *The Politics of Money* from publication. I assured her that Clifford Hugh Douglas and his Social Credit colleagues were on the contrary vehemently *opposed* to fascism, anti-Semitism and any form of blinkered intolerance. But it was only my promise to thoroughly investigate the grounds for the allegations that persuaded her to allow the book to go forward for publication.

It has taken seven years of voluntary, unpaid research to establish the truth behind the writing of Derek Wall's article and the reasons for its subsequent publication in a respectable academic journal in 2003. In January 2009 I started to write up the results of my researches in the form of this book. It is the story of the dedicated commitment of countless individuals to the quest for sane, alternative ways of running the economy for the common good of humanity. It is the story of an experiment in political economy which came close to becoming a practical reality in Alberta during the 1930s, and which remains an example for the future. It is also the story of an intriguing campaign by mainstream academia, politicians and the press to discredit Social Credit in the U.K., in Canada and world wide.

Cock-up and conspiracy

The basis of the disagreement between Mary Mellor and myself was that the former fully and wholeheartedly embraced the cock-up theory of history, and jumped to the conclusion that I was a simple-minded conspiracy-theorist. I am inclined to believe, with Terry Boardman, that the truth lies somewhere between the two. Things do happen because we allow ourselves to be blown along by the force of circumstance, without seeking to understand what we are doing or where we might be heading. At the same time there is undoubtedly evidence that conscious decisions are being made behind closed doors by individuals who *do not have the common good at heart*. Boardman illustrates his point with the following story:

> A young man is walking along the road day-dreaming and looking up at the sky without noticing where he is going. A family relative, a jaded and jealous uncle, for instance, who hates his nephew and wishes him ill, decides to hide in the bushes and throw a banana skin in his nephew's path, so that he will fall and injure himself. The nephew then does fall and nearly breaks his back. Who is the more responsible for the victim's injury, the one with the consciously malicious intention or the one who failed to pay attention to what he should have been doing? Surely, both can be said to be 'responsible'. A comprehensive study of the event would seek to examine the reasons behind the jealous relative's action and for the young man's absent-mindedness.[5]

The story of Social Credit is one of the 'nephew' picking himself up from the 'fall' of the Great War and the following depression years and trying to take active steps to avoid falling on another banana skin.

The threefold social order

A year or two after starting the research I came across the Anthroposophical and Camphill movements which flowed from the work of

Rudolf Steiner, and immediately saw a connection. Both Social Credit and Anthroposophy, in their very different ways, have been major world-wide movements of 'the people' which have been ignored by academia and the mainstream presses. During the year in which I wrote up my researches, I came across a considerable interchange of ideas between social crediters and the earliest proponents of Social Threefolding ideas (see chapter 9) in the U.K. during the 1920s and 1930s.

Rudolf Steiner (1861-1925) was an Austrian philosopher, literary scholar, educator, architect, playwright and social thinker. Initially recognised as a major literary critic and cultural philosopher, at the beginning of the twentieth century he originated the Science of the Spirit, known as Anthroposophy. As long ago as 1919, Rudolf Steiner wrote the following words:

> The economic aspect of life has to a great extent overspread everything, because it has outgrown both political and cultural life, and it has acted like a suggestion on the thoughts, feelings and passions of men. Thus it becomes ever more evident that the manner in which the business of a nation is carried on determines, in reality, the cultural and political life of the people. It becomes more evident that the commercial and indus-trial magnates, by their position alone, have acquired the monopoly of culture. The economically weak remain the uneducated. A certain connection has become apparent between the economic and the cultural, and between the cultural and the political organisations. The cultural life has gradually become one that does not evolve of its own inner needs and does not follow its own impulses, but, especially when it is under public administration, as in schools and educational institu-tions, it receives the form most useful to the political authority. The human being can no longer be judged according to his capacities; he can no longer be developed as his inborn talents demand. Rather, is it asked, 'What does the State want? What talents are needed for business? How many men are wanted with a particular training?' The teaching, the schools, the examinations are all directed to this end. The cultural life cannot follow its own laws of development; it is adapted to the political and the economic life.[6]

The quotation forms part of the lectures and writings of Rudolf Steiner on the 'Threefold Social Order'. First translated into English in 1920, his book, entitled *The Threefold Commonwealth,* explores the relationship between the three spheres of society, the cultural, political and economic. Throughout his works Steiner insists that man is a spiritual being, not in a vague mystical sense but in an exact scientific sense. This being the case, a social system which fails to offer scope for the free activity of man's spiritual nature will end in chaos. The spiritual is not something private, to be set aside from the mainstream currents of the life of society. Rather it is of central importance within all aspects of human social interaction. Without understanding of the spiritual nature of humanity, attempts to reform the political and economic institutions of society will flounder and fail to meet human needs. It is absolutely essential to liberate science, religion and art, *i.e.*, education in all its forms, from dependence upon the corporate political economy.

As Steiner explains, the three elements of society need to form a coherent whole in which each element operates to complement the others. The three spheres can be summed up as:

1. An economic system having to do with 'everything which is requisite for man's regulation of his material relations with the external world'.
2. A political or equity system dealing with 'all that is made necessary in social life by the relations between man and man'.
3. A cultural/spiritual or educational system covering 'all that of necessity proceeds from the individual and must of necessity find its way from the human personality into the structure of the body social'.

Serious students of society in the present time will find themselves obliged to ask further questions about the author of the ideas cited here, and the multi-faceted movement of which he is the originator.

Work and income

The following chapters introduce the reader to several key issues of the early 21st century in such a way that the inter-relationships between finance and politics, production, gender relations, work, income, farming, education, arts, sciences and all forms of human interaction become a little clearer. Inevitably, in order to sustain the argument, sweeping assumptions have been made as to the reader's familiarity with 'alternative' historical thought. I owe a great debt of gratitude to the early readers of the first drafts of these chapters for their forthright questioning of many unsubstantiated statements. One question, for example, was phrased as follows:

Why, in fact, did the peasants throughout the nineteenth century have to move into towns for money wages? Was it the pressure of higher money wages than they could earn as farm labourers, or the promise of a better lifestyle?

The question reveals a great deal about the standpoint of a reader, who has been conditioned by a mainstream education into thinking in terms of 'progress' from rural poverty to urban plenty. From this perspective, Rational Economic *Man*, the hero of economics textbooks, migrates for 'economic' reasons, that is, for the higher *money* wages made available through industrialisation. This is, however, a teleological argument. The emergence of landless labour was a direct result of enclosures, which were undertaken on grounds of financial profitability, rather than the free choice of the 'labourer'. Throughout long ages the right to use a piece of land, together with rights to the resources of commons and waste lands to provide for one's family has been a fundamental human right. The power of moneyed interests to take the land from the people for commercial 'development', as when Shell used Ogoni lands in Nigeria,[7] dates back to the dawn of modern times. From the outset, enclosure of land has been a legal process, endorsed by the force of laws passed by the political sphere of society:

> They hang the man and flog the woman
> That steal the goose from off the common,
> But let the greater villain loose
> That steals the common from the goose.

And men were, quite literally, hanged in considerable numbers, and their bodies left to rot, for attempting to steal food after having been driven off the land to make way for money-making ventures. Rudolf Steiner cites the English author, Thomas More (1477-1535), on the subject of enclosure of land:

> So what happens? Each greedy individual preys on his native land like a malignant growth, absorbing field after field, and enclosing thousands of acres with a single fence. Result – hundreds of farmers are evicted. They're either cheated or bullied into giving up their property, or systematically ill-treated until they're finally forced to sell. Whichever way it's done, out the poor creatures have to go, men and women, husbands and wives, widows and orphans, mothers and tiny children, together with all their employees – whose great numbers are not a sign of wealth, but simply of the fact that you can't run a farm without plenty of manpower. Out they have to go from the homes they know so well, and they can't find anywhere else to live. Their whole stock of furniture wouldn't fetch much of a price, even if they could afford to wait for a suitable offer. But they can't, so they get very little indeed for it. By the time they've been wandering about for a bit, this little is all used up, and then what can they do but steal – and be very properly hanged?[8]

Thomas More, Steiner observes 'found it necessary to draw attention to the fact that people exist who drive the rural population from the soil they have tilled in order to turn it over to sheep', [9] the rearing of sheep having become a financially profitable exercise in early modern times.

Chapter summary

The Agrarian and Industrial Revolutions were necessary stages in the material evolution of humanity. Hence the developments in international finance introduced by families like the Rothschilds facilitated the technological innovation and the material progress upon which 21st century society depends. The first two chapters present an overview summary of the changes in farming, society and the financial system from the earliest times, through the development of city states into the corporate world economy. By early twentieth century it had become apparent that the financial system could produce war, waste and poverty on an unprecedented scale. Social Credit economics is compared and contrasted with the basic tenets of economic orthodoxy in Chapter 3. In Chapter 4, the social origins of Social Credit in the U.K. in the 1920s and 1930s are introduced. The 'Alberta Experiment', the quest by the people of Alberta to acquire political control over finance during the 1930s, is described in Chapters 5 and 6.

The extensive public debate on Social Credit between Douglas and leading figures in contemporary politics and economics is outlined and extensively referenced in Chapter 7. Chapter 8 documents the strenuous efforts made by the Establishment from 1922 until 2003 to discredit Social Credit and eliminate knowledge of the course of events in Alberta from the public consciousness. Drawing very selectively upon contemporary publications, career academics portrayed Social Credit as a rebellion against party politics and legitimate government. During the 1920s Douglas and other social crediters studied Rudolf Steiner's writings on the Threefold Social Order. Although, as is documented in Chapter 9, a number of articles appeared in *The New Age* making connections between the two schools of thought, for a variety of reasons, the dialogue petered out during the 1930s. By the 21st century, the works of Steiner and Douglas remain virtually unknown outside rather narrow circles of aficionados. Fewer still are those able to make a connection between Douglas Social Credit, Steiner's teachings on the Threefold Commonwealth and the various strands of alternative thought in the twenty-first century.

Inevitably, a work of this nature raises a host of questions which cannot be covered in the course of a single volume. Hence the extensive bibliography provides the reader with supporting evidence for the facts outlined in these pages. Douglas' analysis of the workings of global financial institutions has been fully covered in Douglas' own works, which are listed in Appendix 4a, in *The Politics of Money*[10], and in *The Political Economy of Social Credit and Guild Socialism.*[11] Equally, the work of Rudolf Steiner requires to be studied in the original. As far as possible, the reader is provided with references on these and a whole range of relevant texts. Some samples of original material from Social Credit publications which are no longer in print have been reproduced in the form of appendices to the chapters concerned.

NOTES
1   Anielski (2007)
2   See Sutton (1974) (1975) (1976); Preparata (2005)
3   Douglas (1922b) pp4-5
4   Schumacher (1973)
5   Boardman (1998)
6   Steiner (1919/1972) pp21-2
7   Rowell (1996)
8   More (1516) p25-6
9   Steiner (1916/2005) p10
10   Hutchinson, Mellor and Olsen (2002)
11   Hutchinson and Burkitt (1997)

Chapter 1
The Evolution of Urban Society

The history of the twentieth century suggests that human beings are at best an unfortunate accident in an otherwise beautiful universe. From the dawn of the Age of Enlightenment, scientific explanations for observable changes in the mineral, animal and human kingdoms have inexorably deposed religious faiths and superstitious beliefs in the supernatural. As the building blocks of creation are explored, from the atoms to the stars, and no evidence is found of an all-powerful Creator-God, many wonder how an omniscient and omnipotent deity could condone two world wars, Auschwitz, Hiroshima and the rest of man's inhumanity to man.[1] It would seem that an endless series of casual coincidences has resulted in the barbarous course of history. Man's destiny appears to be that of a rational, self-interested creature who seeks to maximize his own pleasure whilst minimizing his own efforts and pains. Logically, leading thinkers of the later twentieth century declaim that the march of progress has led to the 'End of History'.[2] 'Man' is nothing more than a thinking animal about to reach his full potential, at the endpoint of mankind's ideological evolution.

More thoughtful reflection indicates that human beings stand out from the rest of creation through the possession of a spiritual dimension to their nature. Animals do not bury their dead. Archaeological evidence abounds of flower-strewn graves, and adorned bodies buried with reverence, indicating a belief in the after-life from the dawn of prehistory. Although modern 'man' may dismiss spiritual observances as mere superstition, it is apparent that some form of thought inspired by imagination may have been behind prehistoric constructions of stone circles and ancient earth workings.

Humans as spiritual beings

As prehistory merges into the historical period, stories of exceptional people and their relationship with spiritual beings are found to occur throughout the world. The landscape of England offers abundant examples of stone circles and other prehistoric sites dating back to 3000 B.C. Studies of these sites reveal that their purpose was not utilitarian. They rather indicate some form of spiritual activity. Such constructions would have represented expenditure of considerable time and effort on the part of the human community as a whole, suggesting a superfluity of subsistence necessities and the exercise of conscious choice. The constructions appear to relate to the movements of the sun, moon and other celestial phenomena, further suggesting their significance was spiritual in origin.

In modern times myths and legends have tended to be relegated to the nursery 'fairy tale'. As an individual emerges to adulthood, traditional stories appear to have no significance for 'real life'. Writers such as Moyra Caldecott have explained that, in the scientific age, humanity has tended to lose sight of what it is to be human.

> The truth about living in the universe is elusive, exciting, and mysterious, and it is in the pursuit of mystery that we find all that is worth having, including ourselves. If we catch Truth and put it in a cage – it dies. It only flourishes in flight, in splendid flashes of living light briefly glimpsed through revelational vision, mythic story, and deeply profound poetry.
>
> Many have claimed that they have found Truth, and perhaps some have, but when they try to pass it on to their fellows directly, it falls through their fingers like dust. It was not for nothing that Christ spoke in stories and said: 'He who has ears to hear, let him hear.'
>
> We are too often given explanations, not understandings, and are condemned, sometimes even killed or imprisoned, because we cannot accept another's explanation. Explanations govern us, clip our wings and tame us. Stories free us and encourage us to fly. I believe dogma grows from explanation; myth from understanding.[3]

The march of 'progress' may have temporarily drawn a veil over the very meaning of existence. Truth is seemingly reduced to practical reality of hard-headed science, economics and practical politics. And yet, as Caldecott and many others attest, the stories of heroic men and women live on behind the scenes, available to give life meaning and purpose. Furthermore, the ancient tales provide more interesting role models for women than are to be found in many a modern novel. Reading those stories reveals that there is every reason to believe that in the ages-old village community women had to be of strong character to maintain life from generation to generation. Women were very much involved in the observance of the seasonal celebrations and the preservation of consciousness of the spiritual significance of birth and death. No role here for the empty-headed Disney female tottering around helplessly until her 'he-man' comes to the rescue.

It can be stated with absolute certainty that pre-historic 'man' did not spring up fully-fledged and ready for battle in defence of 'his' females. Man the hunter was entirely dependent upon mother the provider for the whole of his long years of infancy and childhood. For a while in adolescence a young male might stand on his own two feet. But in adulthood it was again up to the women to rear and protect the young consistently and all year round, using containers to collect nuts, eggs, fish, roots, leaves, berries, seeds and all manner of seasonal foodstuffs to maintain the group as a whole, so that when hunting forays failed, the group did not starve to death. The early 'capital' of the group was not the spear, container or digging stick, but the *knowledge* of flora and fauna, of the local geography of the land and the location of its produce according to season. From the earliest times, accumulated knowledge of the material world was the essential pre-requisite of human survival, and such knowledge would appear unlikely to have originated from the antics of alpha males.

When mankind turned to the herding of livestock and to settled agriculture, it was necessary to draw upon observations of the life processes in order to tend animals and cultivate the land. As a generalisation, within traditional cultures, certain males developed ceremonial roles, while women and practical men determined policies useful for comfortable survival. Where interests clash, survival of the group depends on the solidarity of the whole community rather than the individual 'success' of leading males in acquiring personal status and prestige. Hence female goddesses are often to be found in traditional stories, offering motherly guidance and providing checks and balances. In these circumstances, women had a structured place in society as queen-mother or priestess. Where the real work of sharing, caring and provisioning was undertaken by co-operative networks of women, the males could be left to develop their personal prestige in activities like hunting and warfare, giving rise to stories of heroism and self-sacrifice.

The evolution of 'economic man'

Writing at the turn of the last century, the American institutional economist Thorstein Veblen traced the origins of the political economy of industrialisation back to the earliest known forms of social interaction. In his first book, *The Theory of the Leisure Class* in 1899, Veblen conceptualised the evolution of the institutions of industrial society as arising from two distinct sets of skills and talents. These he labelled 'instincts', meaning learned patterns of behaviour. The first group of behaviours, associated with caring, nurturing, parenting, provisioning, invention and education, he termed the instincts of 'workmanship'. They are undertaken by women, engineers and practical men.

The second group of skills and talents are not concerned with survival, still less with the development of practical science and technology. Rather, they give 'invidious distinction' – glory, power and status – to the individual practitioner who acts according to his own selfish interests. Thus the 'instinct of workmanship' provides intrinsic satisfaction, is co-operative in nature, and gives rise to technological development through the un-coerced exercise of 'idle curiosity'. Such traits are useful to the community as a whole. Sportsmanship, including prowess in battle, on the other hand, requires no less effort on the part of the individual, yet gives only invidious satisfaction, involves waste of effort and resources, and is a drain on the community as a whole. As human society has evolved, prestige has attached to the predatory and non-creative male-centred activities of war, sport, politics and high finance, whilst the procuring of the basic essentials of life has been avoided by high-status males. As Veblen explains:

> The upper classes are by custom exempt or excluded from industrial occupations, and are reserved for certain employments to which a degree of honour attaches. Chief among the honourable employments in any feudal community is warfare; and priestly service is commonly second to warfare.[4]

Nevertheless, in whatsoever form it might have taken throughout history, the 'leisure class' has always remained dependent upon the on-going existence of the natural world and the skills and talents of parenting and workmanship which have continued to be practised in the rural village by men with a practical turn of mind and by women. According to Veblen, the two basic traits of predation and workmanship were handed on from generation to generation as humanity passed through its history. Hence economic affairs in early twentieth century America were not driven by notions of usefulness, but by social patterns left over from the tribal customs of prehistoric times. People set about the division of labour on grounds which had nothing to do with usefulness. On the contrary, warfare and hunting, which are wasteful of human resources, have been accorded high status. Meanwhile farming, cooking and provisioning, which are essential and useful, are considered of low status, to be undertaken by inferior men and women.[5]

Urban settlements

With urbanisation, the counter-skills of predation, acquisition of material possessions and emulative consumerism came to the fore. However, until the introduction of enclosures at the onset of modern time, empires and urban settlements depended upon the continued existence of a peasant-farming hinterland for supplies not only of food and other subsistence requirements, but also for supplies of slave workers and soldiers. The enclosures were introduced so that land could be used to produce wool, grain and meat for profit. Such practices not only denuded the land of its vitality, but in the process the acquired knowledge of soils, flora and fauna of generations of peasant farmers were lost. To the present day surviving peasant communities across the world continue to be eliminated so that cash crops can be taken from the land to supply distant urban populations.

Evidence of banking in Ancient Greece appears early in the fifth century B.C. Financial transactions were conducted by the holders of positions of authority in Greek temples and civic institutions, as well as in private dwellings. Financial transactions included loans, deposits, currency exchange and validation of coinage. From these very early times there is evidence of dealings in credit, whereby a money-lender would write a credit note for a customer making a deposit, allowing the client to cash the note in another city, thus avoiding the dangers of carrying material wealth from place to place. Many bankers in the Greek city states were foreign residents or slaves, whose wealth enabled them to buy civic rights such as freedom and citizenship.

Evidence of credit-based banking practices has been detected from the fourth century B.C. across the Mediterranean world. When Egypt fell under Greek rule the numerous state granaries were formed into a network of grain banks, centralised in Alexandria where accounts from all the state granary banks were recorded. Again, the banking network was used as a trade credit system, with payments transferred from account to account without the necessity for movement of wealth in kind. The banking practices developed by the Greeks were built upon by the Romans, who perfected accounting and administration, whilst introducing laws and regulations. The practice of making an interest charge for a loan, and paying interest on deposits, was further developed in Ancient Rome. However, the Romans retained a strong preference for cash transactions, so did not develop banking much further. Legislation restricted the charging of interest once Christianity was accepted as the official religion of the Roman Empire. After the fall of Rome banking disappeared in Western Europe, and did not re-emerge until the time of the Crusades.

The pattern for the development of a world economy was set in the ancient world. Powerful individuals like the Pharaoh in Genesis, on the advice of their prototype financial advisors like Joseph, commandeered control over material resources like grain, which they predicted, according to insider information, were likely to be in short supply in the future. When the predictions proved accurate, the now highly desirable commodity could be sold for *money*. It is noticeable that in the Old Testament account, Joseph 'collected' the grain over the seven years of abundance, placing the food from the surrounding countryside within each urban settlement. The suggestion of recompense to the farmers for their work in the fields is left open. Food would appear to have been simply commandeered. When famine raged, however, Joseph 'sold the grain to the Egyptians'. Indeed, people came 'from all over the world to buy grain from Joseph'. This raises a further question: what did people use to 'buy' the grain? The following chapters of Genesis make frequent reference to 'money' being used as the means of purchase. Money would not as yet be 'legal tender', *i.e.*, backed by law. As far as the story of Joseph in Egypt is concerned, money would have merely been another highly desirable commodity, most probably coinage of precious metal.

Kings and jubilee

When the Hebrews moved into the Promised Land, authority lay with the prophets and the priestly class who arbitrated between God and His people. Prior to the coming of the kings and their powerful henchmen, the land was apportioned directly to the families who were to farm the fields and vineyards and pasture the livestock. In due course of time, however, the people demanded kings, desiring to be like other nations in the vicinity who had kings as figureheads as well as their priests and priestesses. The request was granted. However Samuel, the disapproving High Priest at the time, presented an accurate account of the disadvantages of monarchy so far as the common people were concerned. Samuel spelled out the rights of the king who would rule over the people:

> He will take your sons and assign them to his cavalry, and some will run in front of his chariots. He will use them as leaders of a thousand and leaders of fifty; he will make them plough his ploughland and harvest his harvest and make his weapons of war and the gear for his chariots. He will also take your daughters as perfumers, cooks and bakers. He will take the best of your fields, of your vineyards and your olive groves and give them to his officials. He will tithe your crops and vineyards and give them to his officers and his servants. He will take the best of your manservants and maidservants, of your cattle and your donkeys, and make them work for him. He will tithe your flocks and you yourselves will become his slaves. When that day comes you will cry out on account of the king you have chosen for yourselves, but on that day God will not answer you.[6]

The people failed to listen, and Samuel's prophesy was fulfilled. When people give authority to secular rulers, they put themselves into a servile position. Nevertheless until the coming of industrialisation, the rulers and their subjects were consciously aware of the fact that they remained dependent upon the land, and upon the community which tended the land.

Colonisation and peasant farmers

On the occasion of the sixth annual Zionist Conference held in Basle, in 1903, Franz Oppenheimer made the key observation that 'every nation depends on a mass of humanity being rooted in the soil it occupies and such roots are only struck by agriculture.[7] At the time, the Jewish people had spent 2000 years as landless exiles in the nations of the world. Oppenheimer referred back to the ancient agricultural laws of the Hebrew people, handed to Moses on Mount Sinai before they entered the Promised Land.[8] The newly conquered land was to be apportioned out to families under a complex system of rules. Basically, the Law guaranteed rural properties to the families to which they were originally allocated. If the family fell on hard times and was forced to sell the land, or even to sell themselves into slavery, such sales only stood until the fiftieth or 'Jubilee' year, when slaves were freed and land reverted to its original owners. Somewhat different rules applied to contracts in respect of the sale of rights in urban areas.

Maintenance of equality of land tenure would appear to be the key to social stability in any state or area of political jurisdiction. Thus Zionists sought to restore the 'primeval agricultural laws of Israel, which allocated the land for all time to the tribe or village community, which for its part only possessed it in fief from the nation as a whole'.[9] Under old systems of Common Law in Europe something similar had applied, offering the advantages of individual property rights in land, but free from its worst shortcomings. Land held in this way gives security of possession to farming families who, throughout history, have acted as the guardians of resource management which forms the true basis of the economy.

> It bestows the home feeling in the fullest sense and forges an indissoluble link with the soil which roots the soul of the peasant in the fields he tills; but it precludes the mortgaging of the soil, which deprives the peasant of the fruits of his labour throughout all the countries under Roman Law and throws them into the lap of the landlord. Further, it precludes that breaking up of agricultural holdings here, and their accumulation there which divides the village community into an unfriendly aristocracy and

proletariat, and thereby destroys that community of interests which alone, as the history of the world testifies, can make it invulnerable. Moreover, it precludes that proletarization of poor peasant folk who crowd into towns, inflating them to gigantic slums, morally and physically unsound, and by its offer of pittance wages for hired labour calls every horror of capitalism into the world.[10]

Private ownership of land on a massive scale inevitably results in a dispossessed people. One alternative is for local communities to lease out land to individuals on terms agreed by custom, under the general over-lordship of the State, thus removing the hegemony of finance.

For Oppenheimer, 'peasant' agriculture, in the European sense of traditional patterns of Common Law land-holding, is a key factor in creating a viable political entity. Insightfully, he dismisses as impractical the idea of transporting a gigantic population of artisans, shopkeepers and peddlers from one place on the surface of the globe to another, and expecting them to continue to survive as artisans, shopkeepers and peddlers. A sound mix of urban and rural was essential if the problems of capitalist society, with its dispossessed rural populations swelling the slums and shanty-towns of sprawling cities were not to be transferred to the new nation. Oppenheimer's economic studies and observation of the European experience had led to the conviction that 'he who would create towns must create peasants' who have a vested interest in the soil they cultivate. Having studied examples of 'industry-centred land tenure' in the late nineteenth century, Oppenheimer observed that to build a State without a peasantry with security of tenure would be like 'building a house from the roof downwards'.[11]

Landless labour

Until the present day, the development of political and legal rights has been determined by the exercise of predatory activity involving the use of force. Historically, waves of conquest have flowed over settled farming communities, giving rise to a variety of parasitical ruling classes. However, until the agrarian and industrial revolutions, made possible by the evolution of the debt-based money economy, a *permanent* class of landless families, existing from generation to generation totally divorced from the means of subsistence and from indigenous culture, did not exist.

During recent centuries, where no viable peasantry existed, and only roving huntsmen who could not be subdued were to be found, would-be colonists had to resort to the importation from afar of a mass of slaves, as in the West Indies,

South America, Mexico and the Southern States of the USA. The English-speaking colonies of America, Canada, Australia and New Zealand, however, were exceptional in human history in that once slavery was abolished, they were populated almost entirely by a landless underclass. Formed in this way, the United States of America has become one of the most powerful state-formations in all history. Within it, the landless masses are exploited by a ruling capitalist class, itself originating in landlessness, but which has followed its predatory 'instincts' with enthusiasm. This presents something of a paradox. It would appear that the mass of men to be exploited imported itself by migrating *en masse* to escape intolerable conditions elsewhere. Divorced from land and peasant culture, and hence unable to sustain themselves, the masses sought waged employment from capitalists who were only too willing to oblige. Thus was achieved an illusory 'freedom' to work for a money wage on terms dictated by the self-appointed ruling capitalist class capable of dominating the entire political economy through the scarcely-veiled use of force. In this way was created a culture completely divorced from the land, and hence inherently unsustainable. Prairie farming of European grains and cattle has resulted in the dust bowls of the 1930s and the on-going loss of topsoil.[12]

In the early twentieth century, when Oppenheimer was writing, the consciousness that urban life was sustained by the land, and by the practical workmanship skills of all who worked on the land, remained intact. Urban dwellers, even in large cities like New York, could walk out into the countryside amongst the farms which supplied the city with food. Equally, local daily papers carried news of the major players in politics and business, so that public life could be monitored by the community. By the end of the twentieth century self-sufficiency from the land was virtually extinct within the Anglo-American world, as farming families had themselves become totally dependent upon the money economy. Thus the individual became a cog in a vast and complicated mechanism which seemingly defied comprehension. Working for money under orders from above, buying everyday requirements from totally unknown sources, and complying with rules and regulations made by anonymous authorities had come to be regarded as a normal state of affairs. As urban society became the norm in every country of the world, common sense solutions to the everyday problems of life became more and more elusive. It was assumed that in some way those in charge *ought* to be reducing insecurity, but when things went wrong, it was increasingly difficult to detect who was in charge, and hence who ought to be blamed.

NOTES

1   See Gilbert (1999)
2   Fukuyama (1992)
3   Caldecott (1992) pp1-2.
4   Veblen (1899). For introduction to Veblen's work as a whole, including full reference to available texts see Hutchinson, Mellor and Olsen.
5   Veblen's *The Theory of the Leisure Class* needs to be studied in the original, and can only be briefly introduced here.
6   1 Samuel 8 (adapted from CTS – Catholic Truth Society)
7   Oppenheimer (1903)
8   Leviticus 25
9   Oppenheimer *op. cit.*
10 Oppenheimer *op. cit.*
11 Oppenheimer (1908) p72
12 Friedmann cited in Hutchinson, Mellor and Olsen (2002) pp167-8

Chapter 2
The Evolution of the Corporate World Economy

Glyn Davies' fascinating account, *A History of Money* documents the use of money from ancient times to the closing years of the twentieth century,[1] revealing the interplay between actors in the political and economic spheres and the financiers upon whom they relied for the necessary funding for their military or economic operations. According to conventional texts, however, bankers are rarely mentioned in connection with the development of political and economic affairs, whilst the unprecedented institutional changes which accompanied industrialisation are rarely analysed. According to most histories, life was nasty, brutish and short until technological change gave rise to the development of production and trade, leading to material progress and prosperity. Since progress was inevitable, there was little point in questioning the morality or sustainability of big business. However, histories of money and banking reveal a very different story.

Debt and usury

The moral association between financial debt-creation and corruption of social values was less obscure in the early days of the development of banking. Like Judaism and Islam, the Christian Church banned usury because the necessity to go into debt was a sign of misfortune. An individual normally fell into debt only when they hit hard times, through sickness, crop failure or some other disaster. It was considered moral to lend, but immoral to benefit from another's misfortune by requiring the loan to be repaid with interest. The Medici and other bankers of the Italian Renaissance City States found various ways around the Church's ban on usury such as disguising transactions as 'international' currency exchanges between independent states. Banking practices were further developed by the Lombards, who argued that a money-lender who financed a profitable trading venture had a moral right to a share of the profit.

The practice of taking a money reward for merely lending money is so central to the market economy of the present age that its justification needs to be closely examined. The Lombard bankers financed the merchant ships of Venice, Genoa and other Mediterranean ports, the key centres of world trade at that time. A merchant sending a ship out to India might make a profit equal to thirty times the money spent on the outlay. The Lombard bankers argued that if they financed a merchant they were putting their money at risk if the ship did not return. Furthermore, the money-lenders also argued that they could alternatively fund a profitable venture of their own with any potential loan.

This raises the question, how did the Lombard bankers acquire the *finance* capital to invest in risky but potentially highly profitable ventures? They were private individuals, not kings, emperors or other heads of state with the legal right to levy taxes. The question is key to an understanding of the corporate world order. The early Lombard money-lenders were originally craftsmen and traders who employed other people to work in the weaving industry to produce goods for sale. The employment system came about from the desire of some private individuals to acquire material riches so that they could achieve worldly power over resources. Other people took the timber from the land and built the ships, farmed the land to produce food and raw materials, manned the ships which took the gold, spices and silks from the Indian countryside to sell in the growing luxury markets of Europe and fought in foreign wars. From the outset, the growth of the money economy had virtually nothing to do with producing the necessities of life or conserving essential knowledge and resources.

The development of banking

The maritime centres of the Atlantic coast saw Antwerp, and subsequently the British seaports, become the new centres of trade on a worldwide scale in early modern times. The early bankers, the goldsmiths, invested in productive and trading ventures with the objective of building up their personal stores of wealth. They also invested in the State. Kings needed armies to enforce their claims to the throne. They were, however, notoriously unreliable in settling debts incurred in the process of deploying armies. Hence in 1694 a group of London merchant bankers secured their position by agreeing a loan to William III for the purpose of war, on the security of Parliament's legal right to impose taxes. The Bank of England was not, however, owned or controlled by the King or by Parliament, but by a group of six private individuals who stood to gain substantially from the National Debt so created.

Governments have been in debt to the bankers ever since. The Bank of England was from the outset a joint stock company, meaning that it had a *legal* identity in its own right. When the Government needed to raise new loans from the public the Bank acted as its agent. Hence the loans required to fund the costly wars of the 18th century were in effect underwritten by the citizen taxpayer. The world-wide development of merchant banking, and of financial 'services' generally, has been well documented.[2] All that needs to be stressed here is the interplay between the trading activities of private groups of individuals (firms and corporations) and the creation of the legal framework under which such activities were allowed to flourish. Banking and dealings in money have always been debt-based and underwritten by legal statutes.

The 19th and 20th centuries saw unprecedented changes in the social order. As the agrarian and industrial revolutions progressed, developments in the financial world increasingly impacted upon the everyday lives of peasants in the rural hinterland of the cities. Enclosure and the mortgage and sale of land ended ages-old traditional rights of access to the land, creating a class of landless labouring families whose members had no means of support unless they were hired for money wages. Institutions of finance were crucially involved in the changes introduced in agriculture and industry. Hence debt-finance came to dominate policy decisions, not only in matters of preparation for war but also in determining forms of financially profitable production. Military and industrial enterprises waited on the availability of finance for authorisation to proceed, and increasingly such availability of finance was debt-based.

Surprisingly, in view of such massive change in the social order, the teaching of economic history in schools and colleges across the world has dwindled almost to zero. What remains provides at best a series of disjointed 'sound bites' rather than a meaningful account of the transformations in everyday policy formation processes which have occurred over the past two hundred years. Without an understanding of the changes in political and economic institutions of society over the period of industrialisation it becomes virtually impossible to envisage a sane approach to political economy which alone will facilitate the beginning of moves towards a three-folding social order.[3] With some notable exceptions,[4] economic change has been attributed purely to the technical advances, *i.e.*, to the introduction of agribusiness farming techniques and the technological inventions in industry and transport. The key factor in the social changes of the industrial revolution, the development of financial institutions, is rarely, if ever, mentioned. Fortunately, electronic forms of communication have made information about these developments more readily accessible.

One excellent source of information on banking, finance and its international interconnections in the 19th and very early 20th centuries is the 1906 *Jewish Encyclopaedia*, all twelve volumes of which are now available online.[5] Drawing upon this material, it would appear that, at least in the early stages of enclosure, colonisation and industrialisation, international financiers were in an advantageous position *vis-à-vis* the indigenous populations of the individual countries of Europe and worldwide. The *Jewish Encyclopaedia* (1906), here cited, provides a wealth of information on the central role played by named key people in the wars and industrial developments which prepared the way for the history of the twentieth century. The five sons of the Frankfurt-born Mayer Amschel Rothschild are an essential part of that history.

The House of Rothschild

In 1928 Victor Gollancz published the English edition of a two volume history of the Rothschild family. Written by Count (Egon Caesar) Corti and translated from the original German, *The Rise of the House of Rothschild* and *The Reign of the House of Rothschild* offer insights into the social, political, economic, technical and financial changes of the nineteenth century. Like the late twentieth century accounts compiled by Niall Ferguson,[6] the research and publication of the Corti books was aided and endorsed by the Rothschilds. However, although Ferguson's work contains a mass of detail, it is recounted at a journalistic pace so that the significance of the story for the 21st century is, to all intents and purposes, lost.

A mere couple of centuries ago, when the Battle of Waterloo took place in Belgium, the technologies which could support sophisticated financial networks were yet to be invented. The 21st century economy is regulated by a network of national state currencies which could not have been developed under the conditions of technology and communications which existed in 1815. At that time the Rothschild brothers were building up a network of communications between the countries in which they chose to settle. But such communications still depended on horse-power on land, and wind-driven sailing ships at sea. It is recorded that Nathan Rothschild, who had by then settled in London, engineered the situation so that he received news of Wellington's victory at the Battle of Waterloo *a full day* ahead of the official government messengers. At that point in time, messages were carried by word of mouth, or on pieces of paper, written perhaps in code and sealed with sealing wax. Long distance railways, telegraph, the internal combustion engine, steamships, electricity and electronic means of communication were all as yet to be invented. By the outbreak of World War 1, a century later, a very different world had come into existence, one in which the money economy impacted on the everyday lives of people in every nation state across the world. The world had changed out of all recognition.

Corti's first book contains detailed descriptions of the close relationship between the various members of the 'single House' and the key players on the European stage of the early nineteenth century, including Napoleon, Wellington and Metternich. The second book takes up the story of the relationship between the Rothschilds and all the major figures in the history of Europe after 1830, and includes pictures of the opening ceremonies of railways in England, Austria and Germany, portraits of Napoleon III, Bismark and Cavour. Although the second book purports to bring the history of the Rothschilds down to 'the present day' (1928), it in effect ends at the 1870s with the suggestion that the third generation of Rothschilds merged into their host countries, ceasing to maintain their international connections. Written in co-operation with the Rothschild family, the Corti books followed from years of independent research into the widely scattered literature alongside uncollected letters and documents. The dust jackets of these books, published by the highly respectable publishing house of Victor Gollancz, can be read in the appendix to this chapter, Appendix 2a.

From a historian's point of view, the two books are a delight to read, full of detail about the recorded lives of the Rothschilds and their relationships with the leading political figures in the Europe of the nineteenth century. Their role in all the major events in European wars, and all economic and political affairs, is sympathetically but frankly depicted. The reader is left in no doubt about the existence of a 'House of Rothschild' which transcended the boundaries of the individual nation states of Europe while at the same time playing a key role in the wars and developments of the nineteenth and early twentieth century Europe.

Niall Ferguson, a later apologist for the Rothschilds, recounts their pioneering work in banking and communications, laying stress on the ostentatious display of their legitimately earned fabulous wealth. He is dismissive of 'conspiracy theorists' who have 'misunderstood' the nature of the 'network of private financial relationships with key public figures of Restoration Europe'. In a sense, the work of Corti and Ferguson lays the myth of the Rothschilds to rest. Yes, they existed, playing a key role in international affairs in the early decades of the nineteenth century. But by the twentieth century their riches and power had dwindled, and they took their place among the democratic masses of the twentieth century. The privatisation of the control of public affairs through control of finance is quietly presented as a fact of political life, whilst the very mention of the existence of international finance as a force in world politics is enough to bring forth the dreaded accusation of 'anti-Semitism'.

On one page of the Ferguson book are the portraits of each of the five brothers painted around 1836 by the same artist, in the style of the portraits of aristocracy. All were settled in different capital cities, Amschel Mayer

Rothschild (1773 – 1855) in Frankfurt, Solomon Mayer Rothschild (1774 – 1855) in Vienna, Nathan Mayer Rothschild (1777 – 1836) in London, Carl Meyer Rothschild (1788 – 1855) in Naples and James Meyer Rothschild (1792 – 1868) in Paris. As all the biographies indicate, these five men were in close consultation with the leading statesmen of the capitals in which they resided, whilst at the same time maintaining close contact with each other. Alongside the portraits in the Ferguson book is a reproduction of a part of 'One of many thousands of letters in *Judendeutsch* exchanged between the five Rothschild brothers on an almost daily basis.' It is possible to argue that by the twentieth century networks of contacts between powerful banking interests on an international scale ceased to exist. However, that seems most unlikely.

In the work of historians like Corti and Ferguson, six men, all from the same family, are portrayed as playing a key role in the history of Europe, across international boundaries, in the first three decades of the nineteenth century. In total, Mayer Amschel Rothschild had nineteen children, of whom only ten survived. The five surviving girls had no documented part to play in the story. Although her sons became fabulously wealthy and very powerful figures on the international scene, old Mrs Rothschild remained in the little house in the Jewish quarter of Frankfurt where she had raised her family. Except as help-mates to the men, the women were of no account in their own right.

Furthermore, there is documentation of the 'development of the Rothschilds' private postal system which finally covered the whole of Europe and was used by friendly governments for forwarding confidential documents'. The essence of international finance has been secrecy. It has operated behind the scenes, influencing wars, economic development and public affairs, generally without the need for public accountability. Moreover, Corti clearly states that 'the Rothschilds played a part in the defeat of Napoleon at Waterloo'.

According to popular accounts, Nathan Rothschild used his early receipt of the news of Wellington's victory, mentioned earlier, to his own advantage in his dealings on the London stock exchange. Whatever the truth of the matter might be, by the time Corti was writing, well over a century had passed, and the events had been variously told and re-told. In this instance, Corti, an apologist for the Rothschilds, uses a literary device which has since come into common usage. When an event has become public knowledge, and the subject of open and informed debate, it becomes necessary to confuse and defuse the issue, by ridiculing or vilifying proponents of open discussion. Here Corti is implying that Nathan passed the information on immediately to the British Government, although he does not say so directly.

The members of the British Government were enormously impressed by

Nathan's advance knowledge of such an important event; and when this became generally known, the public, who were just beginning to learn of the extent to which Nathan was employed by the English Treasury, began to invent all manner of legends regarding the method by which Nathan had acquired this knowledge, and the manner in which he exploited it. Some said that he had a private service of carrier pigeons, others that he had been personally present at the Battle of Waterloo and had ridden to the coast at top speed. In order to make the story more romantic, he was said to have found heavy storms raging when he reached the channel and to have crossed at the risk of his life. Nathan was also alleged to have exploited the news on the Stock Exchange, thus at one stroke creating the enormous fortunes of the Rothschilds.

Nathan naturally applied the early information that he had obtained to his own profit in his business dealings, but the substantial part of the fortune of the brothers had been amassed through the profits realised in the financial transactions which have already been described; the successful issue of the Battle of Waterloo merely served to increase it, and to open up wider fields for profitable business in the future. This was all the more so as England had been victorious and Nathan had transferred the centre of gravity of the Rothschild business to her side (pages 178-9).

The trend was set. Information secretly obtained could be used by private groupings to advance their own interests, while at the same time influencing public policies to the advantage of the private group. The dust jacket of *The Reign of the House of Rothschild*[7] spells out the 'quite fantastic role played by the Rothschilds, at the height of their power, in *weltpolitik*.'

Absentee Ownership and the Corporate State

The role of international corporations in the conduct of the political and military history of the twentieth century has been thoroughly documented and does not need to be further rehearsed here.[8] A new world order had arisen in which constitutional government is government by corporations, themselves governed by the 'absentee owners' of business interests. As Thorstein Veblen had already observed in 1904:

Modern politics is business politics. This is true both of foreign and domestic policy. Legislation, police surveillance, the administration of justice, the military and diplomatic services, all are chiefly concerned with business relations, pecuniary interests, and they have little more than incidental bearing on other human interests.[9]

Furthermore, Veblen noted that, whatever their original interests might have been, the most powerful corporations such as J.P. Morgan and National City Bank operate across the full spectrum of industrial enterprise and financial institutions.[10]

> The holding-company and the merger, together with the interlocking directorates, and presently the voting trust, were the ways and means by which the banking community took over the strategic regulation of the key industries, and by way of that avenue also the control of the industrial system at large. By this move the effectual discretion in all that concerns the business management of the key industries was taken out of the hands of corporation managers working in severalty and at cross purposes, and has been lodged in the hands of that group of investment bankers who constitute in effect a General Staff of financial strategy and who between them command the general body of the country's credit resources. This general staff, or inner group, command the credit resources of the country at large … the large business financiers and their banking houses own or comprise or constitute the credit resources of the country.[11]

In these circumstances, it is scarcely surprising to find that 'a constitutional government is a business government' in which the money of the banking and business interests is the central feature of their control over the politics and government. The control of business interests over governments is not, however, simply a matter of politicians being corrupted by corporate interests. As Veblen neatly observed:

> Representative government means, chiefly, representation of business interests. The government commonly works in the interest of the business men with a fairly consistent singleness of purpose. And in its solicitude for the businessmen's interests it is borne out by current public sentiment, for there is a naïve, unquestioning persuasion abroad among the body of people to the effect that, in some occult way, the material interests of the populace coincide with the pecuniary interests of those businessmen who live within the scope of the same set of government contrivances. This persuasion is an article of popular metaphysics, in that it rests on an uncritically assumed solidarity of interests. … [Hence] constitutional government has, in the main, become a department of the business organization and is guided by the advice of the businessmen.[12]

In short, the business interests who operate according to patterns of learned behaviour based on the desire to dominate, command and hold power over others, are presently in control not only of finance and economic activity but also of the sphere of law and politics. Public opinion is, as a result, slow to seriously question the situation. It remains content to assume that big business has at heart the general welfare of society as a whole. Furthermore, corporate business holds sway over the institutions of higher learning through its ability to control flows of finance. Writing in 1918, Veblen observed that under the older American universities the governing bodies were almost exclusively drawn from the rank of clergy and were guided by 'devotional notions of what was right and needful in matters of learning'. However,

> For a generation past ... there has gone on a wide-reaching substitution of laymen in the place of clergymen on the governing boards ... This secularisation is entirely consonant with the prevailing drift of sentiment in the community at large, as is shown by the uniform and uncritical approval with which it is regarded. The substitution is a substitution of businessmen and politicians; which amounts to saying that it is a substitution of businessmen. So that the discretionary control in matters of university policy now rests finally in the hands of businessmen.[13]

During the nineteenth century the role of the 'Robber Barons' in American society was publically transparent. More recently, however, the educational establishment presents 'both sides' of the argument. Hence an on-line teaching guide presents students with a potted biography of John D. Rockefeller. He moved from rags to riches, becoming 'one of the richest men in the world in the oil business' by founding Standard Oil, yet he gave away 'half his wealth' in creating a university, an institute for medical research and several foundations.

The teaching guide admits that, although some of his business practices were 'good (he was organised and efficient), some were unethical. He put other companies out of business, prevented competition, and demanded kickbacks'. As can readily be confirmed,[14] the teaching guide presents an accurate review of the ethical standards of a key corporate figure, albeit with the implication that such behaviour was justified by the results. 'During the Gilded Age', students are told:

> John D. Rockefeller brought business practices to new heights – or depths, depending on one's ethical standards. Amassing huge personal fortunes, often through unscrupulous means, Rockefeller dominated the entire oil industry. Rockefeller's Standard Oil was ruthless; it bought off politicians, made secret deals with railroads in order to obtain favourable rates, and destroyed the competition through bribery and corruption. Standard Oil became one of the most hated companies of its time, earning mammoth

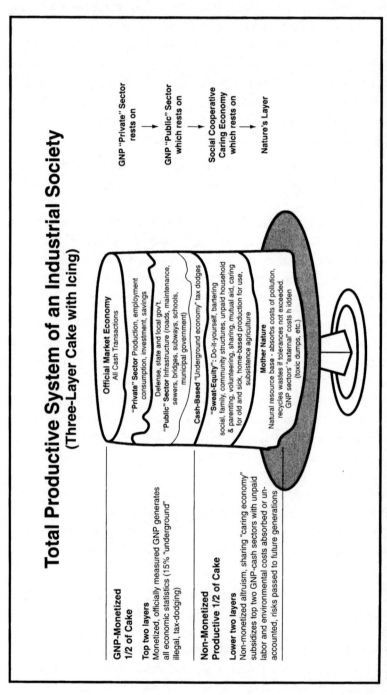

Total Productive System of an Industrial Society
(Three-Layer Cake with Icing)

GNP-Monetized
1/2 of Cake

Top two layers
Monetized, officially measured GNP generates
all economic statistics (15% "underground"
illegal, tax-dodging)

Non-Monetized
Productive 1/2 of Cake

Lower two layers
Non-monetized altruism, sharing "caring economy"
subsidizes top two GNP-cash sectors with unpaid
labor and environmental costs absorbed or un-
accounted, risks passed to future generations

Official Market Economy
All Cash Transactions

"Private" Sector Production, employment
consumption, investment, savings

Defense, state and local gov't.
"Public" Sector Infrastructure (roads, maintenance,
sewers, bridges, subways, schools,
municipal government)

Cash-Based "Underground economy" tax dodges

"Sweat-Equity": Do-it-yourself, bartering
social, family, community structures, unpaid household
& parenting, volunteering, sharing, mutual aid, caring
for old and sick, home-based production for use,
subsistence agriculture

Mother Nature
Natural resource base - absorbs costs of pollution,
recycles wastes if tolerances not exceeded.
GNP sectors' "external" costs hidden
(toxic dumps, etc.)

GNP "Private" Sector
rests on

→

GNP "Public" Sector
which rests on

→

Social Cooperative
Caring Economy
which rests on

→

Nature's Layer

Source: Hazel Henderson, *Paradigms in Progress* (San Francisco: Berrett-Koehler Publishers, 1991).

profits by preventing competition, keeping wages low, and setting prices high. By 1879 – a time when America's appetite for oil to fuel its expanding industry was reaching new heights – Standard Oil controlled over ninety per cent of America's refining capacity.[15]

Thus 'alpha male' behaviour has secured finance, enterprise, politics, learning and industry to the service of the corporate world. Although individuals can no longer be so clearly identified as targets for discontent, the philosophical base of the key institutions of society has continued without deviation.

The Henderson Cake

The corporate world is concerned with the securing of ownership and control so that power can be exercised *without* responsibility. It is not particularly interested in the needs of the poor, the concerns of women or the state of the environment. The whole range of skills associated with what it is to be a mature human being, the skills Veblen termed 'workmanlike', are considered surplus to requirements by the formal money economy. Nevertheless the corporate world, and the political and economic institutions which give it body, remain utterly dependent upon the land and its people for their very existence. During the twentieth century a number of women have written perceptively on the problems caused by irresponsible profiteering, most notably Rachel Carson.[16]

The whole picture has been comprehensively summarised by Hazel Henderson, who likened the twentieth century economy to a layered cake. The top half of the cake consists of the monetised, officially measured forms of national production which generate all economic statistics, plus an estimated 15% of monetised but illegal 'underground' forms of tax dodging. The bottom half of the cake consists of the non-monetised altruistic 'Counter-Economy' of social co-operation, which itself is founded upon the real wealth of the natural world. The two bottom layers subsidise the monetised layers, providing essential unpaid labour and natural resources, with environmental costs being absorbed if possible. Henderson terms the 'Counter-Economy' 'Sweat-Equity': it includes 'Do-it-yourself, bartering, familial, community structures, unpaid household and parenting, volunteering, sharing, mutual aid, caring for old and sick, home-based production for use, subsistence agriculture'.[17] The top monetised half of the 'cake' consists of all activities for which money changes hands. 'Official' market transactions are divided into private and public sectors, with the former taking precedence. Private sector transactions are concerned with production for market exchange, employment, consumption, investment and savings. Public sector transactions are concerned with the infrastructure, including roads, bridges, sewers, schools, defence, and municipal, local and state government.

It is possible to take issue with Henderson's portrayal of the private sector of the cash economy as the top level of the 'cake', suggesting that, like the icing, it is the most desirable yet least sustainable part of the whole. To the simplistic controllers of the corporate world, acquiring more of the monetised 'icing' may well appear to be the only game worth playing. However, it is infants who tend to desire the icing, while rejecting the nourishing richness of the body of the cake. Feminist economist Susan Feiner has perceptively portrayed 'Rational' Economic Man, the key actor in the corporate world economy, as an infant, displaying a set of behaviour patterns associated with siblings vying for the favours of Mother Market.[18] As any parent knows, it is very difficult to reason with an incorrigible infant. So far as the dominant males holding positions of power within the key institutions of corporate capitalism are concerned, there is no earthly reason for them to hold in check their self-centred desires.

Dissent

The corporate world can tolerate a certain degree of dissent. Pressure groups demanding an end to poverty create the illusion that 'something is being done at last', whilst keeping the critics of the system busy raising funds, producing leaflets and giving out speeches which do not raise too many fundamental questions about the causes of poverty amidst plenty. Within the academy, apparent dissent serves the useful purpose of creating the illusion of academic freedom. Marxists can be tolerated because the powerless poor will never rise up in revolution at the injustices of corporate capitalism. In real life they will actually starve to death in their millions, as continues to be the case well into the 21st century. Labour will organise to obtain a better deal for workers *as workers under capitalism*, as Veblen observed over a century ago.[19] Waged labour never organises violent revolution. As Anthony Sutton[20] and others have shown, only corporate elites have the resources to plan and execute violent changes of government. Capitalism, Communism and Nazism are bedfellows arising from the power base of the corporate elite.

The system can tolerate empty-headed dissent. It is content with dogmatic slogans, sound bites and idle speculation as to the causes of disasters, whether man-made, natural or 'economic' (which falls into a category of its own). But it cannot tolerate dissent based upon the systematic and organised study of the social framework of the institutions which govern the social order. In the twentieth century students could be encouraged to read Machiavelli, since the truly powerful *individual* was a thing of the past. Would-be dictators like Hitler might study Machiavelli in order to become effective tools for their masters. But the systematic study of how corporate hegemony over the institutions of society might be countered and successfully reformed is, as yet, nowhere to be found in the institutions of higher learning.

A Machiavellian scheme

In 1920 Eyre & Spottiswoode, a respectable London firm that was the King's printer, published a remarkable document in which a scheme for corporate world control was outlined. Writing about the document in his fourth book, *Social Credit*, published in 1924, Douglas noted that the methods by which the enslavement it describes could be brought about could already be seen reflected in everyday experience.

It was explained in that treatise that the financial system was the agency most suitable for such a purpose; the inculcation of a false democracy was recommended; vindictive penalties for infringement of laws were advised; the Great War and the methods by which it might be brought about were predicted at least twenty years before the event; the imposition of grinding taxation, more especially directed against Real Estate owners, was specifically explained as essential to the furtherance of the scheme. The methods by which the spurious democratic machinery and the journalistic organs of 'Public' opinion could be enlisted on the side of such taxation, and an antagonism between the interests of the town and the interests of the country could be created, were explained with an accuracy of detail which can only be described as Satanic.[21]

The original document can be dated to the late nineteenth century. Published in English for the first time in 1920, *The Protocols of the Learned Elders of Zion* (hereafter referred to as *The Protocols*), was the subject of lively debate, but was soon withdrawn from circulation. Public discussion of the contents of the document was banned on the grounds that it was a 'forgery' intended merely to foster pogroms. As Douglas further commented:

It is quite possible that this document is inductive rather than deductive in origin, that is to say, that some person of great but perverted talents, with a *sufficient grasp of the existing social mechanism*, saw and exploited the automatic results of it. If that be the case, the world owes a debt of gratitude to that mysterious author. He was substantially accurate in his generalised facts, and the inductive prophecies are moving rapidly towards fulfilment[22] (emphasis added).

Little can be said with any certainty about the origins or authorship of the document. It has been suggested that it might be one of a series of fragmentary writings circulating during the nineteenth century. Whatever the origins, the document was placed in the British Museum in 1906, was translated into English, did appear in print in the U.K., and can be obtained both in hard copy and electronic form via the Internet. Perusal of the document will allow the reader to form an opinion as to its possible purpose and authorship. It would appear to be based on considerable observation of the psychology of human interactions, together with firm knowledge of the workings of social mechanisms and institutions. It defies common sense to imagine that a mere rabble-rouser could have produced such a work. A further indisputable fact is that even a passing reference to the existence of the document has been sufficient to stifle debate on its subject matter, by applying the label of 'anti-Semitism' to all who even mention the fact of the document's existence.

Documents such as Machiavelli's *The Prince* and *The Protocols* demonstrate to the thoughtful reader that in order to rule it is essential to make virtually *all the people* into willing subjects. Therefore, it is necessary to control all three areas of the social order: the 'Prince' must provide 'bread and circuses'. That is, the political or law-giving head must control the economic and the cultural spheres of the social order. No sphere can be allowed to function independently of the others.

Until modern times, however, the Prince's rule was not absolute. The lowest slave and the greatest rival could escape into the countryside. Furthermore, both could identify their oppressor, analyse the methods used to oppress them, and observe the roles of key individuals concerned in their oppression. Within the post-industrial corporate world, a general sense of powerlessness may give rise to attacks on Jews or other minority groups who can be identified as scapegoats. Spasmodic bouts of frustration serve as a safety-valve, usefully confusing the issue whilst never leading to the source of the problem. By the time Hazel Henderson came to design her 'Cake' diagram of the industrial world it had become impossible to explain why and how the 'icing' had come to be in control of the whole 'cake'.

Under corporatism, virtually all the people living and working in their local communities know that they are not the Prince, or even a near rival. An individual may pursue a desire for great material wealth, and achieve great riches. Ambition for personal status may enable an individual to head a corporation or even to become head of state. But it would be an illusion to imagine that any personality holds effective power over the political, economic and cultural spheres of a nation state. With nobody to blame, individual citizens turn their dissatisfaction into ambition to creep up another rung of the ladder of wealth and status.

The Protocols is an excellent study of how a property-less, debt-owing, wage/salary-earning proletariat might be discouraged from working towards a threefold commonwealth in which the political, economic and cultural spheres of society could work in independent conjunction for the common good. As with Machiavelli, the use of fear and violence is regarded as a last resort. Rather, control is exercised through enlisting the willing co-operation of the populace by the means noted by Veblen. These include emulative consumerism, in conjunction with patriotism and war. And finally, to make compliance secure, it is necessary to control the 'story', as told by the media, the entertainments and the educational institutions. Social Credit in Alberta broke all the rules, so it had to be eliminated from the public consciousness, as the following chapters demonstrate.

NOTES

1   Davies (1994)
2   Davies (1994)
3   See later chapters for reference to the works of Rudolf Steiner, Clifford Hugh Douglas and others on this subject.
4   See the works of the economic historian E.K. Hunt.
5   Available at http://www.jewishencyclopedia.com/
6   Ferguson (1998)
7   See Appendix 2a.
8   See Preparata (2005) and Sutton (1974) (1975) (1976)
9   Veblen, (1904) p128. See also Veblen (1923)
10   Veblen (1923) p380.
11   Veblen (1923) pp338-9
12   Veblen (1904) pp136-7
13   Veblen (1948) p508
14   See *e.g.*, Hunt (2003) p151-2
15   Freedom: A History of US online.
16   Carson (1962)
17   Henderson (1988) pxviii. (1996) p183.
18   Feiner (1999)
19   Veblen 1906 (1990 reprint)
20   Sutton (1974) (1975) (1976)
21   Douglas (1924) p146-7
22   Douglas (1924) p147

Appendix 2a
Corti Dust Jackets

The Rise of the House of Rothschild
by Count [Egon Caesar] Corti

Translated from the German by Brian and Beatrix Lunn, the book was published in London by Victor Gollancz in 1928. The following texts are taken from the dust Jacket.

Front Dust Jacket:
'On the Stage move the figures of Napoleon, of Wellington, of Metternich; but in the Wings, behind the Scene, and even among the Audience, Members of a single House are together playing one of the greatest Roles of all.'

Inside Dust Jacket Flaps:
'It is scarcely credible that the Rothschild family, which played such an important, even a decisive, part in the history not only of Europe but of the world during the nineteenth century, should have been practically ignored by historical writers of repute. The majority of such works as have appeared consist of either panegyrics or attacks – both equally unreliable and misleading. Here for the first time is an unprejudiced account, on the grand scale, of the lowly origins and meteoric rise of the greatest financial house in history.

'Years of independent research, during which the author has consulted not only the complete and widely scattered literature of the subject but a large number of hitherto uncollected letters and documents, have gone to the making of this work. The tangled threads of international finance and diplomacy are unravelled with a masterly hand, and the intricate activities of the Rothschild family are presented with a clearness and simplicity that come of complete understanding.

'Here are a few of the milestones in this book: The means by which Meyer Amschel Rothschild, founder of the House of Rothschild as we know it, ingratiated himself with the Elector of Hesse; the birth and early years of Meyer Amschel's sons, the famous 'five Frankforters'; the attitude of the Rothschilds to the victorious armies of Napoleon in Southern Germany; subterranean activities of the Rothschilds on behalf of the banished Elector of Hesse; internal organisation of the Rothschild business; the Rothschilds' first transactions as international financiers. The work of Nathan Rothschild in Manchester and London, and of James Rothschild in Paris, the Rothschilds' methods for the wholesale smuggling of English goods to the Continent; the Rothschilds' handling of English subsidies to the allies; Nathan Rothschild enables Wellington to continue the war in Spain; financial relations of the Rothschilds to the governments of England, Austria, Prussia, and Russia; development of the Rothschilds' private postal system which finally covered the whole of Europe and was used by friendly governments for forwarding confidential documents; the Rothschilds' part in the defeat of Napoleon at Waterloo; the Rothschilds' handling of indemnities after the war; their close relations with Metternich and support for his policy; revolutionary troubles in different parts of Europe, notably in Naples and Spain, quelled by the financial intervention of the Rothschilds; the work of Solomon Rothschild in Vienna and of Carl in Naples; achievements of the Rothschilds social ambitions; their practical control over European exchanges; their work on behalf of Jewish emancipation; the great crisis in the Rothschilds' fortunes consequent on the fall of the Bourbons and instable government in other parts of Europe.

'This story of world events is interwoven with the domestic and personal affairs of the Rothschild family.'

The Reign of the House of Rothschild

Count Corti

(Dust Jacket)

Inside Front Flap of Dust Jacket:
'While they can give little idea of the really extraordinary wealth of material which this volume contains, nevertheless a bare recital of the chapter-headings may serve just to indicate the historical importance, romantic interest and 'intriguing' character of *The Reign of the House of Rothschild*.

Weathering the crisis of 1830.

The Rothschild Loans in relation to Home and Foreign Politics, 1832-35.

The Part Played by the Rothschilds in the Early History of the Railways in Europe.

Differences Between the Five Brothers with Regard to Spain.

The Rothschilds' Peace Efforts in the Crisis of 1840.
The Rothschilds Before and During the Revolution of 1848.
Fighting for Position with Louis Napoleon, Cavour and Bismark.
From the Crimean War to the Italian War of 1859.
The Eventful Years: 1866 and 1870-71.
The Rothschilds from the close of the 19th to the end of the first quarter of the 20th century.'

Chapter 3
The Missing Economist

In the immediate aftermath of the First World War the Labour Party was just on the point of emerging as a major political force in U.K. politics. Trade unionists, left-wing academics and potential politicians were being encouraged to study orthodox economics at institutions like the London School of Economics, founded in 1895,[1] so that they could take their place in the establishment institutions of the nation state. At issue was the just or fair share of the proceeds of wealth creation due to the supposed creators of the wealth, the 'workers' on the one hand, or the 'capitalist' owners of land or capital on the other. Thus economics was used as the key to the justification for Labour's claim to a greater share of the wealth created by the capitalist system of industrialisation. The party system lent itself to a polarised debate on the relative merits of the 'working class' or the 'capitalist class'. In this scenario, Clifford Hugh Douglas' predictions, based upon his analysis of the workings of the institutions of finance, of economic depression and further world war were met with little enthusiasm. With hindsight, however, it is clear that Douglas' analysis provides a starting point for a comprehensive under-standing of the workings of the economy-as-we-knew-it in the twentieth century, with all its drives to poverty amidst plenty, ecological devastation, wasteful consumerism, and war.

The financing of the First World War

Douglas' analysis of the relationship between finance and the processes of production and distribution arose from his detailed study of the financing of the First World War. Before war broke out, lack of finance was the major obstacle to construction of socially necessary infrastructure projects. At the same time, goods and services needed by the consuming public could only be produced and distributed on terms dictated by the availability of finance. However, as Douglas observed, war 'is a consumer whose necessities are so imperative that they become superior to all questions of legal and financial restriction'. In the case of war, in order to maintain a connection between finance and production, the situation has to be reversed. Finance has to follow production instead of, as in accepted normal practice, production having to follow finance.

> The extension of production to its utmost intrinsic limits, therefore, involves an extension of finance at a rate out of all proportion to that which obtains in the normal course of events, and this extension reveals the artificial character of normal finance. The Gold Standard, on which British finance was supposed to be based, broke down within a few hours of the outbreak of war. That is important, but it is only the first step, just as the Gold Standard itself is only one aspect of a system of finance in which currency is the basis of credit. What is more fundamentally important, is to observe that immediately production is expanded at anything like its possible rate, the idea that the financial cost of that expansion can be recovered in prices is seen in its full absurdity.[2]

When war broke out, all manner of weapons and munitions necessary for war, plus the millions of articles required by the supply services of the armed forces came into production. All the paraphernalia of war was produced by private firms and paid for by the Government. Normally, a government obtains the money to pay for its services through taxation. To balance the budget, proceeds from taxation must at least cover the expenditure on public services. What actually happened was:

> The National Debt rose between August 1914 and December 1919 from about six hundred and sixty million sterling to about seven thousand seven hundred million sterling. And this rise represents, on the whole, the expenditure over that period which it was deemed impractical to recover in current taxation.

Douglas estimates the average taxation for war purposes over the period 1914-18 at about £300m per annum. Roughly speaking, the amount paid by the public as consumer for the goods and services supplied to it for war, over the period of the war, was about £1,350m. The financial cost of those goods and services was about £8,350m, a ratio of cost to price of 1:6. In other words, goods were sold to the public at one-sixth of their apparent financial value. As Douglas explained, 'a great deal of the necessary money was created by what are known as the Ways and Means Accounts, and the working of this is described in the first report of the Committee on Currency and Foreign Exchanges, 1918, page two'. Douglas' paraphrase of the report appears in *Social Credit*.[3] Writing in 1919, Douglas summarised the situation. A sum of around eight thousand million pounds was spent during the course of the war, on services rendered and paid for, on munitions of all kinds produced and used up, leaving a War Debt to be repaid.

> Now, the services have been rendered, and the munitions expended, consequently, the loan represents a lien with interest on the future activities of the community, in favour of the holders of the loan. That is to say, the community guarantees the holders to work for them without payment, for an indefinite period in return for services rendered by the subscribers to the Loan. What are those services?

> Disregarding holdings under £1,000 and re-investment of pre-war assets, the great bulk of the loan represents purchases by large industrial and financial undertakings who obtained the money to buy by means of the creation and appropriation of credits at the expense of the community, through the agency of industrial accounting and bank finance.[4]

Over the years to come, the loan will have to be paid off in purchasing power over goods not yet produced – it simply represents communal credit transferred to private account:

> For every shell made and afterwards fired and destroyed, for every aeroplane built and crashed, for all the stores lost, stolen or spoilt, the financier has an entry in his books which he calls wealth, and on which he proposes to draw interest at 5 per cent, whereas that entry represents loss not gain, debt not credit, to the community, and, consequently, is only realizable by regarding the interest of the financier as directly opposite to that of the community.[5]

Douglas concludes that the financier is usurping the function of the State in creating, in the form of debt, the credit necessary to fund the war. Credit is the possession of the community as a whole, and not that of a sectional interest group such as the bankers.

From his early observations of the financial mechanisms employed in the funding of the production of goods and services deemed necessary for the conduct of the First World War, Douglas developed his Social Credit analysis of the financing of production and distribution in 'normal' times of peace. Throughout his writings Douglas stressed that blueprints and panaceas were to be avoided at all costs, since 'every suggestion made in this connection has in view the maximum expansion of personal control of initiative and the minimizing and final elimination of economic domination, either personal or through the agency of the State.'[6] That is, Douglas looked towards an end of the necessity for forced acceptance of waged or salary slavery on terms dictated by a private employer or a State institution. In this, he was at complete variance with economic orthodoxy.

Economics in the academy

Economics is the study of the monetised economy, the top layers of the Henderson Cake (see Chapter 2). Thus the student embarking upon a study of economics is taught to distinguish between needs and wants. A need is a matter of opinion. A want, on the other hand, is a need *backed by money* so that it becomes a 'demand', which is something scientifically recognisable. A demand is a measurable, non-normative fact which can be studied by the economics profession and fed into models. Other factors, including human needs and environmental considerations, can be factored in artificially as 'externalities'.

Economics studies the behaviour of 'economic man' in his pursuit of the maximisation of satisfaction and minimisation of effort: it is the science that deals with the production, distribution and consumption of material wealth *as measured by money*. According to economic theory, under division of labour in a perfectly free market, individuals will undertake a series of small tasks according to their skills and resources, combining together to increase wealth. All have an obligation to participate in the general wealth creation, giving a corresponding right to a share of the increased wealth. All schools of economic orthodoxy adhere to the basic assumptions that resource allocations can be taken as read, that the legal/institutional framework is neutral in implications for economic activity, and that technological change can equally be discounted as relevant to the study of the economy.

A number of 'heterodox' schools of economics have evolved to challenge the basic assumptions of orthodoxy. Institutional/evolutionary economists factor in the existence of banking, legal, corporate and other institutional structures. Marxian economics follows Marx's development of the labour theory of value: as the capitalists appropriate surplus value from labour they accumulate wealth for future investment. Post-Keynesian economists explore macro-economic models, tending to reject the IS/LM (Investment Savings/ Liquidity (preference) Money supply) model, but broadly accepting the basic tenets of economic orthodoxy. Feminist economics and environmental economics seek to apply orthodox economic methodology to 'women's' and 'environmental' areas of concern. All these schools have raised fundamental issues about the relationship between the economy, the social order and the natural order. Economists of all types and persuasions have dedicated their lifetimes to the subject, producing a wealth of literature which makes fascinating reading. This all-too-brief summary of the broad field of economics is not designed to dismiss the volume of significant study of the economy which has been produced over the past two centuries. It is rather to place the 'missing link' of Douglas Social Credit economics within the broad context of the study of economics.

The 'circular flow'

Broadly speaking, orthodox economics is the study of the allocation of *scarce* resources to the satisfaction of infinite wants. The economics student is first instructed in 'micro-economics' *via* the concept of the 'Law of Markets', or 'Say's Law which derives from the writings of the French businessman and economist, Jean-Baptiste Say (1767-1832). According to this 'Law', production (supply) creates its own demand: that is, when goods are produced and supplied to the market, the process automatically generates a demand for those goods. This can be illustrated diagrammatically (see above).

Households have what businesses demand, and businesses supply what households demand. People go to 'work', supplying the firms with labour (or land or capital if that is what they own) so that goods can be produced. In return for their labour (or land or capital) they receive money which they spend on the market to buy the goods and services that they have produced. According to this theory, recessions are not caused by a shortage of money, because the production of goods automatically distributes money, in the form of wages, salaries and dividends, with which to buy the goods. As supply increases, so does demand. If demand is not sufficient, it may be because people are hoarding their money by saving it, or taxes are too high. In that event, prosperity can only be increased by stimulating *production*, rather than consumption. The answer is not to create more money, because more money demanding the same quantity of goods does not create a real increase in demand: it merely results in inflation. In the face of the obvious fact of booms and slumps, modern Keynesian macroeconomists have argued that Say's Law only applies when prices are fully flexible. In the short run, when prices are not flexible, a drop in aggregate demand can cause a recession. By the late twentieth century the obvious errors in even this interpretation of Say's original conceptualisation of the 'Circular Flow' have been noted by a few career economists.[7] The circular flow model only conceivably 'works' where both *time* and *money* are eliminated, so that exchange takes place under a barter system in which outputs remain exactly the same as inputs. It is an entirely static model: if anything changes, an entirely new frame has to be drawn.

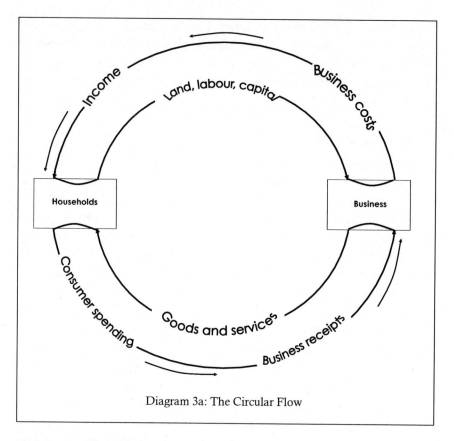

Diagram 3a: The Circular Flow

The A+B Theorem

Douglas pointed out the obvious. Production takes place over *time*, and exchange takes place on the market *for money*. When these two facts are taken into account, it becomes necessary to view the 'circular flow' more critically. At the point in time when businesses send finished consumer goods onto the market for sale, they have merely completed a process which may cover months or even years of the different stages from raw material through to finished product, including the making of machines and the building of factories. Hence the wages, salaries and dividends paid out *at the point* of sale will be less than the total prices of products going onto the market *at that point in time*. Each business must cover the total costs of *past* production, or they will go out of business. The fact that a substantial part of the inputs to the firms do not come directly from the consuming 'households', but take the form of capital or intermediate goods, drastically alters the usefulness of the Circular Flow concept. In Douglas' words:

A factory or other productive organisation has, besides its economic function as a producer of goods, a financial aspect – it may be regarded on the one hand as a device for the distributing of purchasing power to individuals, through the medium of wages, salaries and dividends; and on the other hand as a manufactory of prices – financial values. From this standpoint, its payments may be divided into two groups:-

Group A – All payments made to individuals (wages, salaries and dividends).

Group B – All payments made to other organisations (raw materials, bank charges and other external costs).

Now the rate of flow of purchasing power to individuals is represented by A, but since all payments go into prices, the rate of flow of prices cannot be less than A + B. Since A will not purchase A + B a proportion of the product at least equivalent to B must be distributed by a form of purchasing power which is not comprised in the description grouped under A.[8]

The above statement of the 'A+B Theorem', originally published in 1920, in *Credit-Power and Democracy*, was amplified upon in Douglas' Birmingham debate with Hawtrey in 1933[9] by the use of the Social Credit Analysis Diagrams.

The diagrams can usefully be compared with the conventional Circular Flow diagram. The key difference is that the Bank having been identified as the 'money maker' is shown to have a crucial role to play in the whole scenario. Earners of wages, salaries and dividends get their money from a producer. However, producers do not make money: *banks* make money as loans to productive organisations. Loan money flows from the bank to the producer, who passes on part of the total sum directly to the citizen in the form of a wage or salary which can then be spent by the consumer in that production period. Those 'distributed costs' or 'A' payments are available to be spent with the retailer so that in the course of time they return to the Bank. However, the producer must meet other 'allocated costs' incurred from past stages of production, including costs of plant and raw materials. These 'allocated costs' or 'B' payments are costs which each individual producer must meet over and above any payments distributed by that producer in the form of wages, salaries and dividends. The producer cannot meet all costs until *after* all the goods are sold, *i.e.*, the 'A' payments distributed before the goods are sold cannot be enough to meet the total costs. For the economy as a whole to function, new money has to be constantly produced by the Bank as debt, in

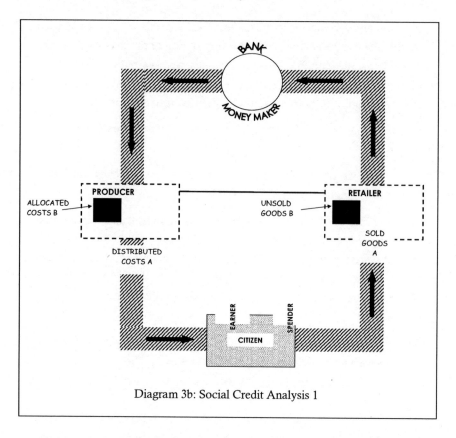

Diagram 3b: Social Credit Analysis 1

respect of capital and intermediate goods which are not available for purchase in the present time period.

For well over two decades Douglas varied his explanation of the basic theme: in an industrial economy production is regulated by *finance* and takes place over *time*. Since production takes place over time, flows of *money prices* do not necessarily match flows of money to consumers *at any particular point in time*. Leaving aside the question of capital equipment for the moment, production can be viewed, perhaps, over five stages:

1. The farmer combines natural materials (land and seed) with labour to produce corn.

2. The corn is sold to the miller, who adds the cost of his labour and materials to those of the farmer.

3. The flour is sold to the baker, who adds further costs to those of the previous stages.

4. The bread is sold to the retailer, who adds further costs.

5. The loaf is sold to the consumer.

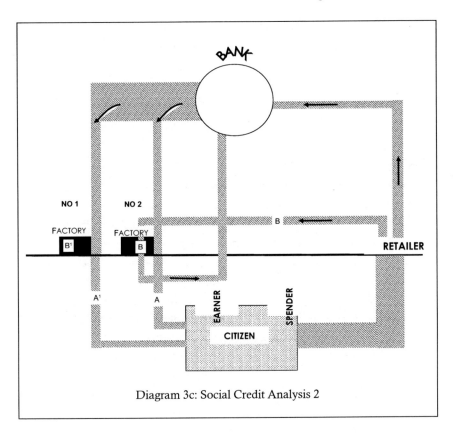

Diagram 3c: Social Credit Analysis 2

At Stage 5, the consumer must pay a price sufficient to cover the costs of all previous stages of production. The wages paid out *at that point in time* form income with which to purchase the loaf. If the only income available was that paid out to the counter staff, only a fraction of the cost of the loaf could be met. Douglas repeated his original explanation in *The Monopoly of Credit*:

> It is irrelevant that in the modern world all of these five processes are taking place simultaneously and that the product may be found in any of the five stages at any moment. It is still true that you cannot bake bread with corn which you are simultaneously grinding.[10]

If the wage-earners in Stage 1 use their current incomes to buy current production, the money they use has been distributed in respect of work done on the production of a product which will not appear on the market *now*, but only in the *future*, which may be months or years away.

The Circular Flow diagram implies that finance has no role to play in the economic processes of production, distribution and exchange. Commodities exchange for commodities, and money merely facilitates as a 'medium of exchange'. However, as any child can tell, there is a very big difference between 'swapping' items on the one hand, and buying and selling for money on the other. One sweet can be bartered directly for one biscuit. However, where money is concerned, child A can sell child B the biscuit for £2, buy the sweet for £1 and end up £1 the richer than before. Far from being incidental, money plays a central role, not only in the economy, but in society as a whole.

Incomes – A payments

According to mainstream conventional theory, all payments to 'households' are being paid in the form of wages, salaries and dividends as rewards for inputs to the productive process. This means that *money incomes* to individual consumers are primarily conceived of as deriving from work undertaken in the service of the *money* economy. The logic of the scenario is that working for money is pure 'disutility', an onerous duty for which a reward is given. In the same way, a dividend is paid to the 'owner' of saved up financial capital which, when it is invested, brings a reward for the disadvantage of abstaining from earlier spending on consumer goods.

Going to work to earn the money to spend on the necessities and luxuries of life had, by the twentieth century, become so ingrained in the cultural psyche that it was difficult for people of *all* political persuasions *who were doing well out of the system* to begin to think laterally. Douglas' analysis was clear and to the point. In days gone by it was necessary to labour for long hours with hand tools in order to produce the basic requirements of human existence. With the new technologies, made possible through the division of labour, the link between 'work' put in and money reward given became indistinct.

As long ago as 1776, Adam Smith dramatically illustrated the principle of the 'division of labour', whereby each worker specializes in one or a few functions of the production process within a particular trade or profession. Smith's example of the pin factory is often quoted but rarely studied for its far-reaching implications:

> ... a workman not educated to this business (which the division of labour has rendered a distinct trade), nor acquainted with the use of the machinery employed in it (to the invention of which the same division of labour has probably given occasion), could scarce, perhaps, with his utmost industry, make one pin in a day, and certainly could not make twenty. But in the way in which this business is now carried on, not only the whole work is a peculiar trade, but it is divided into a number of branches, of which the greater part are likewise peculiar trades. One man

draws out the wire, another straights it, a third cuts it, a fourth points it, a fifth grinds it at the top for receiving the head; to make the top requires two or three distinct operations; to put it on is a peculiar business; to whiten the pins is another; it is even a trade by itself to put them into the paper; and the important business of making a pin is, in this manner, divided into about eighteen distinct operations, which, in some manu-factories, are all performed by distinct hands, though in others the same man will sometimes perform two or three of them. I have seen a small manufactory of this kind where only ten men were employed, and where some of them consequently performed two or three distinct operations. But though they were very poor, and therefore but indifferently accom-modated with the necessary machinery, they could, when they exerted themselves, make among them about twelve pounds of pins a day. There are in a pound upwards of four thousand pins of a middling size. Those ten persons could therefore make among them upwards of forty-eight thousand pins in a day. Each person, therefore, making a tenth part of forty-eight thousand pins, might be considered as making four thousand eight hundred pins in a day. But if they had all wrought separately and independently, and without any of them being educated to this peculiar business, they could not each of them have made twenty, perhaps not one pin in a day.[11]

The passage is revolutionary in its implications. If, by separating into different trades and professions, and specialising within each separate trade, pooling knowledge, expertise and invention, the total wealth of the entire economy is increased many thousand times over, calculation of money wages, the rewards rightly due to *one individual worker* in respect of his personal contri-bution to the total enterprise, must become a major issue for consideration.

The passage cited from Smith is followed by discussion of the degree of adaptability of the different trades to the division of labour and hence to mechanical productive processes. Even at this early stage of the development of modern productive methods, Smith observed that agriculture was less suited to mechanisation than other types of production, since the care of the land, its plants and animals, necessitated a holistic approach which could not be quantified in the same way as the manufacture, *e.g.*, of pins.

The men in the ten-man pin factory cited by Smith were 'very poor', with little inclination to exert themselves. Smith was writing during the eighteenth century, during the early stages of industrialisation, when landless labour was plentiful. Enclosures had continued to force people off the land, from which they had traditionally secured a living, so that men, women and children were employed for a pittance in mines and factories, working under appalling conditions. The *only* incentive to work was the reward, in money or in kind, which would supply the basic necessities of life. Under these circumstances, the demand for a fair day's wage for a fair day's work was logical and entirely reasonable. Workers did quite literally go to work to earn the money to buy the products of the industrial system. Employment was seen as the only way to obtain the living which was now denied to them from the land.

In Smith's day, as outlined in the quoted passage, the *input* of the individual worker to the total productive process had already become difficult to account. The labour of one worker, working alone, could be expected to produce very little more than *one* pin per day. Under the division of labour, using new technologies, ten men could *each* produce an average of *four thousand eight hundred* pins per day. But one cannot eat pins, still less use them for clothing, shelter and other requirements. The pins have to be sold, for the money with which to buy a selection of all the variety of goods and services which a modern economy can supply. Such variety can only be supplied by virtue of the division of labour and the use of mass production technologies. The problem now arises: how much of the value of the four thousand eight hundred pins per day produced should accrue to each individual worker in the pin factory? Without the plant and machinery, and working alone, a solitary pin-maker would find it impossible to create *and sell* sufficient 'pin-value' to exchange for even the barest necessities of life. Other factors would appear to be involved.

According to orthodox theory, each business firm brings together land, labour and capital, seeking to achieve the optimum combination in order to maximise output. The example normally used is that of farming a piece of land. On a given area of land, so the story goes, a number of men (labour) are given a number of spades (capital) to work with. If any one of the three variables (land, labour, capital) is increased without increasing the other two, the initial total increase in productivity will progressively diminish. The trick of the capitalist is, then, to combine the 'factors of production' in optimal amounts to assure maximum output. To do this, he must offer rent (for the land), interest (for the capital) and wages (for the labour) in amounts which will enable him to sell the product on the market at such a price that his costs are covered. In this scenario, 'labour' is a part of the expense of the capitalist, and therefore will rightly receive a part of the financial returns to the firm resulting from the sale of the product. What proportion of the total monetary returns from the sale of the pins on the market rightly went to 'labour', and what proportion to the other 'factors of production' has been, in practice, a matter settled by acrimonious negotiation.

The increment of association

In the Douglas analysis, in addition to the division of labour, two further concepts can be used to interpret the pin factory scenario, the unearned 'increment of association' and the 'common cultural inheritance'. All material wealth is created in community through co-operation. As the industrial revolution progressed, access to the increased wealth was allocated through the money system in a rather bizarre fashion. Those who undertook the physical work in a factory or mine were rewarded with a money wage according to the number of hours worked or the quantity of items produced (piece work). Those who merely *owned* the business, or held a financial share in the business, received a financial reward in the form of a 'dividend'. And those who merely supported the economic system by rearing the children, caring for the land, or managing the food, shelter, clothing and other requirements of the household –without which the economy as a whole would cease to function – were due no share at all of the wealth accounted by the money economy. The situation developed in this way for historical reasons. Without apportioning praise (to the workers) or blame (to the capitalists or men in general) it is possible to review the social framework of industrialisation with some degree of objectivity.

Alone, a single worker would take all day to make one pin, even supposing that he already had the tools, know-how and materials to hand, and a supply of food and shelter to support him whilst he worked. In real life, people work together at an incredibly wide variety of tasks, all of which are interconnected and interwoven into the fabric of what makes up society. Staying with the pin factory in isolation from the rest of society, it can be said nevertheless that a group of ten or more people co-operating on a single task will achieve in total far and away more than ten individuals separately engaged in the same task. In Social Credit terminology, this is termed the unearned increment of association. As Douglas explained in 1922:

> Men associate together in industry because there is a true unearned income in association – a telephone system requires a population to give it a value; ten men pulling on a rope can accomplish that which ten separated men could never achieve. With the growth of machine production and the utilisation of non-human sources of energy, this unearned increment is growing enormously more important than the earned increment about which the [socialist], in particular, is so concerned.
> *This unearned increment rests inalienably on a basis of Capital, not of Labour;* and if Capital derives from, and should be vested in the community, as

is, broadly speaking, incontestable, then it is as members of the community, *tout court*, unconditionally, that individuals should benefit by this unearned increment. The dividend is the vehicle for the distribution of this unearned increment, and it is in the universalisation of the dividend, and not its abolition, that we shall achieve freedom. Only when this is realised will it be grasped that it is better for everyone concerned, and especially for Labour, that the routine operators of the plant of civilisation should be selected solely for efficiency, subject to the most drastic competition, and progressively displaced by machinery.[12]

Since production takes place in community, *i.e.*, within society *as a whole*, all should have a right to a share of the wealth generated by society, regardless of time spent in 'employment'.

National Dividend and the common cultural inheritance

By the 1920s and 1930s, when Douglas was writing, technological developments had reached the point where, in certain industries, machinery could perform most of the mechanical routine tasks previously undertaken by individual workers. The result was a plentiful flow of goods into existence, at prices covering their previous costs of production, but an inadequate flow of the necessary finance as incomes to consumers, with which the products of industry could be purchased. The option was to jettison the labour-saving technologies and revert to manual labour and handicrafts in order to keep the labourers employed. In 1924, Douglas spelled out the necessity to re-think the relationship between finance and the social order:

> The early Victorian political economists agreed in ascribing all 'values' to three essentials: land, labour, and capital. But it is rapidly receiving recognition that, while there might be a rough truth in this argument during the centuries prior to the industrial revolution consequent upon the inventive period of the Renaissance, and culminating in the steam engine, the spinning-jenny, and so forth; there is now a fourth factor in wealth production, the multiplying power of which far exceeds that of the other three, and which may be expressed in the words of Mr. Thorstein Veblen as the 'progress of the industrial arts'. Quite clearly no one person can be said to have a monopoly share in this; it is a legacy of countless numbers of men and women, many of whose names are forgotten and the majority of whom are dead. And since it is a cultural legacy, it seems difficult to deny that the general community, as a whole, and not by any qualification of land, labour or capital, are the proper

legatees. But if the ownership of wealth produced vests in the owners of the factors contributing to its production, and the owners of the legacy of the industrial arts are the general community, it seems equally difficult to deny that the chief owners, and rightful beneficiaries of the modern productive system can be shown to be individuals composing the community, as such.[13]

The 'dividends' paid to owners of capital derive from the unearned increment of association and the common cultural heritage. Hence a recipient of a dividend under the present financial system is a pioneer of the future, when all citizens will have the inalienable right to income security through a National Dividend.

A 'dividend' in its accepted sense, is a payment of money, a 'credit' which derives from the community but is paid through the banking system. The institutions which mobilise the issue of 'credit' are the banks and financial institutions. But what is 'credit'?

Real and financial credit

Throughout the twentieth century individuals spent their lifetimes 'earning' and spending 'their' money. Yet most would find it very difficult to explain exactly what money is, how their employment generates an income, or what forces regulate the circulation and amount of money in existence.

From the outset of his writings on the subject, Douglas distinguished between *real* and *financial* credit. At a point in time a community may have to hand all the physical and practical resources necessary for production, including land, raw materials, factories, machinery, power, skill, organisation and labour. With a continuous supply of the means necessary for production, a plant could turn out a stream of goods. However, a year or two later the same plant could be lying idle, while the 'labour' was said to be 'unemployed'. What has happened to stop the wheels of industry turning? Clearly it is not a breakdown of the productive system, since tomorrow it could be set in motion again without the slightest difficulty. The plant lies idle because orders for the goods have ceased to come in: demand has ceased. The question is, why has demand ceased if the products in question are needed? The problem is that need is not backed by money: it cannot be translated into effective demand. The question then is – why is money at one time plentiful and at another time scarce? Productive capacity certainly does not vary upwards and downwards at regular intervals. On the contrary, the world's productive capacity has steadily and rapidly increased over the decades. The productive capacity of the industrialised world is hundreds of times today what it was a century ago, and is constantly increasing with every new invention. It can be stated with all certainty, therefore, that the variations in the availability of money and its circulation through the economy are not due to variations in productive capacity. Not only are variations in the availability of money independent of productive capacity, they scarcely relate to production at all. The production of goods depends upon the availability of real resources: the production of finance, on the other hand, depends on factors over which the productive processes have little or no control. This discrepancy between goods and finance, between productivity and currency, is the difference between real credit and financial credit. Real credit rests on real resources – materials, power, labour and technology. Financial credit rests, ultimately, upon belief – credo – it is an article of faith. If the ownership of the means of direct production is in the hands of capitalists, the real control still lies with finance, whose ultimate ownership is vested in the financial, and not in the productive system.

Douglas' analysis of the actual role of finance within the real economy of everyday practice was at sharp variance with mainstream neoclassical orthodoxy. Economic 'science' is almost exclusively concerned with accounting the distribution of ownership and income within a business community centred on the market. Thus orthodoxy reduces motivation to the pure calculation of profit or loss: the actions of individuals are informed by a very simple rule of thumb, that of the pain-cost and pleasure-gain of 'Rational Economic Man'. However, although mainstream theorising purports to focus upon the physical processes of production and consumption of material goods it does so in a very confused manner: the theories of supply, demand and price are based upon financial calculations and considerations. Thus businesses do not acquire finance in order to consume, but in order to acquire more finance from further sales, which is a very different matter.

According to orthodox theory capital is an accumulated fund of productive goods in the form of buildings and machinery. However, as Thorstein Veblen pointed out as long ago as 1908, the concept breaks down immediately when it is used, as in discussing the 'mobility of capital' from one industry to another. Veblen cites the shift of investment from a whaling ship to a cotton mill:

> To speak of a transfer of 'capital' which does not involve a transfer of 'capital-goods' [as does the orthodox economist cited by Veblen] is a contradiction of the main position, that 'capital' is made up of 'capital goods.' The continuum in which the 'abiding entity' of capital resides is a continuity of ownership, not a physical fact. The continuity, in fact, is

of an immaterial nature, a matter of legal rights, of contract, of purchase and sale.[14]

In actual business practice, 'capital' is a financial, not a physical, concept, an outcome of the subjective valuation of the valuers. Such capital is a saleable asset which does not possess intrinsic productive value. In orthodox theory, however, this fact has to be overlooked, since it would lead logically to the admission of intangible assets playing a role in the economy. That in turn would undermine the basis of circular flow 'law' of rewards flowing to 'labour' and 'capital'.

The financing of production

Production takes place in factories, that is, in buildings designed to house the machinery necessary to shape raw materials or semi-manufactures into finished products for sale on the market. Before a factory can commence operations it has to be built and equipped with machinery. This requires finance. The method of finance which commonly springs to mind, as a result of orthodox teachings, is that of saving. However, as Douglas explained in *The Old and the New Economics*;

Probably the method by which most modern financing is done, under cover of a smoke screen provided by comparatively small subscriptions from the public, is that some financial institution actually creates the money, taking debentures on the new factories as security. Ethically, there is every difference between money created by a stroke of the pen and money acquired as the result of years of effort, but I am not at the moment concerned with ethics. At first sight it is a better method, considered as an isolated operation. When the new factories come into existence, new money is distributed to the men who built the factories. But there are two practical objections, leaving aside any question of ethics. The new money or credit is claimed by the financial institution as its property, and therefore when it is lent creates a debt against the public. At the same time, being distributed in advance of consumable goods, it tends towards true inflation. The debt differs in nature from the debt created by private finance in exactly the same way that a debt to foreigners differs from an internal debt – its repayment actually takes money out of the country. If a rise of prices has occurred, it [the debt] is repaid twice over, once in increased prices and again on redemption. Secondly, there is no provision in this method of financing for the money to pay the interest on the debentures, which, in fact, can only be paid, if it is paid, by the issue of fresh money to pay it, which, under existing circumstances, comes from the same source, that is to say, the financial system. From this point of view, it is the difference between usury and profit – a difference clearly drawn in the Middle Ages. There is an additional factor, perhaps more important than any of these, and that is that, either by directly calling in the debentures or by selling the debentures to the public and calling in public overdrafts, financial institutions can, and most unquestionably do, recall the money equivalent to the plant value at a greater rate than the plant depreciates.[15]

Under normal circumstances, then, production is initially financed by a loan from a financial institution. As shown in Douglas' two diagrams, (Diagrams 3b and 3c), what happens over time is as follows:

Finance flows from the Bank, the 'money maker' at the top of the diagram, to the producer in the form of loan finance capital. The producer is employing labour, and also buying raw materials or other semi-manufactured goods in order to send the finished goods produced in the factory on to the market. The money distributed to the workers, the 'distributed costs A', forms the income of the workers who, as consumers or 'citizens', spend their money with the retailer. For simplicity in the diagram, the retailer and wholesaler are treated as one, being joined by a single line. Thus the money from the 'A' payments which has been spent by the earner/consumers on the goods sold, forms the income of the producer. From that income, at that point in time, he has to deduct his 'allocated 'B' costs' which are additional to the costs distributed as incomes in the form of wages, salaries and dividends. Since the 'B' costs must be included in the price at which goods are sold, the 'A' payments will not cover the full costs, and a certain amount of goods will remain unsold, to the value of the 'B' costs.

Fig.2 depicts the situation where Factory No.1 is already operating as shown in Fig.1. Factory No.2 is now financed in the way described by Douglas in the quotation from *The Old and the New Economics*. A financial institution creates new money which enters the economic system as a debt: the productive enterprise gives a bond which has to be redeemed, along with interest payments. The new money is distributed to the workers who build Factory No.2. As yet, no goods are flowing from the new factory. So the workers in Factory No.2 must spend their 'A' payment incomes on the unsold goods of Factory No.1. In this way, the economy is driven to the continuous growth necessitated by the workings of the institutions of finance as developed over the period since the onset of the industrial revolution. The system is preserved from total collapse by excessive capital production, production for wasteful consumerism and war, and production for export far in excess of imports. For professional economists, the economy remains a natural phenomenon, to be studied much like the weather. Trends and phenomena can be documented statistically so that likely outcomes can be predicted, but policies must either be left to the free play of market forces, or planned by a centralised 'nanny state'.

Socialism and banking[16]

The capitalist/socialist antithesis was between 'private' administration of business and national or 'State' administration. Stripped of a mass of irrelevances, the debate boils down to a choice between large-scale centralised administration or small-scale decentralised administration. The latter is what advocates of 'private' administration have in mind when they advocate 'capitalism' as opposed to 'socialism'. Large-scale corporate administration of business may be termed 'private', but in reality it is nothing more than centralised, large-scale administration, indistinguishable from nationalised or 'State' administration. Both types of centralised administration lead to a helplessness on the part of individual workers. The powerlessness to put right identifiable defects in the organisation results in constant frustration, coupled with loss of interest in the work in hand. Under these circumstances, employees work for the purely self-interested motive of securing a financial reward, especially where a high salary appears to offer income security merely for working the system. In this scenario, it matters little whether the banks are run as 'private' or as 'State' institutions. Whatever nominal changes are made, the banks continue to be administered with the same degree of efficiency – and workers remain employees.

At issue is the fact that banks deal with public credit, which functions as money. At present, the banking system *lends* credit to businesses. It is assumed that the credit which the banking system deals with *belongs to the banks*. It must be remembered, however, that these loans are *new money* which functions in exactly the same way as new Treasury notes when they are printed. The question to be established is, does this new credit truly belong to the banks, in which case they are correct in *lending* it? Or, on the other hand, does the new credit arise from the organisation of individuals within the national economy? If the latter is the case, the new credit rightly belongs to individual citizens in their capacity as tenants-for-life of the social unit of the nation, and it is not correctly *lent* to them. Rather, in order that the business of the world should be carried on smoothly, it should be *given* to them, the banks being paid for their services as trustees.

If the current system of credit control and distribution is deemed to be functioning satisfactorily, there is a great deal to be said for leaving matters as they are. If however, the ongoing frustrations of working within a debt-financed system which leads to third world poverty, war, environmental degradation and social malaise are recognised as being far from inevitable, it may be time for a critical re-examination of dogmatically held assumptions. A prime example of an assumption providing an intellectual block to methodical thought is the idea that working for money, *i.e*, *employment*, creates wealth.

The practical approach is to consider first the price system, rather than the banking system *per se*. It is through the agency of prices that the credit-purchasing power is returned to the banking system which, according to leading bankers, creates all but an insignificant fraction of purchasing power. Prices have two limits. The upper limit is governed by what the purchaser is able and willing to pay. The lower limit, however, is governed by the cost of production. It is often assumed that restriction of purchasing power to consumers, *i.e.*, deflation, will cause prices to fall. In practice what happens is that when prices have fallen to around the cost of production, any further attempt to depress prices by conventional financial measures merely arrests production and removes articles of production from the market.

Modern productive methods depend more and more on the use of power and machinery, rather than labour. Hence, in addition to the costs of wages and salaries, the cost of machinery is added to the total costs of production. In so far as the cost of the machinery, which goes into the total costs of the articles produced by their use, has been paid for, and the payments used to cancel bank loans, part of the current price of the product is collectively in excess of the ability of the consuming public to pay. In short, in total the rate of flow of prices from the producing system is greater than the rate of flow of purchasing power. The difference is measured by the disparity between bank credits created *minus* bank credits cancelled by repayments, and prices created *minus* price values destroyed. It will be seen that the difference arises fundamentally from the necessity, under existing arrangements, of repaying bank loans.

The economic problem is not a technical matter of an inability to produce goods and services in sufficient quantities as may be required. Since the days of Adam Smith's pin factory, a mass of material goods far in excess of the requirements of a sane and sensible social order can be poured out of the productive system. The problem lies in the social failure to understand the financial mechanics of the distribution system. At present, the individual citizen is locked into an employment system which derives from the requirements of a debt-based financial system. As Douglas never tired of pointing out, however, his technical analysis of the workings of the financial system could be adopted by any type of political system, democratic or otherwise.

Free (social) credit

The essential ingredient for a free society is that blind faith in plans and blueprints be rejected by a well-informed, active citizenship. During the decades in which Social Credit formed a major part of the worldwide debate on alternatives to mainstream orthodoxy, a great deal of confusion arose when individuals committed to some form of 'monetary reform' pedalled ideas which had nothing to do with Douglas' analysis of the workings of the financial system. Often claims were made that Douglas merely advocated the injection of more money into the system. Such misinterpretation can only arise from a failure to engage in the focused study of Douglas' writings. Additional credit flowing into the system on the basis of the debt-financing of production or distribution would merely exacerbate an already precarious situation. From the Social Credit perspective, credit is 'free' or not 'free' according to the conditions of its use when in circulation. Credit can be 'given' in form, and yet may not be 'given' in substance. What is required is the gift in substance.

A credit is 'free' in form when a Credit Authority transfers it to some recipient without requiring the recipient to return it or to pay interest on it. Is such a gift of credit essentially different from a loan in perpetuity to the recipient? It seems the same in effect. If no interest is charged, and if no moral obligation on the part of the recipient to pay interest is recognised, there would seem to be no difference in form, either. However, there remains a big distinction between a loan and a gift. It lies in the attitude of mind.

An issue of credit is a loan or a gift according to whether the recipient is supposed to be under a moral obligation to return it, or has the moral right not to do so. Against this background, the true significance of interest can be seen. Any rate of interest implies an agreement to pay it: and that agreement implies an obligation to return the credit. An interest rate is a visible symbol of a moral obligation on the part of the recipient to the authority issuing the credit. Fundamentally, interest is exactly like the seal on a legal document. It is a recognition in law of the acceptance of the borrower of the moral right of the lender to redeem the pledge. It is not the rate of interest, but the fact of its payment, which is at issue.

The missing link

Douglas, the practical engineer, surveyed the workings of the financial system of the industrial world before, during and after the First World War. He concluded that the indirect financing of distribution (incomes) through the debt-financing of employing institutions was an unnecessarily cumbersome and outmoded methodology. This chapter has provided a brief overview of the substance of his Social Credit thought and analysis of the financial system. There can be no substitute, however, for the critical study of Douglas' original works alongside the many excellent study guides, books, articles and pamphlets written by individuals who have studied Social Credit in depth throughout the twentieth century.[17]

In post-industrial societies money forms the 'life-blood' of the social order. It therefore follows that an understanding of the role of banking and finance within the institutional framework of society as a whole becomes an essential prerequisite for progress towards a sane, just and sustainable social order.

> The most important and fundamental function of a bank should be to envisage the capacity of the community it serves, taken in conjunction with its plant and culture, to meet the demands made upon it; and, under democratic control, to issue purchasing power, on behalf of the community (the true State) up to the limit of this capacity, so that as individuals the units composing the community can set in motion the machinery which will make such demands effective.[18]

From the earliest discussions with trade unionists and the Labour Party throughout the U.K., Douglas constantly stressed the need to distinguish between money values and the practical realities of everyday economics. In this respect, he anticipated the 'Post-Autistic Economics' movement by more than eight decades.

'Is There Anything Worth Keeping in Standard Microeconomics?'

In June 2000, an interview in *Le Monde* drew attention to the newly-formed post-autistic economics (pae) movement. The movement, which evolved from the work of Sorbonne Economist Bernard Guerrien and a number of disaffected economics students in France, the U.K. and the U.S.A., flowered briefly in the early years of the twenty-first century. However, for salaried economists, it held no career prospects under the current climate in the academy. Without access to a body of economic thought which relates to the practical realities of everyday economic life, such as Douglas' work, the mainly negative critiques of current mainstream economics by Guerrien and his supporters were easily dismissed as spurious by the 'powers-that-be'.

Two articles by Guerrien,[19] 'Is There Anything Worth Keeping in Standard Microeconomics?' and 'Once Again on Microeconomics' warrant serious study by all would-be students of economics. However, although Douglas' work can be studied without prior knowledge of 'standard microeconomics', the two Guerrien articles are addressed to a target audience of economists. As such, they were the subject of an intense debate. The gist of the argument was that current teaching of economics is based upon a set of 'stories' or 'parables' which can be 'proved' mathematically, but only if the basic assumptions upon which the stories are based are taken as read. Students and staff sought not more and more of the same, but different theories, comparative histories of economic thought, sociology and moral philosophy to replace the static calculations of the antics of a hypothesised 'rational economic man'. Where the only motive recognised is pure self-interest, real-life relationships, between the firm and the wage-labourer, the landowner and the tenant, and the banker, industrialist and merchant have no place.

A key issue, however, according to Guerrien, is the question of *prices*. How are prices determined? Under micro-economic theory buyers react to price: when the price is low, they buy more; when the price rises, they buy less. The quantities which they buy at the various prices can then be mathematically calculated and set onto supply and demand curves. But the question then arises, who sets the price? Quantities are bought at *actual prices* already set by price-making agents: the buyers are 'price takers' not 'price makers'. In reality, it is not the price that varies, but the quantities or stocks which vary, as Douglas explained so long ago. As we have seen, Douglas observed that stocks cannot be sold at prices which fall below cost unless the business is heading for bankruptcy.

In 2002 Guerrien concluded:

I think that you cannot study economic relations if you don't pay attention to institutional arrangements, customs and traditions, mass psychology, class conflicts, and so on. Obviously, this is very difficult, and you have to be very modest when you teach these things (it is much easier to tell our students that 'theory – mathematical models – show this or that; if you do this, then you will have that, etc.' than to say 'well, I don't really know, but in my opinion ...'

Now we come to the last, and eternal problem of the 'alternative theory'. Well, first we have to be cured of our inferiority-complex with neoclassical theory. If we think that it is a bad, empty theory, then there is no problem: any theory can be at least as good as it is. Classical economists (Smith, Ricardo, Mill) say a lot of interesting things; Marx and Keynes, too; there are some good ideas in 'old macro-economy', in the IS-LM fashion. Leontieff and Sraffa models allow us to think about inter-dependencies in the economy. Economic history is quite fascinating – especially the evolution of capitalism (in the way done, for example, by the French 'regulationniste school').

Neoclassical models – with utility and production functions, and maximizing agents – have nothing to say about all this. And we have to explain why, again and again.

There is no need for a new 'great theory' or blueprint. Without it, noted Guerrien, there are plenty of interesting things to say about how the world works, and how it might be consciously changed: 'Economists always have something to propose.' What is urgently needed is a refreshing plurality in approach to the study of economics.

New Age or 'No-wage labour economics'

What has been attempted here is the briefest of summaries of Douglas' detailed analysis. Douglas' original work is essential reading if a full understanding of the technical details of the analysis of the relationship between the financial and the real economies in the post-industrial era is to be achieved. For Douglas, and also Veblen, the economy functions through a series of man-made institutions, the evolution of which can be studied with a view to the introduction of sane, sensible and considered adaptations which take account of all the factors concerned.

A study of the work of both Douglas and Veblen will reveal no advocacy of impractical, Utopian short-cuts, still less the suggestion of abrupt or revolutionary change. Douglas provided clear and concise answers to the frequently asked questions in respect of the workings of the economy in the twentieth century. He was, however, persistently mis-interpreted by career politicians, academics and bankers. This was particularly true of socialists who were pressing for State control of all large nationalised undertakings, and assumed that Douglas might perhaps be advocating a version of State control of industry in general, and banking in particular. Hence Douglas constantly found it necessary to clarify his stance.

As the following chapters demonstrate, when economists move beyond the pure mystique of mathematical models, they speak a language which can be studied with interest by groups and individuals throughout the social order. Those who advocated the systematic study of Social Credit texts, including Douglas himself, did so for no financial advantage or personal gain. The primary motivation was to see the benefits of industrial civilisation directed towards more desirable ends than war, poverty amidst plenty and wasteful consumerism. They were opposed in the main by individuals who sought to achieve the same ends through the pursuit of a salaried career in politics or academia. As the following chapters demonstrate, without the Douglas analysis, mainstream economic thought in the academy remains to this day little more than an incoherent collection of non-sequiturs. However, the study of Social Credit ideas must be informed by a consciousness of economic thought as taught in the academy in the twenty-first century.

NOTES
1   For more historical detail, see Hutchinson and Burkitt (1997)
2   Douglas (1924) pp135-6
3   Douglas (1924) pp137-140
4   Douglas (1920) pp119-120 (emphasis original)
5   Douglas (1920) p121
6   Douglas (1920) p124
7   For a more detailed analysis, see Hutchinson *et al* (2002)
8   Douglas (1932) p8
9   Hawtrey and Douglas (1933)
10   Douglas (1931) p38 (1979 edition)
11   Smith, Adam (1776) pp4-5.
12   Douglas (1922b) pp13-14
13   Douglas (1924) pp49-50
14   Veblen (1990) pp196-7
15   Douglas (1932) p13
16   What follows is based upon Douglas (1925)
17   See, *e.g.*, Rowbotham (1998)
18   Douglas (1922b) p14
19   Guerrien (2002a) (2002b)

Chapter 4
Social Credit – The English Origins

Throughout the 'inter-war' years (1918-1939), the Social Credit ideas of Clifford Hugh Douglas were the subject of a lively popular debate. In the U.K. and across the world, weekly newspapers brought a Social Credit perspective to discussion of current affairs, scores of books and pamphlets were published, a stream of articles appeared in local and national presses. Mass meetings were held in major towns, in the U.K. and across the world, study groups met regularly and radio broadcasts carried the debate into millions of households. Vigorous attempts were subsequently made to explain away the Social Credit phenomenon as a mere reaction to the hard times of the two decades of peace which separated the two world wars of the twentieth century. Such a misapprehension was strenuously encouraged by academia in the later affluent decades of the twentieth century. But the truth, as revealed by the legacy of an extensive literature of the period, is much more interesting.

Social Credit had its origins in the English working class peace movement which flowed from the trauma of the Great War (1914-18). Douglas' original works formed a part of mainstream culture of the period. His books, published by established London publishing houses, took their place in libraries and collections alongside the works of G.K. Chesterton, Hilaire Belloc, T.S. Eliot, H.G. Wells, G.D.H. Cole and others. Social Credit literature was first publicised in the pages of *The New Age*, the highly influential weekly, circulating in literary and political circles through the force of the personality of its editor, Alfred Richard Orage. The latter's opposition to Labour Party policies based on a bureaucratic worker-state and the centralisation of political power, led the Labour leadership to set up the *New Statesman* as the 'official' socialist weekly in 1913. However, *The New Age* remained a major 'think tank' within intellectual circles throughout the 'inter-war' years. In addition to *The New Age*, a range of other periodicals circulated throughout the English-speaking world during the 1920s and 1930s, as Social Credit became established as an international movement. Appendix 4a: (Social Credit Literature) documents the range of publications on Social Credit.

The English[1] working class

To understand the Social Credit movement it is necessary to appreciate the cultural soil in which it grew. Throughout the nineteenth century, when families like the Rothschilds were funding wars, railways and other profitable ventures, peasant farming families were being forced by economic circumstances to leave their cottages in the English countryside and move into the crowded urban areas as landless waged labour. Early migrants to the towns brought with them knowledge of farming and the countryside, together with a rich cultural history of co-operative customs which dated back to the Celtic past.[2] The practice of being employed *as an individual* for a money wage was alien to the sense of traditional community of the peasant village. The migrants moved from town to town, seeking any kind of 'work' which would keep together body and soul of self and family. The appalling conditions of work, life and 'leisure' in the industrial mills and mining towns of the British Isles have been well documented. Migrants spread across the 'English-speaking world'. As an independent nation state, the U.S.A. gave rise to the full development of corporate capitalism. Meanwhile settlers in Canada, Australia, New Zealand and South Africa tended to maintain something of their English cultural origins.

As the industrial revolution progressed in the U.K., the traditional aristocracy and master-craftsman families were joined by wealthy capitalists and a host of small traders, shopkeepers, schoolteachers, doctors and clergy, all occupying independent households. Urban houses for the middle class were designed to accommodate at least one or two residential servants, so that throughout the nineteenth century, vast numbers of domestic servants were employed in the houses of the urban well-to-do. Cast-off clothing from the higher rungs of society, together with crockery and furnishings no longer deemed fashionable, made its way *via* the servants into the homes of the aspiring working class. With the cast-offs went an appreciation of style, of the arts and etiquette, and a sympathy with the political views of the employing class. Combined with the peasant traditions, this gave rise to an indefinable sense of what it is to be English. The mood of the times was captured by the Savoy Operas of Gilbert and Sullivan as, using Shakespeare's language to full effect, they portrayed the resistance of the English to an emerging social order in which 'economic' considerations were coming to dominate culture and politics. It took a particular social setting to portray the members of the British House of Lords being compelled by law to marry a fairy. In the same comic opera, *Iolanthe*, it is solemnly observed that:

> Nature always does contrive,
> That every boy and every gal
> That's born into the world alive
> Is either a little Liberal,
> Or else a little Conservative!

That the political party system amounts to little more than a matter of exchanging Tweedledum for Tweedledee every now and then, was fully appreciated by English audiences when *Iolanthe* was first produced in 1882.

When the Labour Party emerged to take its place as the 'Tweedledee' to the Conservative 'Tweedledum', in the immediate aftermath of the First World War, the Social Credit movement was perceived as a major threat by career politicians and academics. The founding fathers of the Labour Party set about shaping the party of the *workers* under centralised capitalism and centralised state provision. As the twentieth century progressed, the policies of the national Labour Party were based upon centralised planning and state control, with the entire nation being chained into waged or salaried slavery as the price for gaining an income.

English socialism

In the early years of the twentieth century, according to Alfred Richard Orage, 'every intellectual' was 'some sort of a socialist':

> Socialism was not then either the popular or the unpopular vogue it has since become; but it was much more of a cult, with affiliations in directions now quite disowned – with theosophy, arts and crafts, vegetarianism, the 'simple life,' and almost, as one might say, the musical glasses. Morris had shed a mediaeval glamor over it with his stained glass *News from Nowhere*. Edward Carpenter had put it into sandals. Cunninghame Grahame had mounted it on an Arab steed to which he was always saying a romantic farewell. Keir Hardy had clothed it in a cloth cap and a red tie. And Bernard Shaw, on behalf of the Fabian Society, had hung it with innumerable jingling epigrammatic bells – and a cap. My brand of socialism was, therefore, a blend, or let us say, an anthology of all these, to which from my personal predilections and experience I added a good practical knowledge of the working classes, a professional interest in economics which led me to master Marx's *Das Kapital*, and an idealism fed at the source – namely, Plato.

Writing in the U.S. publication *The Commonweal* in 1926, Orage was describing his fifteen year stint as Editor of *The New Age*. By the early twenty-first century, names cited by Orage would be difficult to trace, were it not for the entries in Wikipedia. A glance through those entries demonstrates that the socialism of the turn of the twentieth century had virtually nothing in common with Communism, whether of the Russian variety or the paternalistic 'gas-and-water' socialism of the Labourist central planners. When he took over the weekly in 1907, it was expected that *The New Age* would follow the Fabian socialism of the statisticians and planners. However:

> Very little was anybody, including myself, aware of the course the *New Age* would take; but of one thing I was certain – no society or school or individual could count on my continuous support. The whole movement of ideas, called Socialism, including of course the then burning question of parliamentary Labor representation, was in the melting-pot; and my little handful of colleagues and I had no intention of prematurely running ourselves into anybody else's mold. The socialists of those days were, in practice, individualists to a man.[3]

Under the editorship of Orage, *The New Age* became the leading English language weekly of politics, literature and the arts. Famous names appeared in the journal, including George Bernard Shaw (who assisted in the purchase of the paper), G.K. Chesterton, Hilaire Belloc, Ezra Pound, Katherine Mansfield, Wyndham Lewis, Herbert Read, T.E. Hulme and Guild Socialist writers such as Arthur Penty, S.G. Hobson, Maurice Reckitt and G.D.H Cole. The periodical reflected the multifarious nature of socialism in the pre-War period (1907-1914). A range of socio-political philosophies reflected the aspiration to do away with all violent and coercive institutions so that each and every person would have free access to the necessities of life. The broad spectrum of anarchist socialism sought the end of centralised, hierarchical institutions through which power over others is exercised, whether in the economic, political or religious/cultural spheres of society.

The socialist anarchist philosophy found its fullest expression in Guild Socialism, which sought to work through decentralised trade union branches of the different trades and local municipalities. Informed by a notion of *service to* the community, Guild Socialists rejected the concept of working for the personal reward of a wage or salary. Work should be freely undertaken, under the control of the producing unit which drew upon the resources of the community it served, and of which the workers formed a part. All forms of production for financial profit, whether of the capitalist or State owner of the means of production, undertaken by colluding wage/salary slaves, were criticised by Guild Socialist writers and thinkers.

Wage slavery in any form was regarded as *the* major evil of industrialisation by a large proportion of activists within the Guild Socialist movement. Where a person is totally livelihood-dependent on the wage or salary paid by an employer, they can be deemed to be a wage slave, no matter how high the payments may be, how agreeable the working conditions or whether the employer is a private individual, private corporation or state enterprise. *All* employment relationships within a hierarchical social environment are ultimately backed by the coercive threat of cessation of the employment, bringing personal financial disaster along with social stigma coupled with social exclusion. Hence many individuals within the Guild Socialist movement of the first quarter of the twentieth century, inspired by the guilds of craftsmen of mediaeval England, sought to introduce decentralised, small-scale administration of trades within the context of modern industry and the community at large.

The adult education movement

The adult education movement was a central feature of social life in towns and cities across the U.K. throughout the first half of the twentieth century. As urban industrialisation evolved, the practice of 'working class' men and women seeking out literacy and numeracy with a view to studying philosophy, history, sciences, theology, politics and the arts can be detected in local papers, social histories and biographical accounts from as early as the seventeenth century. In the years immediately following the First World War, University Extension classes, branches of the Workers' Educational Association, Settlements and Summer Schools were a commonplace feature in most urban areas.

Noting the lack of continuity involved in the University Extension classes, Albert and Frances Mansbridge founded the Workers' Educational Association (W.E.A.)[4] in 1903 to enable workers to study with leading figures in politics, the arts and academia. Throughout the country groups of 20 to 40 adults invited tutors to teach them in evening classes over a three year period. Classes were similarly organised through local branches of trade unions, the Co-operative Movement and Guilds. Study groups were often associated with residential 'summer schools' held at stately homes and attended by people from all walks of life.

University Settlements were frequently to be found in major towns and cities. Founded in the years immediately following the First World War, under the Wardenship of Arnold Freeman, the Sheffield Settlement is one of the few currently documented on the Internet. The Settlement was administered by a

Council of some forty members, including respected local figures such as the Bishop of Sheffield and the Vice-Chancellor of the University, and nationally-known people such as Edward Carpenter and Arnold Rowntree (member of the noted Quaker Family and President of the Educational Centres Association) ... [The] declared and ambitious Object was 'to establish in the City of Sheffield the Kingdom of God'. The Method of achieving this was 'Education'. The definition of the 'Kingdom of God' was spelled out in the Settlement letterhead:

By the Kingdom of God we mean streets along which it is a pleasure to walk; homes worthy of those who live in them; workplaces in which people enjoy working; public-houses that are centres of social and educational life; kinemas that show elevating films; schools that would win the approval of Plato; churches made up of men and women indifferent to their own salvation; an environment in which people 'may have life and have it abundantly'. By 'Education' we mean everything by means of which people may become more spiritual; everything that enriches human beings, with That which described in three words is Beauty, Truth and Goodness, and described in one word as GOD.

The story of the Sheffield Educational Settlement belongs with the history of the University Settlement Movement. Some Settlements had more formal university links, but all sought to bring education, improvement and hope to the lives of the poor and socially disadvantaged in the decades before the development of the Welfare State following the Second World War. The early decades of the Sheffield Settlement coincided with the serious hardship of the post-First World War era, typified by the Depression and mass unemployment.[5]

Far from being a mere matter of gaining paper qualifications for the purpose of following a well-paid personal career, liberal adult education was viewed by students and tutors alike as a means for citizens to grow in authority in order to assume responsibilities, as adults, within the local community and society as a whole. The practice of group study of writings, on all manner of subjects, was found to be beneficial to all concerned, and was undertaken across social and class barriers. Albert Mansbridge, himself self-educated, observed in 1920:

Education and knowledge must not be confused. Knowledge is the instrument in the hands of a man, and if he be educated, and therefore reaching out to the higher things, his knowledge will be used for purposes ministering to the common good. If he be not educated, merely drifting down the streams of opportunity, or aiming at lesser or unhealthy things, then his knowledge will be used for false purposes. The educated man can do no harm to the community. The band of educated work their way to 'Zion with their faces thitherwards.' The field of education is a common upon which all men can meet and exercise rights, no matter what their differences may be in the ordinary activities of life. They may differ in politics, even in religion, but, if they be one in their determination to reach out to the things which are eternal, then they may unite to promote the great democratic adventure which needs the best thought and action of every individual.[6]

The necessity for study, tolerance and understanding of different points of view was widely appreciated in the inter-war years of the twentieth century. William Temple, activist in the W.E.A., supporter of Social Credit, and future Archbishop of Canterbury, observed that it would be useless for men to pool their thoughts unless they differed: he wrote an Introduction to a pamphlet by Mr. Stephen Hobhouse *because he disagreed* with what he said in it:

The whole forward movement of our social life turns on the development among the great mass of the people of that kind of education which makes men eager both to think for themselves and to appreciate the truth in any opinion from which they dissent.[7]

The vital importance of adult education for a healthy society was spelled out in 1941 by Sir Richard Livingstone, President of Corpus Christi College, Oxford. In *The Future of Education*, Livingstone distinguished between primary, secondary, technical and university education on the one hand, and adult education on the other. After fifty years spent 'receiving or giving education' Livingstone was convinced of the importance of higher education in the sciences, literature, history and politics in the years after 18, and better still after 30.[8]

The practice of group study spread throughout the 'Overseas Dominions' which had been settled largely by English working class people during the industrial revolution. In the years immediately prior to the First World War Albert Mansbridge and his wife toured Australia, lecturing at over a hundred different venues on W.E.A. ideals:

The idea of adult education as the development of the being and powers of man, in and through the fusion of labour and scholarship, came as a recreating force to these powerful though young communities. They indeed generated it themselves. Their experience had convinced them that education, if not an end in itself, is a permanent factor in all healthy individual and social life, and is a deeper thing than training for livelihood or even for direct social and political purpose.[9]

When Mansbridge was writing, civic duties and political activities were undertaken from a sense of service to the community, as work was done on a voluntary basis without financial reward or recompense. Following the visit of the Mansbridges, University Extension Courses were set up in every Australian state, with thirty-seven courses operating in New South Wales alone by 1919. Further W.E.A.s were set up in New Zealand, Canada and South Africa. The pre-existence of networks of study groups was a key factor in the spread of Social Credit to Australia, New Zealand, South Africa and Canada.

Clifford Hugh Douglas

The writings of Clifford Hugh Douglas, and what people made of them, form the core subject matter of this book. Throughout his public career and subsequently, Douglas himself has been portrayed as an anti-Semitic, racist, monetary crank in a constant stream of malicious attacks which are far from innocent in intent. Since, at his own request, no biography was written, it is necessary to turn to the testimony of people who knew him personally and worked closely with him over many years to gain a measure of the man himself.

Writing in the New York Catholic weekly *The Commonweal*, in 1926, Orage related the impression made on him by Douglas and his analysis:

He had been assistant-director of the Government aircraft factory during the war: he was a first-rate engineer: he had encountered financial problems practically as well as theoretically; and he appeared and proved to be the most perfect gentleman I have ever met. His knowledge of economics was extraordinary; and from our very first conversation everything he said concerning finance in its relation to industry – and indeed to industrial civilisation as a whole – gave me the impression of a mastermind perfectly informed upon its special subject. After years of the closest association with him, my first impression has only been intensified. In the scores of interviews we had together with bankers, professors of economics, politicians and businessmen, I never saw him so much as at a moment's loss of complete mastery of his subject. Among no matter what experts, he made them look and talk like children.

The subject itself, however, even in the hands of a master, is not exactly easy; and, in fact, it compares in economics with, let us say, time and space in physics. By the same token, Douglas is the Einstein of economics; and, in my judgement, as little likely to be comprehended practically. In other words, a good deal of sweat is necessary to understand Douglas; and, with our absurd modern habit of assuming that any theory clearly stated must be immediately intelligible to the meanest and laziest intellect, very few will be the minds to devote the necessary time and labour to the matter. I was in all respects exceptionally favourably placed to make a fairly quick response. I had time and, from my long experience with literary geniuses, almost illimitable patience; I was vitally interested in the subject, having not only exhausted every other, but being convinced that the key to my difficulties lay in it; and, above all, Douglas himself was actively interested in my instruction. He said many things in our first talk that blinded me with light; and thereafter I lost no opportunity of talking with him, reading new and old works on finance, with all the zest of an enthusiastic pupil. Even with these advantages it was a slowish business; and my reflections on the stupidity of the present-day students of Douglas are generously tempered by the recollection of my own. It was a full year from beginning to study his ideas before I arrived at complete understanding. Then all my time and labour were justified. … Certainly there is no lack of light on the subject to-day; but only the usual poverty of eyes and understanding.[10]

Orage's reflections on Douglas offer a clear picture of a powerful intellect at work. They also give an indication of the stature of Orage himself.

Over fifty years later L. Denis Byrne, another close colleague of Douglas, wrote the following tribute to him:

Notwithstanding a mental stature unusual in any society, Douglas' outstanding characteristic was a profound humility – a humility which was reflected in his writings and in his life [Douglas died in 1952]. Where others viewed the world in terms of mankind's struggles and achievements, and society as the creature of man's brain and behaviour, with the realism of the engineer and the penetrating spirituality of a Medieval theologian, Douglas saw the Universe as an integrated unity centred in its creation and centred in its Creator and subject to His Law.

It was the basis of Douglas' philosophy, of which Social Credit is the policy, that there is running through the warp and woof of the Universe the Law of Righteousness – Divine Law – which he termed the Canon.

He must seek it actively, and to the extent that he finds it and conforms to it, he will achieve harmony with the Universe and his Creator. Conversely, to the degree that he ignores the operation of the Canon and flouts it, he will bring disaster upon himself.

It was inherent in Douglas' writings that he viewed society as something partaking of the nature of an organism which could have 'life and life abundant' to the extent it was God-centred and obedient to his Canon. Within this organism the sovereignty of 'God the creator of all things visible and invisible' being absolute, there must be full recognition of the sanctity of human personality and, therefore, of the individual person as free to live his life, and within the body social, to enter into or contract out of such associations as, with the responsibility to his Creator, he may choose. And no person may deny another this relationship to God and his fellow men without committing sacrilege.

This concept, reflecting the ideal of Christendom as the integration of Church and Society which was the inspiration of European civilisation for centuries, involves adherence to a policy in every sphere of social life, economic, political and cultural. This is the policy which Douglas termed 'Social Credit'.

Looking upon the world with a clarity of vision which was unique in his time, Douglas saw a doomed civilisation committed to the opposite policy, stemming from a conflicting philosophy, a philosophy which deified Man and sought to subjugate the world to him.

The true test of science is consistently correct predictions. Genuine prophets, amongst whom might be counted statesmen, are those who, because of their understanding of Truth, can see well in advance the consequences of certain policies if they are persevered with. In his earliest writings Douglas warned that all attempts to operate the finance-economic system under the prevailing methods of creating and issuing financial credit, must result in inflation. The insidious effects of monetary inflation are destroying Western Civilisation in the same way that it played a major part in destroying the great Roman civilisation.

Douglas predicted the Great Depression and also warned that the Second World War was inevitable unless there was a major modification of orthodox finance-economic policies. Douglas warned that it would be used to break up the British Empire, establish the Political Zionist State of Israel, and centralise all power still further in a bid to establish the World State. Douglas made his predictions before the massive documentation of Dr. Anthony Sutton[11] and others showed conclusively that there was a concrete programme to build up Communism as an essential feature of the programme to create the World State.

Long before ecology and conservation became issues for widespread discussion and resulted in a vast literature, Douglas had warned that to attempt to drive the economic system under the centralised financial policies of debt, heavy taxation and inflation must result in built-in obsolescence and a growing waste of valuable resources. But unlike those conservationists who seek to exploit pollution and associated problems to further more centralised controls over the individual, Douglas advocated policies which would remove the basic cause of pollution and the waste of raw materials.

Douglas insisted that salvation was only possible by going back to basic principles. He stressed that the only hope was what he described as 'practical Christianity.' He shed new light on the Doctrine of Incarnation by stressing that it was not Truth as such which moved events; it is the proper harnessing of the truth so that power was released. Faith without works is death. Faith can only move mountains if the appropriate equipment is used.[12]

During the late 1930s and early 1940s L.D. Byrne was Douglas' representative in Alberta, and advisor to the Alberta Government. The article is cited here with very little abbreviation despite its unfashionable mentions of Empire and Christianity in a positive light, negative reference to Political Zionism, and the use of gendered language throughout. It is hoped that readers from a variety of differing backgrounds will nevertheless find Byrne's picture of Douglas illuminating.

Social Credit on a world scale in the 1920s

Douglas' first book, *Economic Democracy*, written in collaboration with Orage, was serialised in *The New Age* and relayed to study groups in the U.K. and the Dominions in this form. From 1920 onwards, weekly periodicals carried articles by Douglas and others, together with advertisements and reviews of books and pamphlets on the subject of Social Credit. *Economic Democracy* was published in hardback by Cecil Palmer in 1920, followed by *Credit-Power and Democracy* in the same year. The two books were 'set as text books for

Economics Honours at Sydney University in 1921'.[13] *The Control and Distribution of Production*, published in 1922 is largely a compilation of lectures delivered by Douglas, together with articles of his published in *The New Age* and *The English Review*. As a result of his writings Douglas was invited to lecture at a variety of venues throughout the UK and elsewhere.

Douglas' second book, *Credit-Power and Democracy*, carried as an Appendix the 'Draft Mining Scheme', described as 'A Practical Scheme for the Establishment of Economic and Industrial Democracy', together with a detailed commentary by Orage. The Scheme offered the potential to create a guild system free from dependence upon a debt-based, predatory, competitive financial system. The Scheme, written from the perspective of the Miners' Federation of Great Britain, was particularly popular in the Scottish Labour Party, amongst the Scottish Miners and amongst Labour supporters elsewhere in the U.K. As a result, in 1921 the Labour Party hastily convened a sub-committee to consider 'The Douglas-NEW AGE Scheme.' Since the committee was composed of individuals known by Douglas and Orage to be hostile to the political philosophy of Social Credit, it came as no surprise that the committee returned a negative verdict on the 'Scheme'. The official Labour Party Report did not appear until 1922.[14] In 1922 Cecil Palmer published a 46-page booklet by Douglas and Orage entitled *These Present Discontents* and *the Labour Party and Social Credit*. The latter publication recounts the story of the refusal of the Labour leadership to give serious consideration to the Social Credit economic analysis. At this point Orage resigned as editor of *The New Age,* and left the country. He continued to promote Social Credit in the USA, and on his return to England he founded *The New English Weekly* to promote Douglas' work. He died during the night following his delivery of his BBC broadcast on Social Credit on 5th November 1934.[15]

At the request of people who had studied his work, members of the Canadian House of Commons in Ottawa invited Douglas to give evidence to the 1923 Select Standing Committee on Banking and Commerce in Ottawa.[16] In 1929 he addressed the World Engineering Congress in Tokyo on 'The Application of Engineering Methods to Finance',[17] and his latest book, *Social Credit* was translated into Japanese.

A synopsis of 'The Douglas Credit Proposals' published by the International Labour Office in March 1922 demonstrates that in the very early period (1918-1922) Douglas' writings were given serious consideration by mainstream thinkers in the academic world. The text, which neatly sums up Douglas Social Credit, reads as follows:

Supporters of the Douglas 'New Age' scheme argue that the purchasing power in the hands of the community is chronically insufficient to purchase the whole product of industry. This is ascribed to the fact that the cost of capital production, paid for by means of credit created by the banks, is charged into the price of consumers' goods. As a consequence of this lack of purchasing power, industrial communities are faced with the alternatives of continual and widespread unemployment of men and machines, as at present, or of international complications arising from the struggle for foreign markets.

The Douglas 'New Age' scheme proposes to remedy this defect by increasing the purchasing power in the hands of the community to an amount sufficient to provide effective demand for the whole product of industry. It is, of course, recognised that this cannot be done by the mere creation of more money, such a course necessarily giving rise to the 'vicious spiral,' prevalent during the war, of increased currency, higher prices, higher wages, higher costs, still higher prices, etc. The proposal, in its essentials, aims to create more money, but, at the same time, to regulate the price of consumers' goods, basing them on the real cost of production. It is argued that by thus selling goods at the 'just price' [*i.e.*, free from financial speculation] and simultaneously issuing new money to the requisite amount as statistically determined, purchasing power could be increased to, and maintained at, the point where it would be sufficient to exercise an effective demand for the whole product of industry. Advocates of the scheme claim that its adoption would result in an unexampled improvement of the standard of living of the community through elimination of the enormous waste prevailing in industry by reason of the lack of effective demand.

It is claimed that the scheme provides for the control of industry by the community through the control of the credit with which industry is financed. It is also pointed out that, unlike other radical measures, these proposals do not necessitate expropriation in any form, but insist upon the necessity of business enterprise remaining in private hands, steps being taken to ensure that it serves the needs of the community.[18]

The extract demonstrates that the writer had studied Douglas' work, weighing it against his own understanding of the subject. Scholarship of this type in the academy was to become increasingly rare, as career academics followed the 'free market' or 'planned economy' models acceptable to the paymasters – and avoided all serious debate on coherent alternatives.

Social Credit on a world scale in the 1930s

By the 1930s the Depression, which Douglas had long predicted as the inevitable result of the financial policies followed during the immediate aftermath of the First World War, drew further attention to his work. He gave evidence to the 1930 Macmillan Committee on Finance and Industry, being cross-questioned by Keynes.[19] Following the publication of *The Monopoly of Credit* (1931), *Warning Democracy* and a number of reprints of his earlier works, public interest in Social Credit gave rise to a high profile debate, in which expert economists and figures in Labour politics engaged with Douglas on public platforms. The content of this debate is reviewed in detail in Chapter 7. Throughout the 1930s Douglas addressed packed audiences at major venues throughout England, Scotland and Northern Ireland. He also spoke in Oslo to leading public figures, including the King of Norway.[20] Speeches given by Douglas were circulated through the weekly Social Credit publications, being also reproduced as pamphlets.

Sailing from England with his wife, Edith, at the end of 1933, Douglas embarked on a speaking tour of Australia, New Zealand, Canada and the United States. The tour was a resounding success. Over the previous fifteen years Douglas' work had been studied throughout Australia. People flocked to major venues to hear him speak. Although broadcasting was still in its very early days, people sought to catch his words on the radio, Social Credit being a hot political issue. As Douglas himself described it on his return in June 1934 in a speech delivered at Buxton, entitled 'The Nature of Democracy':

> One of the troubles of broadcasting in Western Australia is that during the morning reception is seriously interfered with by a large mill at some distance from the capital which is run by electricity – though in the ordinary way this does not matter, as most people only listen at night, when the mill is not running. When the owners of the mill heard that I was to broadcast during the morning they shut down the mill.[21]

Douglas was entertained by leading public figures at each venue. In Sydney he attended a luncheon meeting of over 900 people, and in the evening he addressed a meeting at the Stadium, Rushcutters Bay, attended by about 12,000 people, with another 5-6,000 listening on outside amplifiers and over a million on the radio. In Australia and New Zealand, Social Credit was a movement of farmers and working people, with governments and officialdom being violently opposed to it. In New Zealand, where it was thought that about one in four of the electorate were committed to Social Credit, the General Election was delayed until after the visit. Already the mainstream press was adopting a hostile position.

The popularity of Douglas' writings throughout Canada, particularly in Alberta, gave rise to the events which are documented in subsequent chapters. In Western Canada Douglas found strong popular support like that in Australia and New Zealand. However, there was 'almost equally strong official support and no press opposition':

> This may be ascribed largely to the antagonism of Western Canada to Ottawa. In fact, although the Southam Press, which owns a chain of newspapers appearing throughout Western Canada, has given us magnificent support for some years, I am sure that if Mr. Southam were here he would not object to my saying that even more space was given us in the opposition papers than his own. The evidence that I gave before the Government Committee of Enquiry at Edmonton was broadcast, but when I gave evidence at Ottawa before the Dominion Government that was not broadcast![22]

From Ottawa, Douglas went to the United States:

> In Washington I think I can say that I saw most of the people that mattered. I broadcast both from Washington and New York, and on the second occasion it was known as a 'coast to coast broadcast'; that means that the broadcast is relayed from all the local stations throughout the United States and would therefore be heard by something like 90 million people.[23]

Subsequently, historians and political commentators have sought to belittle Douglas and the Social Credit movement as a whole. However, Douglas' account can be verified through the documented evidence of contemporary periodicals. There is every reason to suspect that his popularity with farmers, working people and many other thinking people could not be ignored by people holding official positions in the cities which he visited.

The thread running through all Douglas' writings with unwavering consistency is the question of *authority*. The key person is the individual adult citizen who must freely make up his or her own mind as to the ways in which they interact in the life of society. Only a person who is *not* totally dependent upon an income from an employer, in the form of a wage or salary, can be said to be a truly free and independent citizen. When speaking to the Marshall Society at Cambridge Douglas freely admitted that he was no economist - since economists spend all their time trying to prove why theory does not match practice. Nor was he a political agitator, organiser or leader. He was a writer and teacher. His work speaks for itself.

Douglas had genuine respect for bankers, who knew what they wanted to do and in practice set about their work efficiently. Bankers could, and did, provide valuable service to the community as a whole. However, the services of bankers could also be corrupted to the services of sectional interests and conflict. Such conflict would endure so long as individuals continued to conduct their economic, political and spiritual lives as waged/salaried slaves of a system which they did not understand and could not be bothered to study. The dust jacket of *The Monopoly of Credit* (1931) sums up the situation:

> How is it possible for a world which is suffering from overproduction to be in economic distress? Where does money come from? Why should we economise when we are making too many goods? How can an unemployment problem, together with a manufacturing and agricultural organisation which cannot obtain orders, exist side by side with a poverty problem? Must we balance our budget? Why should we be asked to have confidence in our money system, if it works properly? It is hoped that answers to these and similar questions will be suggested by a perusal of this book.[24]

In short, by the mid-1930s Douglas and his worldwide readership were coming to the conclusion that not only economists and politicians, but also the press, media, education and cultural life generally were taking orders from finance. Although the corporate world subsequently described by David Korten[25] was as yet not fully developed, it was already taking a recognisable form. Eimar O'Duffy's presentation of the features of global capitalism in his futuristic science fiction Goshawk trilogy remains a classic fictional overview of the twentieth century political economy. The final volume of the trilogy, *Asses in Clover*[26] followed O'Duffy's comprehensive study of Douglas, Keynes and other leading economists of the time, as set out in his *Life and Money*.[27]

The Social Credit movement

Douglas' books, speeches and articles in *The New Age* and other publications gave rise to a mass of groupings of individuals throughout the UK and the Dominions. Social Credit study groups were to be found in most towns and cities throughout the UK and the Dominions. Many of these had arisen from existing organisations such as farmers' unions, trade unions or the university extension movement. Reading matter for discussion was obtained from Douglas' books and pamphlets published through mainstream presses and made available through the usual channels. In addition, from the early 1920s, small presses such as the Social Credit Press in London started to print introductory educational material, necessitating a degree of organisation. During the 1920s most of Douglas' work was publicised through the pages of *The New Age*, which was edited, after Orage's departure, by Arthur Brenton.

From as early as 1922 books and pamphlets explaining Social Credit began to appear alongside Douglas' original work. Often these were published by small presses which were sympathetic to Social Credit. C. Marshall Hattersley's *The Community's Credit* was published in 1923 by Credit Power Press which shared its business address with *The New Age*. Credit Power Press also published, in cloth and paperback, a verbatim report of Douglas' evidence to the Canadian Parliamentary Committee on Banking and Commerce, under the title *Canada's Bankers and Canada's Credit*. Dozens of minor publications appeared, and evidently found a market as most of them ran to several editions. Although most of this material originated in England, throughout the inter-war years it found its way across the world to Canada, Australia, New Zealand and South Africa, providing the subject matter for informed debate on the crucial issues of the times.

In 1924 *The New Age* appointed an Honorary Co-ordinating Secretary to facilitate the setting up of new Social Credit groups throughout the UK, and to co-ordinate the work of existing groups. Flyers were circulated outlining the objectives of the 'Social Credit Movement':

1. Our ultimate objective is, of course, to secure the adoption of Social Credit principles as an integral part of the economic mechanism of civilisation.

2. Our immediate objectives are (a) to bring home to the public the real cause of trade depression, poverty, and war; (b) to emphasise the enormous potentialities of the national productive capacity; (c) to direct attention to the true nature and function of money as the mechanism of distribution; (d) to press for an immediate and impartial inquiry into the relation of finance to production and consumption; and (e) to familiarise people with the idea of 'consumer credit' as a practical method of satisfying their needs for goods and services, which will at the same time enable finance to steer an absolutely safe course between the rocks and whirlpool – between Inflation and Deflation.

The flyers cite examples of good practice amongst existing groups. Social crediters were already approaching local and national public figures in religious organisations, business, education, politics and other walks of life to enlist their interest in, and support for, the dissemination of Social Credit on the lines indicated in the 'objectives'. The provision of literature, training of speakers, and printing of study material for the formation of new study groups formed part of the service offered. Requests for funds were evidently highly successful. In the June 12, 1924 edition of *The New Age*, activists or groups were listed in over forty towns and major cities in the U.K.

Groups normally met on a weekly basis to study social credit publications and to organise local campaigns. The policy was to work within existing organisations across the full political and religious spectrum of public life, rather than to set up a new political party or sectional interest-grouping. The appeal was to the general good, rather than to factions. By the late 1920s, however, more militant groupings started to appear in the UK, notably the Economic Freedom League, based in Coventry, which had set up its own journal, *Age of Plenty* by 1926. One such group, the 'Green Shirts for Social Credit', set up by John Hargrave in 1933, at first received endorsement from Douglas. Its banners, uniforms and one-line slogans, like: 'We want Social Credit, and we want it *NOW*', had widespread popular appeal throughout the country. Local news sheets such as the *Keighley Green Shirts Review* and *The Challenger,* were printed and circulated. Hargrave, however, sought to put up Social Credit candidates in opposition to existing political parties. Douglas quickly recognised that the polarisation of the debate in this way would prove counterproductive, as indeed the subsequent history of Social Credit in Alberta was to demonstrate.

The Social Credit Secretariat

Pressures for a national movement, not only from Hargrave and the Green Shirts, but also from a northern group based in the West Riding, led to the setting up by Douglas of the Social Credit Secretariat, and to the publication in 1934 of the weekly *Social Credit*. Despite persistent requests for Douglas to assume a leadership role in the activist wing of the movement, Douglas remained consistent in his view that *policy* formation and *administration* were two entirely separate functions. At no time did Douglas seek to set up a formal organisation to dictate *policies*. In his view, confusion in the political sphere had arisen through the persistent inability, on the part of the people and their representatives, to distinguish between the two functions. Hence the Secretariat was set up to be no more than an advisory body, headed by Douglas himself. Throughout its history the Secretariat has been directed by volunteers who had independent means of support. The strength of the movement lies in the freedom of thought and action of its activists who are not dependent on an income from the organisation for which they are working.

The Secretariat was set up as a bureau of information on how political and financial institutions of *administration* could be brought under the control of the will of the people. However, the speed and complexity of events made the situation urgent. There was every chance that significant numbers of Social crediters would in the immediate future be democratically elected, as members of mainstream political parties, both in the U.K. and in the Dominions. Without careful preparation, however, such election successes would be empty victories. If there was no authority like the Secretariat to provide the technical advice necessary to introduce effective legislation for change, elected Social Crediters would soon be subverted to the mainstream party machines. The holders of financial power behind the scenes could not, after all, be expected to relinquish control at the mere say-so of newly elected politicians. Douglas could have written the script for the *Yes, Minister!* television series. Following the events of 1931, when financial pressures brought down the Labour Government, Douglas, like many of his contemporaries, was aware of the constraints which could be placed upon a democratically elected government.

Extracts from Douglas' work, reproduced in Appendix 4b: The Buxton Speech, provide insights into his views on theory and practical organisation at the time when the decision was made to found the Secretariat. From the Buxton speech, it becomes evident that Douglas recognised the difference between putting across the case for a policy such as a National Dividend, and organising the expertise to bring the policy into practical implementation. For the latter to happen, it was necessary for considerable numbers of people to study Douglas' work over a period of time, in the same way as Orage had done in the year immediately following the First World War. Since career economists and politicians were taught the economic theories of orthodoxy, the Social Credit movement had to continue to rely on informal study groups for access to alternative economic theory.

By 1934, sixty study groups affiliated to the Social Credit Secretariat were listed in *Social Credit*, (September 21) in the U.K., with others recognised in the Dominions. Douglas' work was published, debated and reviewed in a range of newspapers and periodicals throughout the inter-war years. A key question in the studies was the feasibility of introducing economic security through a National Dividend.

The literature of economic democracy

A National Dividend would provide every individual citizen with the necessary purchasing power for self-respect and health *as a right,* regardless of the availability of employment, thus stabilising business conditions without the necessity for the generation of waste through activities like consumerism and war. The pensions and National Insurance system already in place form the beginnings of such a system, although their beneficial effects are neutralised by their being based upon taxation and means testing. The case for the National Dividend provided a central plank of the 1935 electoral platform in Alberta, which forms the subject of the following chapters. The Social Credit press was also outspoken about the operations of international diplomacy behind the scenes, and the role of the press in confusing the issues of unemployment, international trade and war. Following the Second World War, Social Credit was denounced as economically unsound, unpatriotic and anti-Semitic, as explained in Chapter 8.

Throughout the 'inter-war years' Douglas, O'Duffy and Social crediters who studied their writings were alive to the follies of an economy based on the principles of artificial scarcity coupled with self-interest. The text of Douglas' BBC Broadcast 'The Causes of War: Is Our Financial System to Blame?'[28] holds all profiteers to account, be they employers *or employees*, prepared to work for a financial reward regardless of the social usefulness of the industry in which they are employed.

At its very simplest, Social Credit literature can be reduced to three basic observations:

1. That finance is a man-made system, and as such can be consciously adapted and made to operate for the common good.

2. That money and work are two different kinds of value which cannot be exchanged.

3. That orthodox economists are hopelessly out of touch with the financial economics of the technological age which has moved beyond simple barter.

As O'Duffy explained with reference to Keynes in 1932:

He [Lord Keynes] looks upon the economic system as a thing existing *per se*; discusses most learnedly its parts and functions; and is deeply concerned that it shall work efficiently. But he seems almost unaware of its real purpose, and fails to observe, or, at any rate, to allow for, external conditions which must radically affect its actions. Thus in the whole of his comprehensive treatise he never mentions the fact that this is an age of plenty, and he thinks in terms of scarcity as tacitly as did Adam Smith two hundred years ago. The *Treatise on Money* is rather like a treatise on bicycles which might be written by a brilliant mechanic who knows all about the construction and working of a bicycle, but has forgotten that its primary purpose is to carry a man, and is imperfectly aware of the improvement of the roads since the eighteenth century.[29]

The subversion of all the value systems of society to financial considerations lay at the heart of the social question. Underlying the whole of Social Credit literature, and especially powerful in O'Duffy's work, is the horror and futility of poverty and war.[30] Controlled by financial interests, the press, academia and the media presented the public with the scenario that wars and periods of economic depression are natural occurrences which, like acts of God, have to be lived through as the price of eventual redemption. As O'Duffy was writing, men and women were vividly conscious of the white feather campaign and other pressures which had sent them to war in 1914, leaving ten million fighting men dead, and many others shell-shocked and maimed, for a cause which nobody could spell out with any confidence. People looked to the National Government of the 1930s to provide national solutions to the problems of unemployment, confident that there was not going to be another war, since peace would surely be negotiated. When war did resume in 1939, pacifists were blamed for delays in the re-armament programme, which was entered into with gusto, thus solving the 'unemployment' problem at a stroke. Over the subsequent decades of the twentieth century global corporatism was able to fend off serious challenges to its authority by mis-representing its opponent's arguments, and then challenging the misrepresentation.

Social Credit and the Labour Party 1934

H. Norman Smith, Prospective Labour Candidate for Faversham, blamed the 'bankers' ramp' (or swindle) for the collapse of the Labour Government in 1931. Writing in the national weekly *Social Credit* in September 1934, Smith summarised the results of the failure of the Labour leadership to adopt a Social Credit approach to policy formation twelve years earlier. Douglas' work would have enabled the Labour leadership to come up with the means to implement sound social policies. Instead, Labour was living in the past, before the power age, when scarcity dominated everyday lives. Labour Party policies flowed from the outdated assumption that in order to give to the poor it was necessary to take from the rich by nationalising everything. Perceptively, Smith observed:

> If you are going to make everyone work or starve you are going to establish the Slave State. I see precious little difference between Mussolini's Fascist Italy and Stalin's Communist Russia. Neither pretends to give the consumer a look-in. To me, if there is to be a decent industrial system, it must fulfil one condition: that any person, if they so wish, shall have the right to contract out of it without being deprived of an income. Only so can a person be truly free. The Work State is not less

a Slave State because slavery is universal. Only Douglas, with his Just Price and his National Dividend, shows the way to an industrial system wherein real freedom is possible.[31]

Nevertheless, Smith remained firmly an active member of the Labour Party because he shared its fundamental policy concerns. He believed that monopoly industries should not be run as private, centrally controlled concerns. He believed in slum clearance and municipal housing which should be freed from the burden of debt and interest charges which drove up rents. He concluded:

> How Social Credit technique would simplify Labour's task! But Labour made an ass of itself in 1931. It would not have made an ass of itself if it had listened to those of us who have learned Douglas.

Throughout the article quoted, Smith could assume familiarity on the part of the reader with Douglas' writings, which were widely discussed at the time.[32] Three years earlier, in 1931, the Labour Government had been brought down, and a 'National' coalition government brought in, because of Labour's inability to understand, and hence to control, international finance. Those who, like Smith, had thoroughly studied Douglas were in a much better position to base policies on sound judgements. As Smith wrote those words in 1934, leading lights in the Labour Party were touring the country, addressing meetings in all the major towns and cities in response to requests for discussion of the writings of Clifford Hugh Douglas. The Labour speakers sought to discredit Douglas because his teachings did not accord with the policies of 'sound finance' being taught in institutions of higher learning such as the London School of Economics.[33]

Social Credit and politics

Douglas insisted that social policies should be determined by the people who had to live by them, as communities of producers, consumers and citizens. Once policies are decided, the technicalities of finance and administration can be worked out. Although the pursuit of 'full employment' was an administrative decision, it was the fruit of a policy which would inevitably lead to waste, frustration and war. These observations, first published in 1919, in the immediate aftermath of the First World War, pre-dated and pre-dicted the depressions of the inter-war years. It was Douglas' contention that depression and war resulted from administrative policies which had their origins in the institutions of 'sound' finance.

Social Credit was never a protest against legitimate government. On the contrary, it emerged in reaction to the spurious internationalism which had spawned international profiteering and war on a world scale. It struck a chord across the world, being opposed to the international solidarity of waged labour, which led to the oppressive violence of the worker-slave state of Communism, and equally to centralised global corporatism. To this day, many misconceptions based upon untruthfulness are being circulated by powerful international interests. Furthermore, it is *only* in the interests of the powerful to discourage study of Social Credit by spreading inaccurate accounts of the world-wide Social Credit movement and the events in Alberta following the election of Aberhart in 1935. The Buxton Speech (see Appendix 4b) encapsulates the very Englishness of the origins of Social Credit, reflecting a true spirit of internationalism which respects the rights of all peoples to live in the harmony of self-determination. It is a declaration of the necessity for legitimate, workable government to be 'of the people, by the people and for the people'.

NOTES

1   What is described here is not the bombastic, patriotic British, but rather the English hobbit of Tolkien's *Lord of the Rings* to which people of peasant farming stock across the world can relate. See Curry (1998).

2   See, *e.g.*, Mabey (1997)

3   Orage (1926) p376

4   Jackson (2009)

5   Sheffield Educational Settlement Papers (2009)

6   Mansbridge (1920) ppxv-xvi

7   Quoted in Baker (1946) pp229-30. See also Temple 1927

8   Livingstone (1941) pviii

9   Mansbridge (1920) p46

10   Orage (1926)

11   See Sutton (1974) (1975) (1976)

12   Extract from an article by L.D. Byrne in *The Fig Tree*, and reproduced in the *Douglas Memorial Issue* of *The New Times*, Australia, 1979, page 4.

13   Gaitskell (1933) p348

14   For a detailed account of the events see Hutchinson and Burkitt (1997) pp95-103.

15   The text of Orage's broadcast is available at www.douglassocialcredit.com

16   House of Commons, Canada (1923)

17   The full text appears as an Appendix to Douglas (1931)

18   Quoted in *The New Age*, September 25, 1924.
19   The text of Douglas' evidence is included as an Appendix to Douglas (1931)
20   See Hutchinson and Burkitt (1997) for details.
21   Douglas (1934 Buxton) p1. See Appendix 4b for the text.
22   Douglas *op. cit.*
23   Douglas *op. cit.* p2
24   Douglas (1931)
25   Korten (1995) (2000)
26   O'Duffy (1933).
27   O'Duffy (1932)
28   Reprinted from *The Listener*, 5 December 1934, in later editions of Douglas (1931)
29   O'Duffy (1932) pp222-3
30   See Appendix 3 Goshawk.
31   Smith (1934)
32   See www.douglassocialcredit.com for access to Social Credit literature currently available.
33   See Chapter 7 for more details.

Appendix 4a
Social Credit Literature

Social Credit Literature to 1952

Social Credit literature can be divided into five categories:
(a) Books by Clifford Hugh Douglas
(b) Pamphlets by Clifford High Douglas
(c) Books and Pamphlets by other Social crediters
(d) Periodicals
(e) Reference material in libraries, *e.g.*, Government Reports.

(a) Books by Clifford Hugh Douglas

Economic Democracy: First published in serial form in *The New Age* (1918/19/20), this key text was published as follows:
Harcourt, Brace and Howe, New York: 1920, First American edition
Cecil Palmer, London 1920, 1921 (reprinted), 1928 (158 pages)
Stanley Nott, London 1934 (fourth, revised edition)
The Social Credit Press, Melbourne, 1930

Credit-Power and Democracy
Cecil Palmer, London, 1920, 1921 (212 pages)
Stanley Nott, London, 1931, 1934 (Fourth enlarged edition)(211 pages)
Social Credit Press, Melbourne, 1933 (1st Australian edition)

In 1922 the publishers, Cecil Palmer, used an extract from a review in *The Times* as publicity:
'Major Douglas's proposals, outlined and explained in this volume, have for some months occupied an important place among the various plans put forward to counter the economic crisis through which the country is passing. It is indeed possible that before many months have passed we may see them proposed. It would surely be a good thing, therefore, in a country which prides itself upon being a democracy, that such ideas as these should be canvassed publicly and some definite opinion formed on them.' – *The Times*

These Present Discontents and the Labour Party and Social Credit
Cecil Palmer, London, 1922 (46 pages)

The Control and Distribution of Production
Cecil Palmer, London, 1922 (175 pages)
Stanley Nott, London, 1934 (revised edition)

In 1922 the publishers, Cecil Palmer, described this book as follows:
'*This book is a commentary and a re-statement from several points of view of the Author's convictions on the credit and price regulation problems, which are now being discussed all over the world, and notably in the Canadian and South African Parliaments, where it is recognised that the problems with which they deal are at the heart of the general and growing unrest.*
'They link up the proposals with the moving tide of events and will be found of much assistance in bringing them into correct relation with the industrial, financial and economic situation.'

Social Credit
Cecil Palmer, London 1924 (1ˢᵗ edition, 223 pages), 1926.
Eyre Spottiswoode London 1933 (3ʳᵈ revised edition), 1934, 1937.
W.W. Norton, N.Y. 1933 (1ˢᵗ American edition)

The Monopoly of Credit
Chapman & Hall, London, 1931, 1933 (128 pages)
Eyre & Spottiswoode, London, 1937 (revised and enlarged)
KRP, Belfast and Tidal, Sydney (1951, 1958)(Third revision) (165 pages)
Centenary Reprint, U.K., Australia, Canada, New Zealand, South Africa
   (1979) (189 pages)

Warning Democracy (1931)
C.M. Grieve, London 1931 (207 pages)
Stanley Nott, London 1934

The Alberta Experiment
Eyre & Spottiswoode, London, 1937 (220 pages)
Veritas, Australia, 1984

Major C. H. Douglas Speaks (1933) A collection of essays and papers by
   Major Douglas. Sydney: Douglas Social Credit Association.

Mairet, Philip (1934) *The Douglas Manual,*
London: Stanley Nott. (HB 116)
Toronto, J.M.Dent 1934
Coward McCann, NY 1935

(b) Pamphlets and Papers by Clifford Hugh Douglas

The Douglas Theory: A Reply to Mr. J.A. Hobson. (1922) London. Cecil
  Palmer.
These Present Discontents: The Labour Party and Social Credit. (1922) London.
  Cecil Palmer. (44 pages). (1938 price 1s)
The Breakdown of the Employment System, (1923), (Newcastle Speech)
  Manchester Economic Research Association. Institute of Economic
  Democracy reprint (1979) (12 pages).
The New and the Old Economics (1932) Sydney. Tidal Publications (1973
  reprint) (28 pages).
The New and the Old Economics (1932) London. Stanley Nott (25 pages)
Reconstruction (1932) (Articles from Glasgow Evening Times) Reprinted
  1943, Liverpool, KRP. Reprinted Queensland. Social Credit School of
  Studies (12 pages).
The Monopolistic Idea (1934) (Melbourne Speech) Institute of Economic
  Democracy reprint (1979) (16 pages).
The Use of Money (1934) (Christchurch, New Zealand Speech) Liverpool.
  KRP. (24 pages) 6d.
The Nature of Democracy (Buxton Speech) (1934) (1963) Institute of
  Economic Democracy 1978 reprint. (12 pages)
Social Credit Principles. 1d
Money and the Price System (1935) (Oslo Speech) London. Stanley Nott.
  (Institute of Economic Democracy 1978 reprint) (16 pages).
The Approach to Reality (1936), London, KRP (27 pages)
Dictatorship by Taxation (1936) (Belfast Speech) Vancouver, Institute of
  Economic Democracy 1979 reprint. (16 pages)
The Tragedy of Human Effort (1936) (Liverpool Address) Liverpool. KRP (16
  pages)
The Policy of a Philosophy (1937) (London Speech) Institute of Economic
  Democracy 1977 reprint, (20 pages).
Whose Service is Perfect Freedom (1939) 1983 Reprint. Western Australia.
  Veritas. (85 pages).
This 'American' Business (1940) Liverpool. KRP (8 pages).
The Big Idea, (1942), Liverpool. KRP. (64 pages)

How Alberta is Fighting Finance (c1940) Liverpool. KRP.

The Land for the (Chosen) People Racket, (1943), Liverpool KRP. (60 pages)

Programme for the Third World War, (1943), Liverpool, KRP. (60 pages)

Brief for the Prosecution, (1945), Liverpool, KRP. (88 pages)

The Realistic Position of the Church of England (1948) Liverpool. KRP. (15 pages)

Realistic Constitutionalism (1947) Liverpool. KRP (12 pages).

Security: Institutional and Personal (1937) Liverpool: K.R.P (12 pages)

Tyranny: Taxation System a Device for Exercising Despotic Pressure (nd), reprinted from *Social Credit,* (January 17, 1936.) London: Social Credit Secretariat Limited.

(c) Books and Pamphlets by Social Crediters

Aberhart, William (1935) *Social Credit Manual: Social Credit as Applied to the Province of Alberta: Puzzling Questions and Their Answers.* (64 pages).

Adams, Capt. W. (1925) *Real Wealth & Financial Poverty,* London, Cecil Palmer. HB (280 pages).

Allen, F. Stanley (1938) *Money: The Question of the Age.* Sydney.

Ashby, Patrick, M.P. (1946) *Electoral and Parliamentary Reform—On Advice of C. H. Douglas.* Edmonton: Pioneer Press Ltd.

Bedford, The Duke of (nd, Second Edition) *Debt-Free Prosperity.* (9 pages)

Bedford, The Duke of (nd, Fifth Edition) *The Absurdity of the National Debt.* Mexborough: The Social Credit Co-ordinating Centre. (7 pages)

Bedford, The Duke of (nd) *Poverty and Over-Taxation: The Way Out,* The Duke of Bedford. (48 pages)

Bedford, The Duke of (nd, Reprint) *The Neglected Issue.* Metarie: Sons of Liberty Reprint. Original publisher unknown.

Brenton, Arthur G (nd) *Through Consumption to Prosperity*

Brenton, Arthur, *The Veil of Finance,* 1926 (1974 Reprint) Dublin: Revisionist Press.

Britain's Changing Economy (1950) Mexborough: Social Credit Co-ordinating Centre. Leeds Conference.

Byrne, L.D. (nd) *Alternative to Disaster.* London: The Social Credit Secretariat Ltd.

Byrne, L.D. (1943) 'The Abomination Which Maketh Desolate.' Reprinted from the Edmonton Bulletin, November 11, 1943.

Byrne, L.D. (1943) 'Battle for Freedom.' Address to Rocky Mountain House Board of Trade, May 10, 1943. Edmonton: The Social Credit Board.

Byrne, L.D. (nd) *Debt and Taxation.* London: The Social Credit Secretariat Limited.

Byrne, L.D. (1941) 'Democratic Victory or the Slave State? Address to Monetary Reform Convention in Winnipeg, October, 1941. Liverpool: K.R.P. Publications Limited.

Byrne, L.D. (1946, 1977 Reprint) *Faith, Power and Action.* Flesherton: Canadian League of Rights.

Byrne, L.D. (nd) *Social Credit and Party Politics – a Warning.* Auckland, Conservative Publications.

Byrne, L.D. (Third Annual Convention of the Alberta Social Credit League) 'The Menace of Dictatorship.' Winnipeg: *The Social Credit Review.*

Byrne, L.D. (1936) 'The Nature of Social Credit.' Address to National Dividend Club of London. Edmonton: Republished by the Social Credit Board.

Byrne, L. Denis (1959, 1970 reprint with Foreword) *Submission made to the Senate Standing Committee on Finance on the Threat of Inflation in Canada.* Ottawa: Queen's Printer.

C.G.M. (1932, Revised 1967) *The Nation's Credit: A Précis of Major Douglas' Proposals.* Leeds: The British Social Credit Society.

Chastenet, J.L. (1926, Translated from the French by C. H. Douglas) *The Bankers' Republic.* London: Cecil Palmer.

Colbourne, Maurice (1928) *Unemployment or War*, New York, Coward McCann Inc.

Colbourne, Maurice (1933) *The Meaning of Social Credit*, London. Figurehead. Reprinted April 1934, March 1935, November 1935. Edmonton. Social Credit Board November 1935 revised edition (284 pages) Formerly *Economic Nationalism.*

Colbourne, Maurice (nd) *The Sanity of Social Credit.*

Corke, Helen (c. 1935) *From Scarcity to Plenty: A Short Course in Economic History: From the 17th Century to the Present Day.* Mexborough. SCCC. (28 pages).

Corky, Rev. Prof. (nd) *Social Credit Restated.* Belfast: The Douglas Social Credit Movement (Belfast Group).

Cousens, Hilderic (1921) *A New Policy for Labour: An Essay on the Relevance of Credit Control.* London: Cecil Palmer.

Day, G.W.L. and G.F. Powell (nd) *How to Get What You Want.*2d.

Dee, Elles (1933) *Economics for Everybody: The Intelligent Enquirer's Guide to Wisdom.* London: 'Social Credit.'(38 pages)

Demant V.A. (nd) *This Unemployment* .

Dobree, Bonamy (1935) *An Open Letter to a Professional Man.* London:
Stanley Nott Ltd.

Dunn, E.M. (c1935) *The New Economics: Social Credit Principles and Proposals.*
London. Credit Research Library.

Edwards, Elizabeth (c1943) *The Planners and Bureaucracy.* Liverpool. K.R.P.
Publications Limited. (30 pages).

Galloway C.F.J. (Chairman of the National Credit Association of Great
Britain) (1926) *Poverty Amidst Plenty: A Scientific Anachronism; Being a
Simple Introduction to Social Credit.* London. (October 1931, Jan. 1942,
May 1932, June 1932, April 1933, and July 1933 reprints in Melbourne).
Total print run to this date: 10,000. (48 pages)

Galway, J. B. (nd) *The Power of Money.* Liverpool: K.R.P. Publications
Limited. (20 pages).

Gibson, A.L. (c1935) *What is this Social Credit?* (nd) A.L. Gibson.

Gordon-Cumming, M. (Jan. 1932) *Introduction to Social Credit.* London.
C.W. Daniel (May 1932, Feb. 1933, Dec 1933 reprints) 40 pages.

Gordon-Cumming, M. (c1935) *Money in Industry.*

Guthrie, James (nd) *To What End? An Analysis of Modern Society.* Melbourne:
New Times Ltd.

Hargrave, John (1937) *Official Report Alberta,* London: Social Credit Party of
Great Britain and Northern Ireland.

Hargrave, John (1945) *Social Credit Clearly Explained: 101 Questions Answered.*
London. SCP. (67 pages).

Hattersley, C. Marshall, *This Age of Plenty* (nd)

Hattersley, C. Marshall, (1937) *Wealth, Want and War.* Mexborough,
England. Social Credit Co-ordinating Centre (1953 reprint). (350 pages)

Hickling, George (nd) *Social Debt or Social Credit.* London: The Social Credit
Press. (20 pages).

Hickling, George (nd) *Social Debt or Social Credit.* (20 pages).

Hollow, Joseph T. (1936) *Capital and Income.* Melbourne: The Advocate
Press. (24 pages).

Holter, E. Sage (c1935) *The ABC of Social Credit.*

Hooke, Hon. A. J. (1945) 'The Eclipse of Democracy.' Address before the
Alberta Legislature at Regular Session, 1945. Edmonton: The Social
Credit Board. (30 pages).

Jones, Tudor (1935) *You and Parliament.* London: Figurehead.

Johnson, Very Rev. Hewlett (Dean of Canterbury) (nd) *Social Credit and the
War on Poverty.*

Joseph, A.W. (1934, 2nd reprint 1971) *The A + B Theorem* (20 pages).

Joseph, A.W. (1935) Banking and Industry. Birmingham Douglas Social Credit Group. (16 pages).

Joseph, A.W. (1935) *Banking and Industry*. Birmingham Social Credit Group. (16 pages)

Jukes, Major A. H. (1943) 'Dictatorship by Stealth.' Address to the Rotary Club of Victoria, July 29, 1943. (20 pages).

Jukes, Major A. H. (1943) 'Straws in the Wind.' Address to Post-War Reconstruction Group of the Vancouver Board of Trade, April 13, 1943. Jukes, Major A. H. (1943) 'The Third Resolvent.' Address to Kiwanis Club of Vancouver, January 14, 1943.

Larkin, J. Crate (nd) *From Debt to Prosperity: The Proposals of Social Credit.* New York: National Social Credit Association. (82 pages).

Macintyre, A. Hamilton (nd) *Social Credit* 3d.

Monahan, Bryan W. (1947) *An Introduction to Social Credit.* KRP/Tidal Publications 1967 reprint. (136 pp).

Moore, T. J. (1936) *Can Gift Money be Cancelled?* Melbourne: New Times Pty, Ltd. (24 pages).

Muir, Edwin (nd) *Social Credit and the Labour Party*

Munson, Gorham, (1945) *Aladdin's Lamp: The Wealth of the American People*, New York, Creative Age Press

Murray, H. Middleton (c1935) *The A + B Theorem*. London. Stanley Nott Ltd.

Murray, H. Middleton (1929) *An Outline of Social Credit*, London. The New Age Press. (52 pages).

Murray, H. Middleton (1957) *The Struggle for Money*. Glasgow. William Maclellan. (93 pages. Hardback)

National Credit Association. *Economics for Everybody* (1933) 37 pages.

O'Duffy, Eimar, (1932) *Life and Money: Being a Critical Examination of the Principles and Practice of Orthodox Economics with A Practical Scheme to End the Muddle it has made of our Civilisation* (1932) London and New York. Putnam. 292 pages. (Revised and enlarged edition 1933)

O'Duffy, Eimar, (1933) *Asses in Clover*. Charlbury. Jon Carpenter (2003 edition) (330 pages)

O'Duffy, Eimar (1934) *Consumer Credits* London. Prosperity League.

Orage, A.R. (1943) *The BBC Speech on Social Credit* and *The Fear of Leisure* Vancouver Institute of Economic Democracy 1977 reprint. (32 pages)

Pound, Ezra (1935) *Social Credit: An Impact*, London. Stanley Nott. 31 pages.

Powell, G. F. (nd) *What is Democracy?* London: J.M. Dent and Sons Ltd.

Rands, R.S.J. (1933) *The Abolition of Poverty*. Ipswich. W.E. Harrison. Reprinted May 1933, July 1933, Revised May 1934, November 1934, May 1935. (22 pages).

Rands, R.S.J. (c1935) *A Simple Outline of Douglas Social Credit*. (5s a hundred, post free).

Read, Herbert (c1935) *Essential Communism*

Reckitt Maurice B., *Faith and Society* (nd)

Southampton Chamber of Commerce Report of the Economic Crisis Committee with Introduction by L. Denis Byrne (1933, 1977 Reprint). Vancouver: The Institute of Economic Democracy.

Rhys, W.H. (1930, Final Edition 1932) *Real Wealth and Financial Poverty: A Synopsis of the Douglas Social Credit Proposals*. Melbourne: Social Credit Press. (68 pages).

R.L. (1933) *The ABC of Finance and Social Credit* (1933) Edinburgh: The Scots Free Press. (24 pages).

Smith, Norman (1944, Reprint of 1946) *The Politics of Plenty,* Nottingham: Social Credit Co-ordinating Centre by arrangement with George Allen and Unwin, Ltd.

Smith, R. Rogers (1937) *Alberta has the Sovereign Right to Issue and Use its Own Credit: A Factual Examination of the Constitutional Problem*. Ottawa: R. Rogers Smith.

Social Credit Secretariat (1946) Elements of Social Credit. Liverpool. Social Credit Secretariat. (HB 130 pages)

Symons, W.T. (c1931) *The Coming of Community*, London: The C. W. Daniel Company.

Symons, W.T. and Tait, Fred (1926) *The Just Price: A Financial Policy for the Independent Labour Party*. London: Published by the authors and obtainable from the Labour Literature Depot and Credit Research Library (35 pages).

Tait, Fred (nd) *The Douglas Theory and its Communal Implications*. 3d.

Tankerville, Earl of (1934, Fourth reprint 1977 with Introduction by L. D. Byrne) *Poverty Amidst Plenty*. Vancouver: Institute of Economic Democracy.

Tavistock, The Marquis of (c1935, 1977 Reprint with Introduction by L. D. Byrne) *Short Papers on Money*. Vancouver: Institute of Economic Democracy.

Tavistock, The Marquis of (c1935) *Poverty and Over-Taxation*.

Thompson, Robert N. (1936) *The Social Credit Handbook*. Winnipeg:

Manitoba Social Credit League.

Venison, Arthur (c1935) *Social Credit Themes (Poems)*

Ward, William (c1935) *The National Dividend: A Symposium by 16 Public Men.* London: Stanley Nott Limited.

Webb, Norman (1937). Reprinted from *The Fig Tree*, September, 1937, *Social Credit and the Christian Ethic.* London: The Social Credit Press.

Webb, Norman (c1937) *The Happy Mean – a Political Pamphlet.*

Wigley, W.H. (1935, Fourth Impression 1942 with Foreword) *Why Tolerate Poverty? Poverty in Gt. Britain is now entirely unnecessary.* Mexborough: Social Credit Co-ordinating Centre. (23 pages) 2d.

Willett, Jean Campbell (nd) *Women and Poverty.* London. The Social Credit Press.

Young, W. Allen (1921, Second Ed.) *'Dividends for All.'* London: Cecil Palmer.

(d) Periodicals

Alberta Social Credit Clarion (1935, Monthly). Edmonton.

Credit Notes (Successor to the *S.C.S. Bulletin* and incorporating *The Social Credit Gazette* and *Credit Times*) Leeds, British Social Credit Society.

New Britain (c1935, Published Quarterly) London: W. H. Smith and Son Ltd. A wide variety of contributors including C. H. Douglas, Philip Mairet, Prof. F. Soddy.

The Free Man (c. 1935) (Weekly) Edinburgh.

The New Age (1907-1938) Weekly 8" x 13" (12 x 33 cm) 12 pages

Social Credit (1934-1938) Weekly. Vols 1 & 2, 8 ?" x 13" (12 x 33 cm) 12 pages. Vols. 3-6, 12" x 18 " (33 x 46 cm) 16 pages.

The New English Weekly (1932-1949)

New Era (Sydney, Australia) c1934 -

Prosperity (St. Peter's Vicarage, Paynes Lane, Coventry.)

Reality, George Hickling

The Age of Plenty (Monthly)

The Social Crediter (1938) Weekly. 8 "x 11" (22 x 28 cm) 12 pages (by 1952, 8 pages)(2002- 12 pages Quarterly.

The Social Credit Standard c1934-

The Fig Tree (1936 – 1939) Quarterly. 6" x 9 " (15cm x 24) c. 100 pages.

The New Era (Australian)

The New Times (Australian)

Abundance (United Kingdom)

The Albertan, Daily (Merged with Alberta Social Credit Chronicle, and fully endorsed by Alberta Social Credit Government. See *Social Credit*, March 13, 1936, p38.

The Canadian Social Crediter, Social Credit Association of Canada.

Today & Tomorrow (Canadian – endorsed by the Alberta Social Credit League, Premier William Aberhart and the Social Credit Secretariat, England).

(f) Reference Material

The Proceedings of the Select Standing Committee on Banking and Commerce of the Canadian House of Commons (1923). House of Commons, Canada, *on Bill No. 83, An Act Respecting Banks and Banking.*

Canada's Bankers and Canada's Credit: Being the verbatim report of Major Douglas's evidence before the Canadian Parliamentary committee on Banking and Commerce at Ottawa (1923) London. Credit Power Press.

Macmillan Committee, (1931) *Great Britain Committee on Finance and Industry, Minutes of Evidence taken before the Committee on Finance and Industry* (1930) *(Macmillan Report)* , London: HMSO. Chairman the Rt. Hon. H.P. Macmillan, K.C. (The Statement of Evidence submitted by Major Douglas, is reprinted as an appendix to *The Monopoly of Credit.*)

Major C. H. Douglas before the New Zealand Government's Monetary Committee, Notes of Evidence and Examinations with Correspondence preliminary thereto (1934).

First Interim Report on the Possibilities of the Application of Social Credit Principles to the Province of Alberta submitted to His Majesty's Premier and Legislative Council of Alberta, at Edmonton, Alberta May 23, 1935 by Major C. H. Douglas.

The Douglas System of Social Credit, evidence taken by the Agricultural Committee of the Alberta Legislature, Session 1934.

The Existing Financial System in Relation to Post-War Reconstruction being the Interim Report by the Sub-Committee on Finance of the Alberta Post-War Reconstruction Committee, December, 1943.

Appendix 4b
The Buxton Speech

Extract from
The Nature of Democracy: Address at Buxton, June 9, 1934
By Clifford Hugh Douglas

On 9th June 1934, Douglas gave the following address at Buxton. Part I, in which Douglas gave details of his recent world tour, has been omitted, but can be read in full on www.douglassocialcredit.com .

PART II

The Social Credit Movement has three aspects which are quite distinct and require different treatment. The first is persuasive, the second is educative, the third militant. The first assumes a large body of uninstructed individuals having certain desires, of which, for our purposes, economic security and abundance are primary, and our persuasive activity is in the nature of explaining that these desires have a realistic basis and can be satisfied. It should be predominantly a description of the results of a Social Credit policy as compared with the present. The second aspect is more precisely technical, and is properly addressed to a much smaller audience, and has to do with the technical means for embodying the desires of the majority of the population. It assumes a willingness on the part of special technicians to embody the desires of the majority, when satisfied that this is physically possible. The third aspect assumes the existence of a powerful resistance to change, a resistance which, while relying for its effectiveness on the uninstructed majority, rests ultimately on a conscious desire to preserve certain unjustifiable privileges at the expense of the general population.

We have now sufficient troops who want to be led. I think it can be said with regard to the persuasive and educative aspects that we have not made big mistakes; in fact our progress has been phenomenal. Nowadays much of our propaganda is being done for us by the references, which cannot be kept out of the Press, to the existence of abundance in all directions.

To carry out any big operations, such as the realisation of Social Credit, a mechanism is necessary, and our choice lies between using the existing mechanism or inventing a new one. I think that it is true to say, that for any practical policy, at least the embryo of a suitable mechanism exists, even though it may be in a distorted form, and to suppose that you can invent an entirely new mechanism in the face of custom and habit and use it for introducing a new system of society is just plain, bald nonsense.

It has frequently been alleged of the Social Credit Movement that it mixes politics with economics. If the foregoing phases of the Movement be accepted as legitimate, such a combination is necessary and inevitable. No fundamental changes in mechanism can become a part of the daily routine of this or any other country except with the aid, passive or active, of the sanctions of government ultimately residing in the armed forces of the Crown.

The theory of the British Constitution, which is a democracy, is that the armed forces of the Crown exist to ensure that the will of the people should prevail. No convention or laws can stand for any length of time against the will of the people, and anybody who is acquainted with the theory of international law will know what I mean when I refer to the 'right of eminent domain', which is simply that if any law or convention is operating in defiance of the will of the people it will inevitably be modified.

During the trip around the world which I have just completed I was able to obtain what may be called a bird's-eye view of world events. It is possible, of course, that I may be mistaken, but I do not think I am. What I found was all over the world there is an organised campaign in progress to discredit democracy, and when I say 'organised' it does not necessarily mean that it emanates from some particular source. The method used in this campaign is to point to the chaos which, as we know, is unquestionably due to finance, and to start by substituting for democracy a form of administration either under the name of Communism, Fascism, or a National Recovery Administration,[1] or rationalisation or planned economy, all of which are fundamentally similar, in that they aim at thwarting the public will.

The form that any of these methods takes is the employment of a number of second-rate experts who proceed to tell a number of first-rate experts how to run their business, with the inevitable result that the second lot of experts eventually refuse to co-operate.

The allegation, then, is that democracy is ineffective and that the interference of governments in business is the cause of the present breakdown of business. The remedy put forward at this point is dictatorship.

The drive behind the desire to substitute various forms of dictatorship for the democratic machine is the desire to employ the forces of the State to impose the policy of international finance and trustified [corporate] industry upon the general population.

PART III

In order to understand the unquestionable failure of present democracy it is necessary to understand its nature, what it can do from its nature, and what it cannot do. The literal meaning of the word is, of course, 'rule by the people', but I should prefer to call it the will of the people. It is not rule by the majority, an important distinction to note. The idea of party government is comparatively modern, probably not ante-dating the Wars of the Roses, and contains in itself a subtle perversion of the democratic idea.

Now 'the people' is a collective term which, in order to make its nature clearer, may be translated as 'the mob'. I am not substituting what may appear to be a derogatory word for one which appears to be more respectable, with a view to expressing contempt for the population considered collectively, but because a good deal of attention has been devoted to the psychology of mobs, and the conclusions, where they are sound, are obviously applicable to democracy. The outstanding feature of a mob is that it does not reason, or certainly does not reason effectively. Its conclusions as based upon reason can be stated, with confidence, to be almost invariably wrong. A mob feels, it does not think, and consequently by whatever mechanisms we represent a mob, we can represent only a desire, not a technique. It is, of course, possible to contend that the desires of a mob are always and frequently wrong. ... It is quite certain that desire, emotion, or feeling, however you wish to phrase it, is plastic and possesses from its nature a strong desire to clothe itself in forms, so that if a mob shouts 'We want food and shelter' it is easy to get it to translate that into a cry 'We want work', which is, of course, not at all the same thing.

Now in this country we have evolved a mechanism of election which is alleged to be for the purpose of making the will of the mob evident. But the most cursory examination of the slogans on which elections are fought is sufficient to show that the machinery has been completely perverted. We elect Parliamentary representatives at the present time to pass laws of a highly technical nature, not to ensure that certain results are achieved. As a result of this, not merely in this country but everywhere in the world, so far as my observation takes me, we are witnessing a set of second-rate experts in the seats of governments ineffectively endeavouring to give technical directions to a set of first-rate experts who are actually carrying on the functions by which society lives.

Perhaps the most outstanding and possibly the final instance, under an alleged democracy, of this process can be witnessed in Washington at the present time, where may be found previously unemployed individuals expressly appointed and busy, generally for fourteen or sixteen hours a day, in inquiring into how each separate trade and industry in the United States is run, and instructing the directors of businesses in that trade how to do it some other way from that which has up til now proved successful. This is not quite so true in regard to finance as it is in regard to other businesses, but it is beginning to be true in regard to finance.

PART IV

Now I have no doubt whatever that that select group of international financiers who desire to rivet the rule of finance upon the world are observing this process with complete satisfaction, and they are using the situation which they themselves have brought about, and with which governments are effectively meddling, to support the idea that the whole cause of the trouble is the meddling in business of governments and government officials who do not understand business. They are using this argument most effectively as an argument for sweeping away that control over their destinies which people were in process of obtaining through the centuries, and substituting a dictatorship which will enthrone an international oligarchy permanently. I have no doubt also that this is the vital problem which concerns all the people of the world at this moment. To put it another way, *while nothing but Social Credit will provide a mechanism, nothing but the rehabilitation of democracy in a genuine sense, and with an understanding of its limits, will enable Social Credit to become an actual fact* [emphasis added].

There is a key word which forms the solution of this, perhaps the greatest of all problems which confront the world at the present time. That word is 'responsibility'. We have got to make individuals bear the consequences of their actions.

Instead of electing representatives to inform bankers and industrialists (who understand the technique of their jobs perfectly) how to do them, and to pass a multitude of laws which, while providing unnecessary jobs for large numbers of people who could be better employed, still further impede industry, the business of democracy is to elect representatives who will insist upon results, and will, if necessary, pillory the actual individuals who are responsible for their non-attainment. It is not a bit of use asking democracies to decide upon matters of technique, and it is quite certain, as has already been demonstrated, that if you throw a plan to a democracy it will be torn to shreds.

It is not the business of the Parliamentary machine to reform, for instance, the financial system. It *is* the business of the Parliamentary machine to transmit the desires of the people for results (which at present the financial system is not producing) out of the financial system, and to transmit to the people the names of individuals who are responsible for the financial system, so that by the exercise of the right of Eminent Domain, which has undoubtedly been established as vested in the representatives of the people, they may, if necessary, take steps to remove those responsible for impeding the will of the people. If it is pleaded in extenuation, that those in charge of any particular function of State, such as finance, do not know how to produce the desired results, then it is the business of Parliament to provide them with the advice available. But if they will neither take action within a reasonable period of time, and will not accept advice if provided, then it is the business of the representatives of the people to remove them, whether they are alleged to be operating under a system of private enterprise or as public departments.

PART V

The application of these principles to the policy of the Social Credit Movement is, I think, clear enough, and follows much along the lines of the three aspects of the Movement that I have previously discussed. It does, in fact correspond not unsatisfactorily with the activities of the Movement up to the present time. One section of the Movement, the largest, has been charged with the task of clarifying the desires of the general population, by which I mean the integration of popular will to a united objective without specification of mechanism. One of the most effective methods is by explaining what would be the result of Social Credit as compared with those we know to arise out of the present system. I think that most admirable work has been done along these lines.

In another, necessarily smaller, section of the Movement those of us who are sufficiently fortunately placed to devote a large portion of our attention to the matter may legitimately qualify to be experts on mechanism.

From now on, however, I believe that the most immediately important aspect of the matter is the formulation of methods for bringing Parliament itself, and consequently the forces of the Crown, which Parliament controls, under popular control in regard to objectives, I would again repeat, and not in regard to mechanics. This amounts to bringing pressure to bear upon the individual Member of Parliament, and he is interested in only two things: the first is in keeping his job, and the second is in knowing how much voting power is behind any demand made upon him.

I think in every part of the country where a Social Credit Group exists, or can be formed, an organisation should be set up at once for the systematic presentation of the situation to every voter in the district. One by one the voters should be asked whether they are in favour of a larger personal income, with absolute security, via the National Dividend. Sufficient information should be placed before them to show that this is possible. This is a job for the rank and file. The electors should then be asked for a pledge to vote for no candidate who is not prepared to demand that dividend. Every sitting member of Parliament should be notified at a suitable time of the number of individuals whose support has been obtained, and should be asked whether he is prepared to proceed along certain lines which will be explained to him, and informed that he will not be supported unless he is. If any sitting Member of Parliament is not willing to give such an assurance, a new candidate should be nominated.

Although this policy has been sketched only in outline, I am fully conscious of the magnitude of the task that I am laying upon you. You will be advised on tactics by the Secretariat from time to time. To say, however, that it is a matter of life and death is to underestimate the case. If civilisation, not merely for this generation but for many generations to come, is to be saved for a tolerable existence, it requires primarily a tremendous amount of collective will, such as perhaps the world has never seen in peace time, although it is not unknown in times of war. If this collective will can be mobilised in times of so-called peace, as it has been mobilised in times of war, nothing can resist it. If it cannot, then we have indeed lost the peace, whatever we did with the war.

Chapter 5
The Run Up to 1935 in Alberta

On 22nd August 1935 the citizens of the Canadian Province of Alberta elected a Social Credit Government by an overwhelming majority. Out of a total of 63 seats in the Legislative Assembly, 57 were taken by Social Credit members. None of those elected, including the Premier, William Aberhart, had ever previously run for election, still less held political office. The event was of such significance that it was reported in local and national newspapers across the world. Over subsequent decades vast sums of money were expended in presenting the event as a rebellious act against legitimate government, a mindless reaction to the poverty amidst plenty caused by the economic depression of the times, which hit the prairie provinces particularly hard, and a dangerous heresy which must not be allowed to set a precedent. Although their democratically elected representatives were frustrated at every turn in their attempts to introduce practical legislation consistent with Douglas' economic theory, the people of Alberta refused to buckle down to the finance-controlled party system. Time after time they re-elected Social Credit representatives at the polls. Eventually, the so-called 'nonsense' was stamped out, as the Albertan 'Douglasites' were removed from office and the remaining politicians could be described as 'Social Credit' in name only. Although Social Credit was a political force in other Canadian provinces, in the Canadian Federal Parliament, in Australia, New Zealand and elsewhere, including the U.K., the democratic challenge to the conventional party machines was never as great as in Alberta between 1935 and the death of Aberhart in 1943.

The pioneers of Alberta

In 1901, the population of Alberta was 73,022, rising rapidly to 185,000 by the time the state joined the Confederation in 1905. Of these, the majority, 127,000 were farmers and ranchers. Alberta's first citizens were characterised by a strong democratic spirit. In the decision to make their new home in the undeveloped country that was the West of Canada, they sought the democratic freedoms and economic security denied to them in the social environments which they left behind. The story of the rural and urban poverty which accompanied the growth of agribusiness and industrialisation in Europe is well documented. Alf Hooke, who subsequently became a leading member of the Albertan Legislative Assembly, provides some indication of the circumstances which led his own family to migrate to Alberta.[1] The independence of spirit of the prairie farmers is demonstrated by the problems they tackled in seeking to farm unfamiliar soils under very different climatic conditions from those traditions in which they had been reared as children and young people.

From the earliest years of the twentieth century, Alberta's pioneer settlers took command of their institutional framework with a view to protecting the interests of the local rural population. The establishment of a Provincial Legislature in 1905 was paralleled by the establishment of the Society of Equity and the Farmers' Association. In 1909, these bodies amalgamated to form the United Farmers of Alberta (U.F.A.). As early as 1913 attempts were made to overcome some of the commercial hazards confronting the growing farm population in their grain marketing problems. Modelled on similar ventures in Manitoba and Saskatchewan, the Alberta Co-operative Elevator Company was founded with this end in view. At the outbreak of the First World War in 1914, the municipal franchise had already been extended to women. Shortly afterwards Alberta led the world in electing women members to the Legislature.

In 1921 the United Farmers of Alberta took the decisive step of becoming a political party, going on to elect a Government to replace the Liberals who had been in office since 1905. The U.F.A. had originally been organised as a non-political group. The decision to enter politics followed the realisation of members that the traditional two-party structure of Liberals and Conservatives from the old country was ineffectual in dealing with the economic and financial problems of the productive farmers in the West of Canada. In view of later events, this decision was of major significance. Within the ranks of the U.F.A. were a sprinkling of immigrants from the U.S.A. who were followers of the monetary reformer William Jennings Bryan.

Study of monetary reform ideas

The notion that the study of economics, finance, politics and related issues should be confined within a university curriculum did not have common currency in those early pioneering days in Alberta, or indeed in Canada as a whole and the rest of the English-speaking world. In the 1920s and 1930s ordinary men and women took it upon themselves to organise self-help study groups, drawing upon the writings and lectures of leading authors and experts in the chosen field of study. Study was not confined to economic issues, but covered the full spectrum of knowledge, from fine arts, liberal arts, politics, philosophy, law, history, sociology, psychology to alternative medicines and nature therapies. Here, however, we are concerned with the growth of study groups, not only in Canada but also on a world-wide scale, concerned to gain an understanding of social credit economic philosophy and other related issues.[2] In many European countries study groups and libraries were established around trades unions. In Canada, study was largely focused through farming associations.

From 1913 onwards study groups within the U.F.A. focused their attention on financial and economic systems. Led by such people as George Bevington, a farmer of Winterburn, Alberta, who was a member of the U.F.A. Board of Directors, study groups re-examined the causes of wars and other important historical events. The relationship between the people and the system of banking and taxation which led to the American War of Independence (1775-83) were the subject of informed, although informal, study throughout the Province. As happened elsewhere in Canada, parallels were drawn between the role of finance and the economic trends leading to war, poverty and economic depression.

In the years immediately following the cessation of hostilities in 1918, when the early Social Credit writings of Clifford Hugh Douglas became widely available on a world scale, they were studied by students of economics and finance throughout Canada as a whole. From the outset there was a general recognition that Douglas' teachings offered a basis for the establishment of a more meaningful economic democracy than that presented by the established party system. Although as yet there was no formal organisation, from those early days, men and women of all walks of life, teachers, members of the clergy, business and professional men joined with farmers and ranchers in the rigorous consideration of the operation of the financial system, and studied workable alternatives.

Two very distinct agenda appear here. On the one hand the people seek to put their life's energies into working as farmers, miners, teachers or shopkeepers. They need finance if they are to provide for the needs of their families. On the other hand, financial interests seek to take control over the land, its resources and the products which result when resources are combined with human labour. There is no reason in theory why the two different agenda *should* be in conflict. However, the history of events in Alberta provides solid evidence that a conflict of interests can occur.

Alberta's resources and infrastructure

As early as 1885 a well drilled for water at Medicine Hat led to the first discovery of natural gas. Later, the Turner Valley oilfield was discovered, and the Calgary Petroleum Products Company began drilling on the original 700 acres of land. Documentation of the rich resources of the land of Alberta was and remains available for scrutiny. The reserves of oil, natural gas, coal, precious minerals, water-power and farmland were described, for example, in *The Case for Alberta*.[3] Less fully appreciated was the powerful position of the financial and oil interests which drove the economic exploitation of those resources from outside the Province, and outside the Dominion of Canada.

From the outset, the settlement of the Province was facilitated by the development of a system of finance and communications which was not under the control of the settlers themselves. Between 1905 and 1922 extensive telephone and railway networks were developed in the Province by powerful extra-governmental corporations who sought to exploit the resources of the territory. The system of railway guarantees through which the developments were funded led in large part to the financial problems which faced the Government of the Province in the 1930s.

At issue, for the men and women of Alberta, was the need for a financial infrastructure capable of ensuring that they and their children could access food, shelter, fuel, clothing and education – the essentials of life. Also necessary was an infra-structure of transport and communications, the provision of which was also dependent upon the availability of finance. For the ordinary voter, the route to good government of society lay through the ballot box. As far as the farmers, ranchers, miners, small businesses and professional people (doctors, teachers) were concerned, the economy was subject to the sphere of politics. Eastern financiers and other 'outside interests' should have no legitimate role to play in determining legal and political outcomes in the Province. In Alberta, the producers of wheat, meat and coal sought good prices for their produce, preferring to supply the 'home' market directly as far as possible, while building up local industries. The ordinary family, having migrated to Alberta to farm, was conscious of the vast potential wealth of the province, and found the methods of financing production through externally owned debt beyond their comprehension.

From his brief visit to Alberta in 1936/7, John Hargrave[4] provided a useful summary of the actual and potential wealth of the province, drawing upon officially documented sources. These sources included the Bureau of Statistics, Ottawa, the Canadian Institute of Mining and Metallurgy, reports of the Dominion Mines Branch, the United States Bureau of Mines, the United

States Geological Survey, the Chief Geologist of the Imperial Oil Company (Standard Oil) and the Research Council of the University of Alberta.

According to the company's official history as currently presented, the Imperial Oil Company started operations in 1880 in Ontario, coming to be 'a major contributor to the growth of the petroleum industry and to Canada's economic and social development for more than 125 years:

> Imperial's landmark discovery at Leduc, Alberta, was instrumental in the creation of the modern Canadian petroleum industry. The company also pioneered development of the oil sands of Alberta, both through its leadership role in the creation of Syncrude and the development of large-scale in-situ bitumen recovery at Cold Lake.

> Through such initiatives, Imperial has grown to become one of the largest producers of crude oil in Canada and a major producer of natural gas, as well as the largest refiner, with a leading market share in petroleum products and a significant presence in the petrochemical industry.

> Imperial has operations in every part of Canada and our Esso retail outlets are a familiar part of the Canadian motoring scene. Major concentrations of employees are found at our office locations in Calgary, Toronto and Montreal; as well as refinery and plant locations in Dartmouth, Nova Scotia; Samia and Nanticoke, Ontario; Edmonton and Cold Lake, Alberta.

> Imperial has more than 65,000 direct registered and non-registered shareholders, most of whom are resident in Canada. Many others have a stake in the company's share performance through ownership of mutual funds or participation in pension plans that hold shares in the company. The majority shareholder is Exxon Mobil Corporation, which holds 69.6 percent of Imperial shares.

> The company's stock trading symbol is IMO. Our shares are listed on the Toronto Stock Exchange and admitted to unlisted trading on the American Stock Exchange.[5]

In the years immediately preceding the Second World War, when the Social Credit Government was elected, coal was still a major fuel industry on a world scale. The powerful oil companies were just emerging towards the full potential of their monopoly position. Already oil rigs and pungent gas fumes were creeping across the former pasturelands of Alberta. The population as a whole, however, remained largely unaware of the historical significance of these developments.

Social Credit in Canada

The year 1921 brought a sharp economic depression as a direct result of the decrease in the demand for wheat and other farm products as hostilities ceased and exports were no longer required. As the First World War ended, the resultant drastic drop in farmers' incomes brought incredible hardship to thousands of new and established settlers. Hence further attention was focused upon the role of banking and finance in the Province and on a world-wide scale. It was increasingly apparent that money had flowed in abundance when it was 'necessary' to finance the devastation of World War. Yet there was no money to finance the peace. Under the existing system, in peacetime the financial system sanctioned poverty amidst plenty. For thinking people, there had to be some sane alternative.

At this time, a group of farmer representatives was elected to the Dominion House of Commons under the 'Progressive' banner. The group was instrumental in the setting up of a Parliamentary Committee on Banking and Commerce in 1923. Douglas was invited to appear before this Committee. His 'Evidence before the Banking and Commerce Committee', delivered in response to questions and entirely without notes, remains to this day a valuable documentation of the guidelines by which reform of the financial system might be approached.[6] Evidence to the Committee was also invited from Professor Irving Fisher, Sir Frederick Williams-Taylor of the Bank of Montreal, George Bevington of the U.F.A., and Henry Ford (although the latter did not appear).

Reaction sets in

Meanwhile, in Alberta, a number of resolutions relating to the control of finance were brought to the U.F.A. Conventions over the years. They gave rise to intense interest, and involved prolonged and well-informed debates. However, as time went on, the U.F.A. officials, like their counterparts in political and union circles across the world, were becoming increasingly orthodox in their outlook. Frank and open discussions on matters of finance were viewed with increasing disfavour, while the U.F.A. Government itself became increasingly reactionary.

Meanwhile, the rank and file farmers in the organisation continued their quest to become thoroughly well-informed on the subject. They sought to open public debate between the leading thinkers on monetary reform and the bankers in Alberta. With this end in view, they sought to arrange debates under the auspices of the U.F.A. Convention. It soon became apparent that bankers were not willing to engage in open and public debate. Furthermore, private consultations between the U.F.A. Provincial Government and a bankers' representative brought the realisation that it might be difficult for the government to get future 'financial accommodation' if demands for such debates were further entertained.[7]

Farmers resist reaction

Informal discussion of Douglas economics and monetary reform generally continued to increase at the U.F.A. Conventions, despite the hostility of the U.F.A. leaders. On one occasion the President of the U.F.A., Henry Wise Wood, was pressed to give his opinion on a resolution advocating an official enquiry into the workings of the financial system. He is reported to have declared: 'I know nothing about money, and I don't believe anyone else does. This question has been a hardy annual; and it has now become a noxious weed; my advice to you, is to kill it.' He thumped the table, bringing an end to the debate. The motion was defeated, but left many wondering how to evaluate the judgement of a man on a subject about which he openly admitted he 'knew nothing'.

From that time, the U.F.A.'s official policy was to support the formation of commercial co-operatives for the buying and selling of farm produce, but to officially ban all discussion on Douglas economics and financial reform. Similar policies were followed by practically every official organisation of farmers. The U.F.A. leadership had thus chosen to ignore the fact that commercial co-operative methods alone can bring very limited improvements in the absence of co-operative financing. In other words, the real credit generated by co-operative methods must be balanced by co-operative finance if the members are to derive any realistic power over their enterprises within the Province. Although the political leaders allowed themselves to be led into orthodoxy, ordinary men and women continued their quest for enlightenment and understanding of a seemingly incomprehensible financial system.

In due course, the restriction of financial credit to businesses and industry led, as Douglas had long foretold, to the 1929 Stock Market crash. The crash resulted in even more stringent restrictions upon agricultural credit, followed by hazardous economic conditions. Destitution and acute privation became commonplace in a land blessed with vast natural resources and the skills and talents to exploit them. Unemployment, bankruptcies, idle manufacturing plants together with farm and home foreclosures were the result. The consequences of economic stagnation were an evident feature of everyday life. Economic stagnation was triggered entirely by the action of the banks, who were calling in existing loans whenever possible and refusing to grant new ones in defiance of the evident abundance of opportunity for new development on every hand. Real resources, need and know-how required to be brought together by finance, and finance was found wanting.

The Hungry Thirties – a first-hand account[8]

In 1937 Douglas wrote *The Alberta Experiment*, to record the events as they had occurred between 1930 and 1937:

The early 1930s provided ample evidence of the failure of the orthodox financial system to meet the real needs of humanity in Alberta. In January 1932, No. 1 Northern wheat sold for as low as $0.20 per bushel, which was the lowest price reached in 400 years. Prime hogs of 200 lbs. sold for $5 each. Farmers with supplies of near-worthless wheat burned it in their stoves because they could not afford coal. Stockmen shot cattle that were only worth $0.75 per 100lbs on the hoof, to salvage the hides, which brought better returns than the meat. Cases are on record of cattle being shipped to market and their owners being billed for shipping expenses after the sale because the returns from the cattle were insufficient to cover the freight charges. A well authenticated case tells of a farmer who shipped a number of hides to a dealer and later received a bill from the dealer for $1.50 to pay the difference between the market value of the hides and the freight charge on the shipment. The farmer replied that he had no money, but he could send the dealer a few more hides.

At the same time miners walked the streets because there was no demand for coal, and lived on subsistence relief rations because there was no money to buy the beef and wheat which was rotting and burning on the prairies. On every side, the grim spectre of poverty stalked through a land of potential abundance.

The pioneers had built what they imagined was a new empire of freedom in a land teeming with natural resources. But, their attempts to wrest even a bare living from the elements at hand were frustrated. They wrapped their feet and legs in gunny sacks because they had no money to buy socks and rubbers, while they dined off gophers which had got fat on the unsaleable grain lying in the fields. These people wanted to produce, and they wanted to consume the fruits of their production, but they were thwarted on all sides. They turned to their leaders in the farm movement and found them divided. On the one hand, talk of socialization was offered as a palliative. On the other hand, talk of foreign markets and restriction of production was prescribed as a remedy.

In those times the people of Alberta were not so greatly concerned with the selling on foreign markets. Their concern was with markets at home, where people were suffering from semi-starvation in the midst of plenty. They questioned the wisdom of selling the major part of their produce in order to bring in the money to buy the minor part for their own consumption. An ever-recurring 'why' swept the country.

The farmers looked in vain to their own Government for some forthright effort to solve the problem. Instead of action, their ears were assailed at frequent intervals over the radio with a message from Premier Brownlee constantly repeating the idiotic phrase: 'Prosperity is just around the corner'. How far off the corner was, or how long it would take to get there, nobody seemed to know. The Government did nothing.

A spirit of desperation now seized the farmers. This was their zero hour. At their conventions there was apparent a seething spirit of discontent directed towards the apparent unwillingness of their farmer Government to do anything effective for the protection of their people from the debt-based legal rampages of the orthodox financial system.

Many farmers, some of whom had seen service in World War I, stood up in Convention to declare that 'things had gone too far to be cured by peaceful means'. They were ready to turn to arms again in a last desperate attempt to defend their homes and their families from being rendered destitute in the land they had made habitable and productive with infinite dedication and toil. Few realize today just how close Canada was to bloody revolution in those stark days of the early thirties, during the Great Depression.

It was not because the farmers were inefficient as producers that they could not pay their debts, nor because of drought or other natural causes. Many of them had harvested big yields of grain, the sale price of which was so low that even the out-of-pocket costs of production could not be recouped, without making any allowance for wages for the farming families. The records show that more wheat was produced during the five-year depression period (1931-5) than during the more prosperous five-year period from 1926-1930.

It appeared to most Albertans that finance and economic orthodoxy lay at the root of the problem. There was no shortage of goods and services. Labour, machinery and power were available. The fields, forests, mines and fisheries were awaiting development. Only lack of money prevented access to the goods and services which spelled economic security. Since the money problem loomed so largely in their affairs, it was inevitable that Albertans should focus upon it. The educational preparation of the early study groups meant that a considerable number of people were already familiar with the processes of the debt-financing of production, and the overall control over social and economic policy which could be traced to the system of finance. All that was lacking was a focus or figurehead to bring a viable politics to life.

William Aberhart

William Aberhart was a charismatic, in the sense of 'grace-filled', figure. L.D. Byrne, who worked closely with him from 1937 until Aberhart's untimely death in 1943, later observed:

> When I first came out [to Alberta], Mr. Aberhart was inclined to treat me with natural suspicion. However, I gradually gained his confidence and we became firm friends. I found him to be a man of complete integrity and deep and sincere religious convictions. He had a boyish mischievous sense of humour which he combined with an utter fearlessness in clashing head-on with his opponents.[9]

By all available accounts, Aberhart was neither a puppet of powerful interests, nor the self-serving demagogue of later hostile accounts. In 1933 he was the headmaster of Crescent Heights High School in Calgary and Dean of the Calgary Prophetic Bible Institute, in which latter capacity he gave regular religious radio broadcasts, becoming a popular figure throughout the Province. As Byrne noted, 'he had the reputation of an outstanding teacher'.

Both Aberhart's religious conviction and his deeply ingrained sense of justice were offended by the spectacle of his students leaving school educationally equipped to take their place in the world, yet having to join the bread lines. He was greatly saddened when one of his best students committed suicide in despair. Like many others at the time, his reason baulked at a state of affairs in which idle men and idle machines existed side by side with poverty and want. When a colleague of his lent him an interpretation of Social Credit economics by the English actor-playwright Maurice Colbourn[10] – a popular and reasonably accurate outline of the subject – he lost no time in coming to grips with Douglas' work.

The effect on William Aberhart was spectacular. Single-handedly he began to mobilise support for his new-found economic doctrine, spreading the 'good news' through his Sunday religious broadcasts which enjoyed a wide audience, and later held meetings throughout the province. The local study groups set up by the United Farmers' Association provided the basis for informed discussion and further study. The version of Social Credit adopted by Aberhart, following from his reading of Colbourne, was inevitably somewhat at variance in its detail with that of the Social Credit Secretariat. Nevertheless, Aberhart successfully adapted the fundamental philosophy of Social Credit, making it relevant to the people of Alberta.

Aberhart did not aspire to become a politician, still less the leader of any political movement. He recognised that many individual members of the U.F.A. movement were able exponents of financial reform. At this stage in his career, Aberhart saw the U.F.A. as the correct vehicle for progressive reform, making frequent reference to the U.F.A. in his Sunday radio broadcasts and offering them every support. Aberhart urged people to study Social Credit and, if they were satisfied that it provided a route out of their economic ills, to press for Social Credit to be adopted by their U.F.A. Provincial Government.

The Alberta Social Credit League

The response to Aberhart's message of hope was overwhelming. It was a call to the social pioneers of Alberta to organise for their common welfare. As a result, the Alberta Social Credit League was formed as a body of citizens committed to the study of the philosophy and practice of Social Credit principles. The President of the League was Orvis A. Kennedy, and the National Leader Robert N. Thompson. The League was entirely initiated and financed by individuals and groups of ardent seekers after social justice. *No outside funding whatsoever was involved.* Individuals pooled their time, talents and meagre incomes in the fight for economic democracy. William Aberhart acted as the catalyst for this movement, as his dynamic personality, energy, courage and vision galvanised men and women to join the League. Through it thousands were able to study Douglas' economic teachings with a view to putting theory into *informed* practice. Throughout the Province more than 2,000 study groups were set up, many of them reconverted U.F.A. local groups.

In time it became evident that the U.F.A. administration would not take any positive direct action to secure social credit legislation. Indeed, some members of the U.F.A. Provincial Government openly supported socialist planning measures, which were considered to be the direct antithesis of Social Credit. Hence the Social Credit League campaigned through all political parties with a view to obtaining pledges of support for social credit measures. The reaction of all existing political parties was negative. Therefore it was decided to take direct action. Through his radio broadcasts Aberhart announced his intention of leading a Social Credit party into the next election. Such was the enthusiastic support for the new party that pressure was put upon the governments in Edmonton and Ottawa to take Social Credit into serious consideration. The strength of opinion was such that the administrations called on Douglas to visit Ottawa and Edmonton.

Clifford Hugh Douglas called

Douglas had appeared before the Banking and Commerce Committee of the Dominion Parliament in April 1923. In Edmonton in 1934, he was invited to the Agricultural Committee of Provincial House. William Aberhart and a number of others holding opinions, both favourable and unfavourable to Social Credit, were also invited. Following this hearing Douglas was officially appointed as Reconstruction Advisor to the U.F.A. Government which, at the time, was the democratically elected government. That Douglas was so appointed at this stage was entirely down to Aberhart's radio campaign.

A month later, on 23rd May, Douglas submitted his first Interim Report to the Albertan Legislature.[11] In his report, the Reconstruction Advisor stressed the distinction that should be drawn between any programme for the practical utilisation of public credit, and the strategy required for acquiring the power to deal with public credit. Accurately, he warned even at this early stage that every step taken towards the emancipation of credit from its monopoly control by international finance would be opposed. Additionally, he advised that the news media should be under the 'unchallengeable control' of the Province. In view of the subsequent history of Social Credit over the intervening decades of the twentieth century, it is worth studying this document in considerable detail. It has been available, in full, across the world ever since it was first published in 1937.

Preparation for the 1935 election in Alberta

At the time in question, 1935, the UK Government held jurisdiction over a land mass of less than 80,000 square miles (200,000 square kilometres) with a population of around 50 million. Although nominally under the British Empire, New Zealand was in effect a self-governing territory of 103,738 square miles (268,680 square kilometres) with a population of 1.5 million. And Alberta, with a land mass of 255,541 square miles (661,848 square kilometres), with a population of 740,000, was one of the ten Provinces within the Federal Dominion of Canada. Hence in 1935 the chances of successfully introducing Social Credit measures were much greater in New Zealand, which was itself a Dominion, than in the Province of Alberta, which, despite its size, remained under the jurisdiction of the Federal Parliament in Ottawa. Throughout the history of Social Credit in Alberta, however, there ran in parallel a Social Credit movement which was active throughout the Dominion of Canada. Elected Social Crediters were a substantial force within the Federal Parliament in Ottawa, in British Columbia, Saskatchewan and elsewhere. In many parts of Canada, especially in Quebec, Social Credit literature continued to be produced for the rest of the twentieth century. From the date of the first election of a Social Credit Government in August 1935, two contrasting versions of the story have run in parallel.

When the election was called by the U.F.A. government for August 22nd, 1935, the Social Credit League placed candidates in every constituency. In view of the considerable costs in terms of time and money involved in running candidates and producing publicity with no outside funding whatsoever, this was no mean organisational feat. In June 1935 Aberhart published his Social Credit Manual: *Social Credit as applied to the Province of Alberta*. The so-called 'Blue Manual', ran to 64 pages (12cm x 16 1/2cm). At least half of the space in the booklet is taken up with advertising, enabling the booklet to be circulated cost-free. The advertisements themselves make interesting reading, not only for the glimpses they give of life in Alberta at the time, but also as an indication of the widespread support for Social Credit amongst the small businesses who were prepared to take out advertisements.

Organised opposition

Predictably, the U.F.A. candidates regarded the inexperienced Social Credit candidates with derision, and in the run-up to the election confidently foretold utter defeat. However, Douglas' warnings of the existence of another agenda operating behind the scenes proved to be timely. In the U.K. the question of financial backing for political figures was frequently the subject of observation by Social Crediters in the U.K. Two years earlier, Hitler's sudden rise to power was the subject of perceptive comment in *The New Age*.[12]

During the campaign the first signs of an organised opposition to Social Credit became evident. Press and radio facilities were utilized on a grand scale in a well-financed and organised attempt to discredit a body of political philosophy which had by this time become the common currency of everyday conversations within the Province. Cartoons started to appear, depicting Aberhart as a bumbling fool peddling nonsensical policies. The 'Economic Safety League' was one of several mysterious organisations which sprang into life, with plenty of money at their disposal for circulating well-produced literature and sending letters to the press in a concerted campaign against Aberhart. About a month before the election a substantial booklet produced by the Economic Safety League, Calgary, flooded the province. Entitled *The Aberhart Plan: A survey and analysis of Social Credit Scheme as placed before the electors of Alberta*, by W.M. Davidson, it appeared at first glance to be written as a frank and honest explanation of the Social Credit position. However, close reading of the publication confirms that it was part of the concerted campaign to discredit Aberhart. On page twenty-seven the conclusion is entitled 'The Immediate Danger':

> If any person reading these articles believes that William Aberhart has organised a political party, with a sensational slogan, merely to get himself into the centre of the stage, or even to sweep into office, he should abandon the idea for there is nothing further from the truth. If anyone has an idea that after reaching office, he would quickly shed the more extravagant parts of his program, that person is also very wrong. If any party leader has any hope that the Social Credit party, with a band of elected members – not a majority, say, but a group – would make a worthwhile ally in the general mix up that may follow an election, he would be well advised to abandon the dream.

> Mr. Aberhart is resolute, determined and inflexible and will fight unswervingly and without compromise for that program, such as it is, caring not a brass farthing for parties, groups, associations or alliances. If he should be placed in office he will move towards the goal without regard for cost or consequences to province or people. If he should hold the balance of power in a much divided house, he will see to it that the party that rules will accept his mandates, with perpetual turmoil and confusion as an alternative. It would be the alliance of the Nazis and the German Nationalists over again.

Nevertheless, certain local papers such as *The Ottawa Citizen* and *The Western Producer* did give support to the Social Credit campaign, encouraged to do so through Aberhart's broadcasts.

When the election returns were completed, Albertans had elected 56 Social Credit members in the 63 seat legislature. Not a single U.F.A. candidate was elected. Thoroughly rejected by an indignant electorate, the U.F.A. movement, originally inspired by democratic ideas of freedom, died. In the short space of 20 years it had become orthodox, unable to recognise that the key to economic freedom was financial reform along true Social Credit lines. In due course, history was to repeat itself, as those elected on a Social Credit platform were persuaded to reject Douglas' teachings and pursue Social Credit policies in name only.

For the time being, however, the success of the candidates Aberhart had helped to select was overwhelming. Aberhart himself had not been a candidate, but now came under pressure to become the leader in the legislature. He complied with the request and accepted a vacated seat in the Okotoks constituency. He thus became Premier of the first Social Credit government in the world. The Government was destined to last for more than a quarter of a century without a single electoral defeat.

Democracy in Alberta

Aberhart's hurriedly produced election manifesto would have benefited from being thoroughly edited by leading Social Credit thinkers, in so far as matters of debt and finance were concerned. Nevertheless, it contains valuable insights into the essence of the *political* argument in favour of Social Credit in 1935 Alberta. Aberhart states the basic premise of Social Credit, which is that:

It is the duty of the State through its Government to organise its economic structure in such a way that no bona fide citizen, man, woman, or child, shall be allowed to suffer for lack of the base necessities of food, clothing, and shelter, in the midst of plenty or abundance. The Province of Alberta is wealthy enough to carry out this proposal.[13]

The statement is followed by statistical evidence of the wealth of Alberta, and a version of the argument for the payment of a National, or 'Basic' Income on the basis of the common cultural inheritance. The people, it was claimed, had a political right to the resources of the land in which they lived, that is, a right to political and economic self-determination free from artificially created debt which brought with it control over the people and their resources by extra-territorial financiers. Citizens had a right to a share in the unearned increment of association. The latter term is explained as follows:

This expression means exactly what it says. There is an increment or increase in price, and this increase is not earned by the owner or the producer of the goods. ... A Coal Mine situated far from civilization or without transportation would be of little value to anyone except in so far as it could be used for personal needs. If ten people lived near it, it would be more valuable. If a thousand people were within reach of it, there would be that much greater demand for the coal, and, therefore, it would be a greater price. Thus the price of the coal above the cost of production is largely dependent upon the demand caused by the association of individuals in its immediate vicinity. Neither the owner nor the miners are responsible for this increased price. It is an unearned increment which accrues from the association of the people within the bounds of the land controlled by them.[13]

In answer to the question as to the difference between the Social Credit System and a Social Credit Plan this response was drawn:

The Social Credit system is the setting forth of the principles involved in the philosophy of Social Credit. A Social Credit Plan is one method of adapting it to any *State, community or industry*. The principles of electricity are the same wherever it is found. The plan of lighting a room may differ with the style or kind of room or with the whims or the artistic taste of the owner. It is the business of our experts to formulate and devise our own particular plan for this Province.[14]

The entire work is an open and honest demonstration of the potential for democracy in action. In likening the role of finance in the state to that of electricity within a building, Aberhart neatly presents the heart of the matter not only with regard to the Province of Alberta, but also in so far as the world as a whole was and is concerned. It is for this reason that the election of the Social Credit Government in Alberta brought forth decades of negative critiques. Hence *The Times* article was the first attempt of many to argue that the election victory was in some peculiar way a *denial* of democracy. Strenuous efforts were made to thwart the will of the electorate in Alberta. Over the final decades of the twentieth century Social Credit was explained away in the academy as an aberration, a deviant attempt to discredit legitimate finance (See Chapter 7).

The 1935 election in the world context

As *Social Credit* commented in the immediate aftermath of the election in Alberta:

Although 'Dog Bites Man' is not news, but 'Man Bites Dog' is, where Social Credit is concerned a man has to bite twelve dogs before the London press will notice it. Mr. Aberhart has done the equivalent. Every paper of any consequence in London and the provinces has given the utmost publicity to his remarkable achievement, which only those who realise the turmoil of a Canadian provincial election can assess truly.[15]

On August 31, 1935 *The Times* concluded its report on the events in Alberta with a 'warning' that 'it is to be hoped that nothing will be done either by the hotheaded reformers or wild scaremongers to destroy the credit or future prospects of the province'. According to this report, Alberta 'has gained sudden notoriety through electing the first Social Credit Government in the world'. The single word 'notoriety', used to describe the democratic election of a government outside corporate controls, sums up the concern felt by commentators in the mainstream press. The account printed in *The Times* on August 31, 1935 is reproduced in full as Appendix 5a: Poverty in Plenty.

Social Credit was a political issue in a number of electoral constituencies in Canada. The other western states, British Columbia and Saskatchewan also fielded a number of successful Social Credit candidates for the 1935 provincial elections. Later in the same year 17 Social Crediters were elected to the federal Parliament in Ottawa, forming the second largest opposition grouping after a mere six weeks of campaigning. None of those elected had experience within existing party machines.

Elsewhere in the world, Social Credit economic analysis and political philosophy made such good sense that considerable headway was being made throughout the UK and the other dominion electorates. In November 1935 a general election in New Zealand brought in a Labour Government for the first time in its history. Writing in 1937 on the subject of *The Alberta Experiment*, Douglas attributes the election success in no small part to the support given by 'the Douglas Social Credit Movement'.[5] At the time of the elections in 1935, Douglas was aware that the chances of introducing practical policies informed by a Social Credit analysis of the political economy were far greater in New Zealand than they were in Alberta. New Zealand had been settled by Europeans during the first half of the 17th century. It was named 'Nova Zeelandia' after the Dutch province of Zeeland, but Captain Cook, the British explorer subsequently Anglicised the name to New Zealand. During the nineteenth century British rule was established over the territory, and New Zealand became a Dominion in its own right, with the seat of government in Auckland (later moved to Wellington). Representative government for the colony was provided for by the passing of the 1852 New Zealand Constitution Act by the United Kingdom Parliament. The New Zealand Parliament met for the first time in 1854. In 1907 New Zealand become an independent Dominion of the British Empire, under the constitutional authority of the British monarchy on the same lines as the Dominion of Canada. Since the 1870s New Zealand has had no sub-national representational bodies such as provinces or sub-states, apart from local municipalities. From that time also, the currency has been the New Zealand dollar. Hence the people living in the area of land known as New Zealand were, in 1935, in a constitutional position which offered the possibility of giving serious consideration to self-determination of finance.

The policy of supporters of Social Credit throughout the UK, Canada, Australia and New Zealand was to seek political authority by working with candidates seeking election under the banners of existing political parties. If sufficient elected members were convinced of the good sense of Social Credit policies, the members would be in a position to meet the wishes of the electorate. If the elected members failed, succumbing to the pressures of big business and finance, it was up to *the electorate* to secure their replacement.

The outright election of a Social Credit government in Alberta surprised Douglas and the Social Credit movement every bit as much as it surprised the rest of the world. From the outset, Douglas appreciated that the failure of the Social Credit Government to implement the policies upon which it had been elected could, in the long run, prove to be a major setback to Social Credit on a world scale. From their earliest years of collaboration in the writing of Social Credit texts (1918-1922), Douglas and Orage were fully aware of the three-fold characteristics of the social spheres which regulate human interaction. The 'economy' which produces goods and services for exchange on the market does not operate in splendid isolation from the political and cultural spheres of society. Without the inputs of artists, engineers, farmers, craftsmen, technologists, inventors, carers, spiritual thinkers, educationalists and story-tellers, all acting in co-operation, economic activity simply would not happen. Equally, without the sanction of law, determined through the political sphere, finance and all economic activity would rapidly disintegrate.

The Social Credit press for 1935, including the *Social Credit, The New Age, The New English Weekly*, and many other weeklies across the world makes demanding but fascinating reading. It demonstrates that, for a brief period in 1935, there was a very real chance that the forces of reaction might be defeated so that poverty amidst plenty, and its consequences, waste and war, might be defeated. It is not surprising that the forces of reaction swung immediately into action.

Without the resources of big business and international finance at their disposal, the Social Credit Movement had established a substantial body of knowledge on the threefold nature of the social commonwealth, with study groups in towns and cities throughout the UK, the Dominions and elsewhere. As demonstrated in Chapter 7, the published texts of Douglas and others stood up to the most rigorous intellectual scrutiny. By December 1935 it appeared that electoral campaigns could achieve a new era of true democracy. New Zealand, for example, which had recently elected a Labour Government on the strength of Social Credit support, 'could enjoy a universal standard of living such as the world has never known *within a year*' if they could avoid being side-tracked by financial interests.

As reported in *Social Credit* in December 1935:

> The people of New Zealand, like the people of all other democracies, have been taught to vote solemnly on certain technical questions about which they can have no kind of clear opinion, every four or five years, and then to sit back and trust the new government until it so obviously fails to deliver the goods that an election is necessary. They then troop obediently off to the polls once again and vote on the same set of technical questions, slightly rehashed. This is the theory; in practice, of course, the majority either vote on the principle of 'turn the government out,' or else vote for people rather than policies. In either case they get exactly what they asked for, in the first place a new set of dummies, in the second a mixed set of dummies.

> An M.P. is a dummy only because he is not allowed to be anything else. Nothing in democratic government is more striking than the contrast between the personal intelligence and the public impotence of Members of Parliament. I am not necessarily suggesting that the average member is more intelligent than his constituents, but why in the name of democracy need he be? Is he the master, or the representative of the people? The point is that his constituents are intelligent, too, in the sense that they know very well what they want, when (and if) they are given a real chance to say so. The member's proper business is to act as the mouthpiece of their will, and to see that their desires are carried out by the experts he appoints in their name.[16]

The writer of the article was optimistic that the study of Social Credit in New Zealand had given rise to a body of candidates with the potential to break free from the traditional party straightjackets, particularly on the question of nationalisation which is 'so much beside the point and therefore so acceptable to the money monopoly'. The predicted danger was that of skilful compromise, of the piecemeal introduction of selected Social Credit measures. It was clear that the financiers would tolerate 'a great deal of tampering with orthodox financial principles, provided only that *an unconditional money payment regarded as a universal right*, is not seen to be the fundamental question' (emphasis original). The new Government would be put under great pressure to make no reforms of any significance. The Independents, at least eight of whom were known to be firm supporters of Social Credit, were insufficient to hold the balance of power, and the Labour Party itself was divided on Social Credit. Hence it was up to the electorate to put continuous pressure on their individual members between elections, as well as at election times, pressure for desired practical *results*, not vague 'Social Credit' ideas. The writer of the article reflects that:

> even in the Dominions people can often be persuaded to beg for what is their own, and so with the best intentions in the world put themselves in a false position. To petition his majesty King George V., however, adds to this the onus of putting *him* in a false, an impossible, position. When kings were in fact 'sovereign,' the case was clearly very different. But under a democracy, whether one likes it or not, the people are, or should be, sovereign, and for the sovereign people to appeal to what has been described as the 'hereditary presidency' is to do justice neither to it nor to themselves.

> The fate of a petition depends in practice on the recommendation of the Home Secretary to the King, and the opinion of the Home Secretary at present is, and must be, as every Social Crediter knows, at the mercy of finance. If any petition does not traverse their interests, it may be judged on its merits, otherwise, it has about the same chance as a snowball in hell. The so-called 'King's Prerogative' is to-day a legal fiction, and any reliance on it only serves to conceal and strengthen that false basis of power which is at the root of our troubles.[17]

The people are, or should be, sovereign. Hence petitions provide the powers-that-be with exactly the opportunity they require. They offer the opportunity to influence the personnel of any Committee of Enquiry, in such a way as to set its agenda so that the evidence put forward will ensure that the ends of the petitioners are not attained. The findings are then used in 'evidence' against future agitation for reform. The writer cites in evidence the Majority Report of the New Zealand Monetary Committee, the personnel of the Australian Monetary Committee which was currently sitting and the personnel of the Irish Monetary Committee. Finance welcomes such investigations, 'undertaken in all good faith, costing money and energy, rousing false hopes from which the reaction, according to temperament, would be either hopelessness or violence'. In the opinion of the 1935 journalist, such machinations belonged to 'a past age'. Unfortunately, such optimism was misplaced.

NOTES

1   Hooke (1971). This book is available electronically. See
    www.douglassocialcredit.com

2   See Chapter 4. To date little research has been undertaken into the self-
    help study groups, extra-mural classes and summer schools which were
    a feature of life in the 1920s and 1930s throughout the U.K. and the
    Dominions. Archives of local newspapers and other periodicals hold a
    wealth of information on the non-vocational studies of groups of
    citizens.

3   Government of the Province of Alberta (1938) *The Case for Alberta:
    Dominion-Provincial Relations, Addressed to the Sovereign People of Canada
    and their Governments*, Edmonton. See www.douglassocialcredit.com.

4   Hargrave (1937)

5   See http://www.imperialoil.ca/Canada-
    English/People/Campus/P_C_History.asp

6   See *Canadian House of Commons, Select Standing Committee on Banking and
    Commerce*, (1923), Canadian House of Commons, Ottawa, Appendix 1.
    See www.douglassocialcredit.com.

7   See Douglas (1937).

8   The following section is taken from Douglas (1937)

9   L.D. Byrne 'A Background Picture' in *The Alberta Experiment* (1984
    edition, p xxiv). See also depictions of Aberhart by Alf Hooke (1937).

10 Colbourne (1933)

11 Reprinted as Appendix 1 in Douglas (1937)

12 The New Age, 'The German Election' Notes of the Week, March 16,
    1933, p229. Reproduced on www.douglassocialcredit.com

13 Aberhart (1935) pages 5-17

14 Aberhart (1935) page 59, emphasis added.

15 *Social Credit*, 30 August 1935. p1.

16 J.D.B. 'Overseas Notes: New Zealanders Can Do It', *Social Credit*, 6
    December 1935, p113.

17 J.D.B. *op. cit.*

Appendix 5a
Poverty in Plenty

The Plight of Alberta

The Times, August 31, 1935

Alberta, one of the youngest Canadian provinces, which has gained sudden notoriety through electing the first Social Credit Government in the world, has always been a pioneer in progressive legislation.

Birth of a Province

It was created out of the old North-West Territory along with the adjoining province of Saskatchewan nearly 30 years ago, and as a Liberal Government at Ottawa had given it its charter, the first provincial Government was Liberal in name and in policy and held sway until a few years after the War. For most of that time the Premier was the late Arthur L. Sifton, the elder of two brothers who did so much for Western Canada. He had vacated the office of Chief Justice to guide the destinies of the young province, and under his wise and far-sighted rule lasting progress was achieved.

Those were stirring days. Immigration was at its height. The scattered trading posts of the old frontier days where few but half-breed voyageurs, Indians, Mounted Police and the Hudson Bay factors were known to go, soon became thriving centres of trade as the country filled up. At first old country stock predominated, and the older settlements such as those around Calgary, High River, and Macleod, are still in the main of pure British blood.

Boom and Slump

As the number of immigrants increased so the stock became more varied. Thousands of farmers anxious to better their condition left their homes in the Western States, and, bringing their all with them as in the old prairies schooner days, migrated across the frontier to settle in the new country where land was either free or dirt cheap. They brought with them as well many of those new-fangled notions of democracy such as primary elections, the initiative, the referendum, and the recall which already found much favour in some of the Western States, particularly in Oregon, which was always held up as a model of what a modern democracy should be. Before long Alberta was experimenting along the same lines.

The Melting Pot

In the years just before the War the character of the immigrants changed greatly. They were more and more recruited from Eastern and South-Eastern Europe. Galacians, Bulgars, Poles, Rumanians, Italians, Greeks and even Syrians flocked into the new districts as they were being opened up for settlement. Edmonton, the capital of the province, which had been thought by many to lie too far away in the north, was now seen to be in its true place in the centre. Vast new areas were thrown open to the west for agriculture along the new trans-continental railways that crossed the Rockies by the Yellowstone Pass and even further north, where experiments had shown that wheat could be grown, in the region of Athabasca and Peace River. The throngs of new settlers pouring through Edmonton day after day, drawn from nearly every nationality under the sun, often recalled the rush to a football match. Hotels were always crowded out, people sleeping in baths, on billiard tables, in corridors, anywhere they could lay their heads.

Then came the slump in railway construction, and the War. Immigration ceased, and though attempts were made to revive it by public assistance, it never became again what it had been, and at last died down altogether. Business began to dwindle, and people had time to meditate on their hardships. Great discontent prevailed.

Farmers' Despair

Many had settled in distant regions where they had been promised railways, but the tracks never came near, and they were left out in the wilderness with little prospect of marketing whatever crops they raised. In the southern part of the province there was a wide belt of land that was burnt up by drought year after year. The verdure of the spring soon gave way to a deep *terra cotta*, and crops were ruined in a dry spell to which there seemed to be no end. Huge irrigation ditches helped only those along their immediate course, who had to pay highly for their lands. The price of everything the farmer wanted rose, and kept on rising. Most of them had to face heavy mortgages with extortionate interest, liens on their land for machinery they had been inveigled into buying, though they could have got along well enough without it, and burdensome and often crushing contracts, which became so prevalent that laws had to be made declaring them to be legally void unless they had been ratified by a Judge of the county court.

The U.F.A.

Such grievances led to the formation of the United Farmers' Party [UFA], who succeeded the Liberals in 1921 and remained in office until their defeat at the present election. Hard times and the latest slump have swept them away, as they did the Liberals before them. Alberta and Saskatchewan, as the most recently settled parts of the Dominion and the furthest distance from great centres of population and industry, have suffered first and most of all.

With vast stores of unmarketed grain reposing in the elevators with little chance of ever being sold and fields lying idle and untilled, the farmer of the prairies is able to realise as few others can the meaning of the words 'poverty in plenty.' His desire is for more secure markets, steadier prices for his products, and fair charges for the supplies, services and goods he requires, as well as cheap and easy loans to tide him over such hard times as he is now experiencing. He wants simply a secure livelihood. Schemes of co-operation, restriction of production, regulation of markets, financial aid from Governments: all these have been tried, but nothing has staved off the evil day. It is no wonder that these people in their despair have clutched at any straw. Whether social credit can solve their difficulties will not be known until some definite scheme has been presented and tried. Many will feel that no system can make matters worse.

A Warning

In the meantime it is to be hoped that nothing will be done either by the hotheaded reformers or wild scaremongers to destroy the credit or future prospects of the province.

Chapter 6
Alberta 1935+

In August 1935 the vast yet sparsely populated Province of Alberta, in the West of Canada, was big news on a world scale. Over the subsequent decades of the twentieth century volumes of academic works were written to explain away the aberration of a popularly elected government attempting to buck the trend by introducing revolutionary legislation in defiance of the colonial constitution and the conventional party system. Although the events in Alberta gave rise to an immense literature, the full history of events is told here for the first time.

Official version of history

In brief, the history presented by career academics is as follows. The depression years of the 1930s hit the farmers of Alberta particularly hard because the prices they could get for grain and cattle would not enable them to meet their debts to the banks. In the dire poverty which resulted from forces beyond human control, they clutched at a straw. The straw which just happened to be lying around was a watered down version of the teachings of the quack economist, Major Clifford Hugh Douglas. And so a populist movement was born, headed by the Bible-thumping fundamentalist preacher, Aberhart, who knew nothing of economics, and still less of politics. Aberhart and Douglas immediately fell out. Douglas refused to accept Aberhart's invitation to take up the role of economic advisor to the Social Credit Government in Alberta because, so the 'official' version goes, Douglas knew that his economic theories were so theoretically flawed that they could never be implemented in practice. Sensibly, therefore, Aberhart set out on the 'right' path. When Douglas refused to go to Alberta following the election victory, Aberhart called for financial support from the Federal authorities in order to clear the provincial debt, and appointed Robert Magor, the nominee of the recently-created central Bank of Canada, as official advisor to the Government of Alberta. About eighteen months later diehard supporters of Douglas amongst the ranks of the Members of the Legislative Assembly revolted against Aberhart, bringing about the so-called 'Insurgency'. The result was a renewed request for Douglas to go to Alberta in an official capacity as Advisor to the Government. Douglas again refused to give his personal assistance. So instead, according to the authorised version of the story, he sent two representatives, G.F. Powell and L.D. Byrne, in an attempt to force *anti-Semitism* upon the population of Alberta, there being no other substance or meaning to Douglas Social Credit. Aberhart died in 1943, so that after World War II his successor, Ernest Manning, was able to purge the Province of anti-Semitism by removing all supporters of Douglas Social Credit from the political scene. Thus the Province of Alberta was brought back into the fold of respectable, right-wing economics and politics, helped in no small measure by the subsequent exploitation of the vast oil and mineral resources of the Province. This 'official' story-line has been maintained into the twenty-first century.

As this chapter will demonstrate, academics writing the official story were highly selective in the material they cited. The extensive Social Credit literature from which the 'official' story was drawn so selectively, remains available to the present day in reference libraries and private collections. Blocks of writing on Social Credit are therefore reproduced in full, as originally published, in the series of Appendices attached to this chapter. Although the Appendices are not all directly referenced in the text, they serve to introduce the wealth of material available on the subject of Social Credit.[1]

As far as the world was aware, in 1935, the key actors were the 56 Social Credit Members of the Legislative Assembly (M.L.A.s) who had been democratically elected to government by the electorate of Alberta. The elected representatives themselves believed that this was the reality of the situation. All they had to do, they thought, was to follow the mandate upon which they had been elected, by introducing legislation to give the people of the Province the financial security which they lacked. The electorate had a right to control its own affairs, rather than remain powerless. The rich resources of the Province, and the skills and desires of the people should be capable of providing goods and services for the welfare of the community as a whole free from debt and other external financial pressures.

Poised for battle

The September 6, 1935 edition of *Social Credit* announced the election victory and appraised the news in very different terms from those subsequently mapped out by 'orthodox' historians. It carried the headlines:

ABERHART FORMS HIS CABINET:
Determined to Maintain Credit and Meet Obligations.
GOOD LUCK!

Mr. William Aberhart	Premier and Minister of Education
Mr. John W. Hugill, K.C.	Attorney-General
Mr. William N. Chant	Minister of Agriculture and Minister of Trade and Industry
Mr. C.C. Ross	Minister of Land and Mines
Mr. W.A. Fallows	Minister of Railways, Telephones and Public Works
Dr. W.W. Cross	Minister of Health
Mr. E.C. Manning	Provincial Secretary

The front page quoted from Aberhart's campaign speeches:

'We will make a plan for Alberta as soon as we get the facts, and it cannot be done until then. We must get the facts first.

'You don't have to understand electricity before you make use of an electrical system, as it is installed by experts.

'If we are so foolish and fanatical as they say we are, why don't they let us hang ourselves?'

The same issue of *Social Credit* (September 6, 1935) carried a number of informative articles on the significance of the election, including:

(1) Douglas' summary of the situation to date, reproduced in full as Appendix 6a: Douglas on Aberhart.

(2) A prophetic article entitled 'Coast To Coast: Canada and Electoral Policy', reproduced as Appendix 6b: Coast to Coast.

(3) Comment on the stance adopted by *The Economist,* in Appendix 6c: *The Economist.*

These texts are reproduced in full in order to give the reader an opportunity to make a personal evaluation of the mood of the times. In view of the subsequent history of Social Credit in Alberta, these news reports are amazingly perceptive of the roles of the key players and the issues at stake. Also included in the September 6, 1935 issue of *Social Credit* was a long article by Denis Byrne who, as events unfolded, was to play a key part in the history of Alberta. For further illumination of the atmosphere at the time, the reader is referred to the biographical account of a leading Member of the Legislative Assembly (MLA), Alf Hooke, *30+5: I know, I Was There.*[2]

From the outset the battle ranged far beyond the bounds of the purely economic questions of income security in Alberta. By raising the legality of the claims of financial institutions to the assets of the indebted Province, the electorate of Alberta were throwing down the gauntlet to the powers of international finance on a world scale. As stated elsewhere in the September 6, 1935 issue of *Social Credit*:

> The Social Credit case, therefore, points out that, since the banks create money on the basis of (1) a functioning industry, (2) a consuming public, and (3) stable government, which together may be defined as the 'Social Credit' of the community, repayment of bank loans is impossible, unless the community is credited with the monetary value of the created resources. ... The defective system of bank-loan accountancy has reduced all industrial communities to a condition of perpetual scarcity, despite the potential abundance made possible by modern science. It has further involved them in a load of fictitious debt to the banks which can never be paid off.

Around this time, the population of Alberta, men, women and children, was about three-quarters of a million, a little more than half the population of Northern Ireland in an area 50 times as large. Douglas' researches had established that Alberta's capital wealth was in the region of forty-six thousand, two hundred million sterling (£46,200,000,000), or in the region of well over £50,000 for every man, woman and child in the Province. It could be presumed that the greater part of the population of Alberta, that is, the citizens, should be the legal owners of the Province of Alberta. As Douglas later explained:

> I am not saying that there is £50,000 potentially in the pockets of every man and woman in Alberta, but the debts of the population amount to about £400 a head; nevertheless, all their debts together do not present a hundredth part of the capital wealth of Alberta; but since they are money debts, and the wealth in Alberta is real wealth, and not money wealth, civilised life in Alberta is becoming impossible.[3]

Douglas argued that debt should be an asset of the citizens, not the banks. Put simply, a community such as the population of the Province of Alberta could be regarded as an association of individuals seeking to achieve the political, social and economic conditions of life which cannot be obtained without some form of organisation. It is an association through which people can work effectively together, in order to achieve a desirable quality of life and leisure. The wealth of such a community consists of its physical assets in the form of the natural assets of soils, timber and minerals, coupled with capital assets created through modern industrial methods. The greatest asset of all is, however, the population itself, according to 'their state of education, intelligence, morals, health and social well-being. That is to say, "wealth" is not "money".'[4]

At this point in time it was undeniable that an unusual event had taken place. The world's press may report a revolution in Russia, or the outbreak of a war. It does not normally report on the election results of a province in the West of Canada with a population of three-quarters of a million. The correspondent 'J.D.B.', in the September 6, 1937 edition of *Social Credit* by no means overstated the case by declaring: 'Canada is World Centre';

> At this moment, ludicrous as it may sound to those who have not considered the matter, the centre of the world's stage is not Geneva, or Rome, or Moscow, but in Canada. There the battle is joined which will decide the fate not only of nations, for they do not matter, but of men and women and children who do.[5]

The citizens of Alberta would not have voted in 56 Social Credit Members of the Legislature (out of a total of 63), none of whom had previous experience as politicians, were it not for the determined dedication of two very different individuals, William Aberhart and Clifford Hugh Douglas. The latter had, over a period of sixteen years, published books and articles giving rise to public debates with leading economists across the world. Although virtually unknown to the world outside, Aberhart was a famous and popular figure throughout Alberta. As the two men were essential to the election victory, their co-operation would be vital to the successful implementation of the election mandate. From the outset, Social Credit commentators were aware that determined efforts would be made to ensure that such co-operation did *not* take place:

> It seems to me ... likely, however, that they will try to split them in the popular mind, by magnifying the importance of any discussion of technical discrepancies, where they exist, and ignoring the fact that the two men are essentially at one in objective and increasingly so in strategy. There have already been signs in the London press that this course is being pursued.[6]

Those were prophetic words indeed. Considerable effort was taken to ensure that apparent differences of opinion between Douglas and Aberhart were publicised. Furthermore, having met only twice, and very briefly, before the election, they were never to meet again. As the correspondent

J.D.B. pointed out (in the September 6, 1937 edition of *Social Credit*), as things stood at the time, Douglas was already appointed advisor to whichever government was in power in Alberta. Aberhart, meanwhile, had clearly stated his intention to re-affirm the appointment in order to draw upon Douglas' expertise. Douglas was scrupulously careful to distinguish between the *political* campaign to determine the wishes of the people as to *policy*, which was Aberhart's task, and the *technical* advice on *finance* in the Province, which he (Douglas) could supply, if requested to do so *by the legitimate government*.

The question then arises as to who would attempt to keep the two men apart, and why? What issues transcended the boundaries of the Province of Alberta so that an election there had to be intervened in? At that point in time, the politically aware readership of the world's press knew that a major issue had been raised, that of the relationship between an electorate, the voting citizens of a political entity, who in theory determine policy under a democracy, and the 'government' of a nation which determines which policies are 'practical' or 'feasible' – and which are not. Quite plainly, the issue was primarily a *political* one, with the *economic* policies being secondary. As Aberhart noted in his election statement in respect of the latter: 'If we are so foolish and fanatical as they say we are, why don't they let us hang ourselves?'

Castle warfare

Within days of the election victory in 1935, Douglas observed:

Students of politics recognise that, for the first time in modern history, a Government has been elected against the wishes of those financial powers which, for the most part, control all Governments; while the general public senses instinctively that the problem of poverty amidst plenty is about to be tackled (perhaps for the first time) without fear of vested interests.[7]

At the very same time, a correspondent in *The Economist*, observed:

But how is Mr. Aberhart, as Prime Minister of Alberta, to create new money without transgressing the limits set by Canadian banking law?[8]

The comment raises the issue of the *creation* of 'Canadian banking law': how is that done, and by whom? Under a totalitarian government, people expect to be told what they can do, and what they cannot. However, under democracy the citizens expect to determine policy, with the implication that if they do not like the 'limits' set by previous administrations, they can set about changing them through the due process of democracy.

Published in *The New Age* (April 1, 1937), the following diagram provides an overview of the relationship between 'democracy' and 'banking law' as it had evolved at that time.

The diagram represents the clash between two 'wills': the 'Will of Finance' to economic scarcity, and the 'Will of the People' to economic plenty. Progress in the 'industrial arts' has brought about the situation where ample material goods can be produced and distributed without fear of scarcity. However, as the case of Alberta in 1935 amply demonstrates, that plenty cannot be freely distributed – because of 'banking law'. The Will of Finance is conscious, but concealed from the people. The will of the people is subconscious, concealed even from themselves. People are prone to studiously avoid admitting to themselves that what they really want is to take advantage of abundance within a free community. This is the psychological result of the subtle educational forces of academia, the world's press, religious and other 'authorities' who are controlled by finance with the force of legal compulsion. As the diagram illustrates, Parliament is the 'buffer state' between the two opposing wills or policies. It can also smooth over inconsistencies between the two wills. Members of Parliament, however, are no more aware of the clash of interests than are the electorate. Hence they are drawn into the whirlpool of cross-purposes, becoming the unconscious instruments of Finance. Created before World War II, and pre-dating the setting up of the United Nations, the World Bank, the International Monetary Fund, the European Commission and other like-minded bodies, the World Government Diagram indicates an awareness of the nature of the relationship between the individual citizen and the 'authorities' who determine banking and other legal restrictions on elected governments.

Arthur Brenton, Editor of *The New Age*, suggested that politicians might perhaps be prepared to come forward with personal guarantees which they would forfeit if their policies proved impossible of implementation:

'But things like that are not done' will be the first reaction of most people to this idea. No; and this goes a long way to explain why other things are not done – why the ministerial *crapaud* [toad] is able to croak: 'Pie in the sky by and by and a peerage for me while you die.' It is regarded as a symptom of irresponsibility, as well as being in bad taste, to take politics seriously. We grant that there is a rational basis for this attitude on the part of politicians, though few are aware of it, and it is that the bankers have reserved to themselves the last word on major policy leaving the politicians only parish-pump issues to settle by debates and division-lists, and even as regards those, confining the matter of their

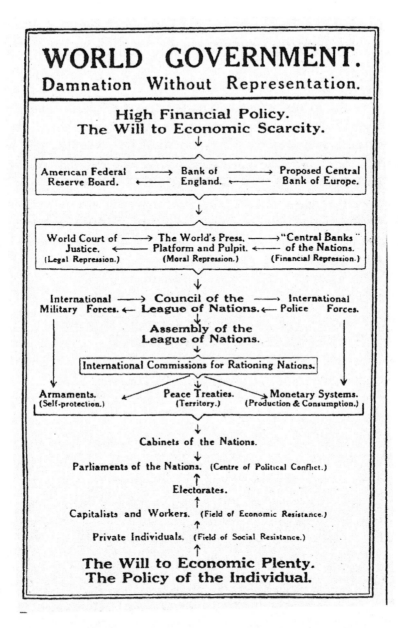

WORLD GOVERNMENT.
Damnation Without Representation.

High Financial Policy.
The Will to Economic Scarcity.
↓

| American Federal Reserve Board. | ⟶ ⟵ | Bank of England. | ⟶ ⟵ | Proposed Central Bank of Europe. |

↓

| World Court of Justice. (Legal Repression.) | ⟶ ⟵ | The World's Press. Platform and Pulpit. (Moral Repression.) | ⟶ ⟵ | "Central Banks" of the Nations. (Financial Repression.) |

↓

| International Military Forces. | ⟶ ⟵ | Council of the League of Nations. | ⟶ ⟵ | International Police Forces. |

Assembly of the League of Nations.
↓

International Commissions for Rationing Nations.

| Armaments. (Self-protection.) | ⟵ | Peace Treaties. (Territory.) | ⟶ | Monetary Systems. (Production & Consumption.) |

↓

Cabinets of the Nations.
↓

Parliaments of the Nations. (Centre of Political Conflict.)
↑

Electorates.
↑

Capitalists and Workers. (Field of Economic Resistance.)
↑

Private Individuals. (Field of Social Resistance.)
↑

The Will to Economic Plenty.
The Policy of the Individual.

settlement within the framework of their *faits accomplis*. To fight for the rich man's castle is compatible with self-esteem, but to fight over the crumbs from his table is humiliation.[9]

In 1935 Aberhart, Douglas and the bulk of the Social Credit movement were well aware that they were joined in battle for the 'rich man's castle.' And they were battling against amazing odds.

Democracy frustrated

In the immediate aftermath of the election, Aberhart was faced with the organisational tasks of a political leader for the first time in his life. Inevitably he made mistakes. Without experience of the world of politics, he was an open target when 'sensible' advice was offered to him by the Federal 'Authorities.' Instead of calling upon Douglas first, he committed himself to a course of action which was in direct contradiction to Douglas' analysis of the situation. Although the two sides did eventually work together, from June 1937 until Aberhart's death in 1943, the initial delay ultimately proved fatal.

In the days immediately following the 1935 election, moves were made to thwart the Social Credit initiative. Sir Montague Barlow was in Alberta during the election and its immediate aftermath, in the role of Chairman of the Coal Mines Commission in Alberta. Speaking at the Canadian Chamber of Commerce in London on March 6, 1936, Barlow, former Minister of Labour, summed up the situation:

> I have a high opinion of his [Aberhart's] courage and sincerity. He did two very remarkable things while I was there. He appointed as Minister of Mines Mr. Ross, who was not a politician and not, so far as I know, perhaps even a Social Crediter. He is a man thoroughly competent for his work and a first-rate administrator. That was the act of a statesman on Mr. Aberhart's part.

> Equally, when he found the treasury empty and he had to be prepared to get large sums of money to pay interest on the provincial bonds, he met the bankers, asked for a financial expert, Mr. Magor, one of the ablest financiers in the East who was called in to help Newfoundland out of its difficulties, and Mr. Magor, at Mr. Aberhart's request, addressed the Social Credit party in the state legislature.[10]

The 'two very remarkable things' certainly did not arise from Aberhart's own political judgement or experience. According to Alf Hooke's autobiographical account, it was because Mr. Aberhart appreciated the vast potential of natural resources, especially oil and gas, that he 'invited Mr. Charles C. Ross, and engineer well qualified in this field, to become Minister of Lands and Mines.'

> It is interesting to note that Mr. Ross had never been known as a Social Crediter and, in fact, had no connection whatever with the Aberhart movement. Mr. Ross, however, accepted the invitation and the Athabasca constituency was made available to him following the resignation of Mr. Tade, who had won the election.[11]

After the election Aberhart became fully aware of the gravity of the Province's debt to external financial institutions. The Treasury was empty, the bond interest was overdue and civil service salaries were unpaid. Revenue was totally inadequate to meet the commitments of the Province. Aberhart went to Ottawa to seek assistance in obtaining a loan. The loan was granted, on the condition that Robert Magor should become the financial and economic advisor to the Government of Alberta. The Governor of the Bank of Canada recommended Magor, the intention being to discredit Social Credit and bring down the Government in Alberta. For the following sixteen months Aberhart followed policies which were acceptable to the Federal 'authorities', as also to established banking interests. Measures adopted on the advice of Magor included the dismissal of civil servants, a steep rise in income tax and the suspension of bond interest. The measures brought the Social Credit Government into disrepute with the electorate.

In December 1936 John Hargrave, leader of the Green Shirts and Social Credit Party of Great Britain and Northern Ireland, which operated independently from the Douglas Social Credit Secretariat, travelled to Alberta alone and uninvited to assess the situation for himself. Hargrave's visit was a key factor in triggering the 'insurgency' of Members of the Legislative Assembly three months later, and the subsequent appointment of George F. Powell and Leslie Denis Byrne as Douglas' representatives to work with the Aberhart administration.

On December 17, 1936 Hargrave had a lengthy interview with Premier Aberhart during which the technical inconsistencies between the proposals outlined in Aberhart's *Manual of Social Credit* and the National Dividend and Just Price as explained by Douglas, were discussed. It became apparent to Hargrave that Aberhart did not understand the Douglas analysis: he had yet to move beyond the conventional assumption that a 'basic dividend' would have to involve re-distribution, *i.e.*, taxation in some form or other. Hence his gradualist approach.

The next day, Hargrave addressed a meeting of Social Credit Cabinet Ministers in the following terms:

Alberta is the key to the world situation.

What happens in Alberta can affect the destinies of Europe and the rest of the world. If Social Credit is able to show even a modicum of success in Alberta, not only will the other three Western Provinces – Manitoba, Saskatchewan, and British Columbia –'go' Social Credit, and then the whole of Canada, but New Zealand and Australia, already ripe, are certain to follow. The Irish Free State, now striving for economic self-sufficiency, would swing into line. The other parts of the British Isles – England, Scotland, Wales and Northern Ireland – could not resist the 'pull' exerted by a Social Credit Federal Union of Canada, reinforced as it is bound to be, by a Social Credit Commonwealth of Australia and a Social Credit New Zealand. Nothing could stop this politico-social-economic landslide, which would result finally, in a Social Credit World Order in which poverty and war had been eliminated for ever.

The United States of America, at this moment struggling towards economic freedom through a maze of New Dealism, would look across the boundary-line of Montana and begin to move towards Social Credit.

At the first sign of success in Alberta, the eyes of all the people of war-doomed Europe would turn away from the developing Right-Left conflict – they would look up and see, not a theoretical argument printed in a book, but the actuality of 780,000 Albertans using their own real wealth and living debt-free. And they would say to themselves, over there in Europe, 'If the Albertans can live in peace and prosperity, why should we live in poverty and the fear of war – why should we starve amidst plenty – why should we slaughter each other? Let us beat our tanks into tractors and follow Alberta's lead.'

What happens here in Alberta, therefore, can actually slow down or stop the Gadarene rush towards the Next Great War that may at any moment overtake Europe and let loose such a hell upon earth as has not been seen since the beginning of the world.[12]

Hargrave's summary provides a fair assessment of the significance of the events in Alberta as perceived by many within a world context. His address was followed by a number of questions, during which the Social Credit Attorney-General, Mr. Hugill, stated that 'in his opinion there were legal, constitutional restrictions and limitations that would effectually prevent Social Credit from being put into force in one Province alone.'[13]

Soon after his arrival Hargrave had a personal interview with the Hon. C.C. Ross, whom Aberhart had appointed as Minister of Lands and Mines:

Mr. Ross was a science graduate of McGill University, Montreal, and for a number of years had served as a mining engineer for the Dominion Government. He explained at this interview that he was 'not a Social Credit man,' and that, as a mining engineer, he attended to his work in the Department of Lands and Mines from a purely technical point of view. He had been following a particular policy in his Department, and would like to have Hargrave's opinion of it from a Social Credit point of view.

The policy, which the Minister proceeded to outline, was: to develop the natural resources of the Province by encouraging outside capital to come in and get to work on production, especially in the Turner Valley oilfields, some 45 miles southwest of Calgary. Outside firms were thus enabled to lease holdings, and, in return, undertook to pay certain sums and royalties on output to the Government. In this way the Government, financially in a difficult position, would be able to tap a steady source of revenue, while at the same time areas that would otherwise remain more or less wastelands would be developed.

The significance of this policy will not be seen in its proper perspective unless it is remembered that an 'oil boom' was, and is now, in full swing in Alberta, and that fact must be related to the vast real wealth resources of the Province. ...

It was clear that the Department of Lands and Mines, covering the greater part of the natural resources of the Province, was working quite separately from what might be called 'the Social Credit part' of the Government. The Minister made a particular point of this. He explained that his department 'just went on with its job,' and was not concerned with attempts to find some way of putting Social Credit into operation. Premier Aberhart and other members of the Cabinet were trying to solve that problem. This, of course, was a perfectly natural standpoint for a non-Social Credit Minister to take up, and Hargrave did not comment upon it.

Alberta had, therefore, a Social Credit Premier who had promised $25.00 a month 'basic' dividend, but who could not now find out how to 'get it back' if he attempted to keep his promise; a Social Credit Attorney-General who held that it was illegal to issue any such dividend, whether it was possible to 'get it back' or not; and a Social Credit Minister of Lands and Mines who frankly admitted that he 'was not a Social Credit man,' and was just going on with his technical work leaving Mr. Aberhart and his colleagues to find out whether anything might be done along the lines of Social Credit.[14]

Hargrave came to the conclusion that the element of surprise had been lost. Since the election, matters had simply been allowed to drift. The Members of the Legislative Assembly (M.L.A.s) who fully understood the aims of Douglas

Social Credit were aware that a great deal was being done to confuse the issue, in the hopes that Social Credit would simply fade away. However, the people of Alberta were conscious of the exceptional platform upon which their Social Credit Government had been elected, and were closely monitoring their M.L.A.s

One-way government

In his autobiographical account of events in Alberta, published in 1971, Alf Hooke presents a clear statement of the reality of the situation:

> During these years Alberta's legislation was subjected to the most careful scrutiny by those whose powers were being challenged. Political opponents ridiculed, high-priced lawyers argued, banking institutions sponsored broadcasts and newspaper advertising, all designed to destroy the confidence the people of the Province had placed in William Aberhart and his followers on August 22nd, 1935.[15]

By early 1937 it was obvious that, although the Social Credit Government in Alberta had been democratically elected, like all Governments it was nothing but a one-way street. That is, elected governments are only permitted to exist, vested with the panoply of power, supported with money, and their ways made smooth by the press, so long as they do not rock the boat of international finance. So long as it was prepared to follow financial orthodoxy by increasing taxes and using the greater part of the increase to pay the interest on bonds held by financial institutions, the Social Credit Government of Alberta drew no opposition from the Dominion of Canada Government at Ottawa. It was allowed to experiment with measures which, although they infringed Dominion prerogatives, were judged by the orthodox financial advisor as being incapable of leading to any effective challenge to the monopoly of credit held by the banks. At least two Bills became law in spite of the fact that they exceeded the boundaries of authority of the Province, including the 'Prosperity Certificates', a form of disappearing money modelled somewhat on Silvio Gesell's[16] notion of making money *lose* value so that people spend their way to prosperity as conventionally understood. No action was taken by the Dominion to frustrate the issue.

The Insurgency

During the run-up to the election, Aberhart had repeatedly stressed his intention to bring Douglas to Alberta as technical advisor to the government.

The exchange of twenty-five cables and twenty-seven letters between August 1935 and March 1936, published in Douglas' *The Alberta Experiment*,[17] shows that both men fully intended to work together. However, each had definite views concerning their roles. Douglas, the originator of the whole body of socio/political/economic thought, was conscious of the world-wide significance of the 'Alberta Experiment'. Aberhart, on the other hand, genuinely believed that Magor, skilled in orthodox financial and economic techniques, was the right person to sort out the immediate problems facing the newly elected Government. Douglas' *Interim Report to the United Farmers of Alberta Government* on May 23, 1935, made before the August election, contains his recommendations for necessary steps to be taken towards control of financial policy. The document demonstrates Douglas' thorough appraisal of the legal, political and economic situation in Alberta.[18] Hence Douglas had reason to suspect that the visit of Montague Norman, Governor of the Bank of England, to the Governor of the newly constituted Bank of Canada, in the fortnight immediately prior to the Alberta election, was not unconnected with the subsequent appointment of Magor as advisor to the Alberta Government. Hence the ensuing delay in the issue of a formal invitation to Douglas to resume the official position of Advisor to the Government of Alberta.

Throughout 1936 dissatisfaction amongst the M.L.A.s at the lack of progress towards meeting the election promises began to surface. The exchanges between Douglas and Aberhart, and the full text of Douglas' Interim Report to the U.F.A. Government were not as yet available to the M.L.A.s. A debate therefore arose between the M.L.A.s who were keen to see genuine Social Credit measures introduced, and the Cabinet, some members of whom argued that Douglas should be 'entirely ignored'.[19] As discussions became more focused, those members of the Cabinet who had never been committed to Social Credit resigned, including the Minister for Land and Mines and the Provincial Treasurer. The debate culminated in the 'insurgency' over the Budget of March 1937, details of which are documented by Alf Hooke.[20] The 'insurgents' refused to vote the money supply to allow the Government to continue, after which both sides agreed to set up the Social Credit Board to advise the Government on Social Credit policy.

At this point Aberhart agreed to send Mr. Maclachlan, the Chairman of the Social Credit Board, to invite Douglas to join the Board as official advisor to the Alberta Government. The upshot was the arrival in Alberta of the two Douglas nominees, George Powell and Denis Byrne in June 1937. According to the author of *30+5: I know, I was there*,[21] the following five years turned the Aberhart administration into an 'exciting drama, the like of which I am sure has never occurred in modern history'. An exaggeration, perhaps? Yet it certainly makes very interesting reading.

Denis Byrne, who was from this point at the centre of the action in Alberta, takes up the story:

> Powell preceded me to Alberta. By the time I arrived I found that he had succeeded in bringing the two opposing Government factions – the Cabinet supporters and the insurgents – together on the understanding that there would be speedy action to further Social Credit policy. In the economic field the issue was centred in the control of the real credit of the Province – that is in its ability to produce the wanted goods and services which would lift its people out of the conditions of poverty which prevailed. This real credit was, in turn, controlled by the monetary system – which was constitutionally the responsibility of the Federal Government because of its jurisdiction over banks and banking. Therefore any action to bring the real credit of the Province - involving fundamental property and civil rights under the exclusive constitutional jurisdiction of the Provinces – under the Provincial control required of the banks to conform to the policy laid down by the Provincial Government. As the policy being pursued by the banks under the Bank of Canada was diametrically opposed to Social Credit policy and was inherent in the system, therefore such action was bound to bring the Alberta Government into conflict with the banks, financial institutions, and through them the Federal Government.

> Having explained this to the Cabinet and, at their request, to the Caucus, I recommended with the concurrence of my colleague Powell and the approval of Douglas that a special session be called immediately to pass legislation requiring the banks to implement the measures required by the Government. No sooner had the session been called than press representatives, officials of the Bankers' Association and others poured into Edmonton. The legislation which was introduced – specifically 'The Credit of Alberta Regulation Act' – was the object of violent attack by the financial powers-that-be in Canada, England, the U.S.A. and several other countries. It was promptly disallowed by the Federal Government – notwithstanding the fact that the then Minister of Justice had stated shortly before he doubted that the Federal Government had the constitutional right to disallow Provincial legislation.

> I went back to England with a pressing request by the Alberta Government to take up an appointment as their economic adviser. In

my absence my colleague Powell was arrested on what I am satisfied was a trumped up charge of defamatory libel. I returned to Alberta to take up my appointment with the Government and shortly afterwards, following a farcical trial before judge without jury, Powell was sentenced to six months imprisonment and ordered to be deported. After serving three months he was released and died shortly after returning to England from the effects of his experience. ...

From early 1938 until his death in May, 1943 I worked closely with Aberhart as advisor and confidant, so I got to know him intimately. One of the strongest aspects of his character was his passionate loyalty to the Crown – the full implications of which he understood and cherished dearly.[22]

Disallowance

Following the arrival of Powell and Byrne a series of Acts were passed by the Albertan Legislature designed to implement the wishes of the electorate by introducing measures compatible with Aberhart's electoral platform. When the 'Credit of Alberta Regulation Act', the 'Bank Taxation Act', and the 'Reduction and Settlement of Debt Act' were passed by the Alberta Legislative Assembly in a four-day session in August 1937, the Dominion Government, backed by the financiers, reacted at once. Amidst a storm of controversy, the Prime Minister of Canada, Mr. Mackenzie King, 'disallowed' the Acts. For details of the Acts 'disallowed' by the Dominion authorities, see Appendix 6d: How Alberta is Fighting Finance.

As the Social Credit Board subsequently explained, in their 1939 Annual Report to the Legislative Assembly of the Province of Alberta, in respect of the Credit of Alberta Regulation Act:

It is questionable whether any single piece of legislation had commanded such universal attention. Alarm was evident in the banking centres of London and New York. The financial press of the world hurled abuse at the Government which had dared to challenge the sover-eignty of finance. The disallowance of this legislation was demanded.

And all this excitement was caused by the simple act that merely required the banks operating within the Province of Alberta to order their administration of the financial system so as to give the people of the Province access to their own resources within their own boundaries. This legislation did not interfere with the banks, banking, coin, currency, or any administrative matter coming under the federal jurisdiction. It only provided that the banks operating within the Province could not continue violating the property and civil rights of the people by so manipulating the operation of the monetary system as to deny the people access to their abundant resources.

It was an act establishing the base democratic right of the people to determine the results which should accrue to them from the administration of their affairs by the responsible authorities.[23]

Since it was recognised that these three acts, like any other action designed to be effective in fighting 'the authorities', would be violently misrepresented, a further Act, the 'Act to Ensure Publication of Accurate News Information' was debated and passed. This Act was portrayed by the press as 'censorship', although it was the very opposite, seeking to guarantee publication of sources of information and make certain opportunity for corrections was given. It was designed to ensure that 'the same information which every publisher demands from correspondents to columns, *i.e.*, the names of contributors of articles, would be available to The People when demanded by their representatives'. In theory, a central plank of democracy is freedom of information: in practice, the Act was disallowed.

In his 1954 study of the relationship between Social Credit and the Federal Power in Canada, Mallory explained that the assent of the Lieutenant-Governor of the Province was necessary before the legislation passed by the Aberhart administration in August 1937 could take effect. And the Lieutenant-Governor would rely on the advice of the Attorney-General, Mr. John Hugill, whose position, therefore, was 'a difficult one'. In Mallory's own words:

The original Aberhart cabinet had included at least three members who were 'moderates' and whose adherence to social credit doctrine was questionable. They were Mr. C.C. Cross, the Minister of Lands and Mines, Mr. Charles Cockcroft, the Provincial Treasurer, and Mr. John Hugill, the Attorney-General. Differences with Mr. Aberhart had led to the resignation of Mr. Cross in December, 1936, and of Mr. Cockcroft in the following month. Mr. Hugill remained. One can imagine the discomfort of an experienced barrister, the product of an English public school and a university in the Maritime Provinces, moderate in his political views and absorbed principally in his departmental duties, confronted by a cabinet of hot gospellers, presided over by the messianic Mr. Aberhart.[24]

The 'differences' between Aberhart and the two members of his cabinet, Cross and Cockcroft, lay in the dawning realisation that the two 'moderates' were working with the Federal administration to circumvent the introduction of Social Credit policies. Mallory's study, from which the above is cited, formed part of the series of academic research projects on 'Social Credit in Alberta', commissioned by the Social Science Research Council of Canada and funded by the Rockefeller Foundation. The publications are described in Chapter 8. Thus, in Mallory's study, the democratically elected Premier is described as 'messianic' and his cabinet as 'hot gospellers' in contrast to three of his original cabinet who were 'moderates' just trying to get on with their jobs by ignoring 'social credit doctrine'.

It is curious that three key members of Aberhart's seven original cabinet turned out not to be committed to Social Credit. Equally curious is the sequence of events which led to the 'disallowance' by the Governor-General, as described by Mallory. When asked in the House by a member of the opposition whether the government had the power to legislate on banks and banking, Mr. Hugill would not commit himself, but merely referred to section 91 of the British North America Act. Recognising that the assent of the Lieutenant Governor was essential, the Premier himself asked:

> So that we may be certain of our Bills receiving the assent of the Lieutenant Governor, we suggest that the Attorney-General assures us that he feels in a position on every count to recommend that the Lieutenant-Governor gives his assent to every Social Credit Measure.[25]

Mr. Hugill did not give this assurance. When he accompanied the Premier in an interview with the Lieutenant-Governor he was again asked whether the bills passed by the Legislature were within its constitutional competence. As Attorney-General his advice to the Lieutenant-Governor was 'that the proposed enactments were not within our legislative competence. ... The acceptance of such a formula would be and the acquiescence in the enactment of such legislation, is tantamount to shaking the very foundation of our constitution and national unity.'[26] This disagreement with the elected Premier made Hugill's resignation inevitable. However, this was not an end of the matter, since the Lieutenant-Governor, Mr. J.C. Bowen, 'bowed to the wishes of his cabinet and assented to the legislation', ignoring the advice of the Attorney-General. Mallory excuses the Lieutenant-Governor's action on the grounds that he was new to the job and was uncertain 'what course to pursue'. His assent certainly 'came as somewhat of a surprise'. Since his assent was perfectly legal, according to the constitutions of both Provincial and Federal governments, fancy footwork was necessary to undo the decision which would have allowed the legislation passed by the democratically elected government to take effect. Within ten days the Federal Government 'disallowed' the legislation.

Constitutional framework

Writing in the December 10, 1937 edition of the *Social Credit Supplement*, Douglas explained the constitutional framework under which the Provinces and the Dominion of Canada were governed, pointing out that the Constitution of Canada was formed by the British North America Act, (B.N.A. Act), an Act of the British Parliament of 1867 which conferred certain rights on the Dominion and on the Provinces, including rights regarding disallowance. Having gone into the matter with Constitutional lawyers during his stay in Alberta in May 1935, Douglas was well versed in the subject. For a detailed description of the constitutional position, see Appendix 6e: Douglas on Constitutions. In brief, the ability of the Federal Prime Minister to 'disallow' legislation stems from the Royal Prerogative of the reigning U.K. sovereign being vested in the Governor-General of Canada, who was at that time Lord Tweedsmuir, and the Lieutenant-Governor of a province such as Alberta.

Mallory follows Hugill's justification of his advice to reserve assent 'on the ground that the Attorney-General was the official legal adviser of the Lieutenant-Governor and if his duty as legal adviser conflicted with the principle of cabinet solidarity he must choose to uphold the law as he understood it and risk severing his connection with the cabinet. He also argued that his professional oath as a barrister made it necessary for him to uphold the law and prevented him from giving advice contrary to what was to him the plain letter of the law'.[27] With the resignation of Hugill, 'the last of the moderates in the cabinet' the 'policy of the administration headed into a direct challenge to Dominion authority'.

Overview

The events in Alberta are a test case, demonstrating how the man-made rules of politics and finance can be used to frustrate the will of the people. To understand what is happening it is necessary to view World Government Diagram 6:a. Ultimately, power rests with *the people*. However, the weight of 'The World's Press, Platform and Pulpit' is thrown into shielding the people from knowledge of the truth. In theory, The People form the electorates who democratically vote in the 'Parliaments of the Nations'. In practice, only those policies which maintain 'The Will to Economic Scarcity' of the corporate world, or which do not seriously threaten the *status quo*, are allowed. Anything which does threaten the *status quo* is 'disallowed', and the power of the world's press, the entire academic world, and all moral teaching is ranged against the 'heresy'. 'Of course, people have got to go to work to earn the money to buy the goods produced by other people going to work. If people did not work for money there would be no production, and hence nothing to buy.' That is the message of 'The Will to Economic Scarcity' which is the policy of 'High Finance'. In view of the power of orthodoxy to present lies and half-truths, a debt of gratitude is owed to the prime movers in the story of Social Credit in Alberta, including Douglas, Orage, Aberhart, Byrne, Brenton, the Social Credit M.L.A.s, the electorate of Alberta and Social Crediters across Canada and throughout the world for seeing through the fog of untruth and refusing to remain silent.

The story of Social Credit in Alberta provides a working demonstration of the way forms of legal and financial repression work in co-operation. In 1935 the August Provincial election which brought in Aberhart's administration was followed by the Federal election of the same year which brought in Mackenzie King's administration. As leader of the Liberal Opposition contending for power during the election campaign, Mr. Mackenzie King, said at Saskatoon on September 21, 1935:

> Canada is faced with a great battle between the money power and the power of the people, a battle which will be waged in the new Parliament. I plead for a sweeping Liberal victory to carry out my policy of public control of currency and credit.

> Until the control of currency and credit is restored to the Government all talk of the Sovereignty of Parliament and democracy is idle and futile.[28]

When the Liberals defeated the Conservatives, so that Mackenzie King became the Canadian Premier after the Federal elections, the 17 Social Credit Members of Parliament formed the second largest opposition group. This fact, together with Mackenzie King's campaigning speeches, led many to suppose that Federal policy would have been sympathetic to the Provincial Government in Alberta. In disallowing the Albertan legislation which threatened to empower the people of Alberta, Mackenzie King demonstrated that he was powerless to act against the control of international finance over the political process in Canada, and by implication across the world. As Douglas demonstrated, the authority for 'disallowance' was based on the legal fiction of the Royal Prerogative vested in the Lieutenant-Governor of Alberta, Mr. Bowen, who was appointed by Mackenzie King in 1935.

Lord Tweedsmuir (John Buchan) wrote in *A Prince of the Captivity*, published in 1935:

> There is a great and potent world which the governments do not control. That is the world of Finance, the men who guide the ebb and flow of money. With them rests the decision whether they will make the river a beneficent flood to quicken life, or a dead glacier which freezes wherever it moves, or a torrent of burning lava to submerge and destroy. The men who control that river have the ultimate word.

Thus is indicated the spurious nature of a democratic system which separates principles from *actual policies*, and emphasises the importance of *principles* as if they have a separate existence. Moreover, as Douglas frequently pointed out, *individuals* must be held responsible for the systems they operate. One cannot fight burglary, only burglars.

The 1940 Alberta election

After five years in office William Aberhart, Premier of the Province of Alberta, sought re-election – and won it. Douglas commented:

> After years of careful preparation every trick that is known to the underworld, and some that are not, has been employed, to confuse, intimidate, and bribe the electorate into 'ridding the Province of Social Credit.' They have all failed. Rivers of dollars have poured into the towns for the same purpose—and have, it is hoped, permanently added to provincial purchasing power.

> It is, of course, perfectly well understood in Wall Street, Lombard Street, and Moscow that a world issue was at stake in Alberta—and Liberals, Conservatives, Socialists and Communists all disappeared to be replaced by 'Independents,' each with a nice little local policy for election purposes—to make it impossible for a Government not controlled by Finance ever to get back in power, Radio, Press, Pulpit—all were manipulated. The Alberta Electorate remained almost completely silent—and then voted the Social Credit Party back to power with a majority, which is probably stronger than ever before.[29]

The achievements of Aberhart and his Social Credit Government in its first term of office are remarkable. As Hooke records:

It is normal during a four-year term of office to hold four sessions of the Legislature, or five at the most, if the government remains in office for a five-year term. However, during the first term of the Aberhart administration, nine sessions were held altogether.

Before the arrival in Edmonton of the Douglas appointees, special sessions had been held as afore-noted as a result of the insurgency. Shortly after the arrival of Powell and Byrne, recommendations were made to the government by the Social Credit Board that legislation be passed which would have the effect of challenging entrenched finance. Special sessions were called for the purpose of enacting such legislation and these, together with the regular sessions up to and including the Session of 1940, witnessed what no doubt was one of the greatest battles ever undertaken by a provincial government. ...

Some of the provocative legislation did not get beyond the Legislature, as the Lieutenant Governor of the day, the Honourable J. C. Bowen, refused assent. Other legislation was rejected by the Courts. In some cases the Federal government of the Honourable Mackenzie King exercised the power of disallowance. This despite the oft-repeated promises made by Mr. King that his policy would always be 'hands off Alberta.' In order that my readers will better understand the nature of the battle in which the Alberta Government was involved, I shall outline briefly some of the legislation and indicate its fate. The Bureau of Information and News, which had been established by the government in order that accurate information could be given to public from time to time, summarized these legislative enactments under three headings: 'Why Passed'; 'What Happened' and 'What it would have done.'[30]

Further detail of the achievements of the administration are included in Appendix 6d: How Alberta is Fighting Finance.

The 1940 election was the last one Aberhart was to fight. He died in May 1943. His final broadcast, An Aberhart Broadcast,[31] is available electronically. His successor, Ernest Manning, adopted policies more in keeping with orthodoxy. Although Byrne continued to work with the Social Credit Board until 1948, supporters of Douglas Social Credit policies were progressively eliminated from the Cabinet. Although the Government of Alberta continued to be re-elected by the people of Alberta under the name of 'Social Credit', the policies pursued were indistinguishable from those of political parties endorsed by the financial authorities.

Did Social Credit fail?

Far from having 'failed', Social Credit achieved success, against over-whelming odds. In spite of systematic misrepresentation by mainstream press, media and academia, Social Credit literature was studied throughout the British Commonwealth, the United States and elsewhere. For decades Social Crediters continued to contest provincial elections in Saskatchewan, Manitoba, Ontario and French-speaking Quebec, and achieved political power in British Columbia (1952 – 1991). They also continued to contest Federal elections, achieving continuous representation in the House of Commons.

However, the mainstream was successful in representing Social Credit to the public as a dangerous heresy, economically unsound and politically steeped in anti-Semitism. To the extent that thinking people have allowed themselves to be convinced of the 'official' version of the story, Social Credit could be said to have 'failed'. In March 1934, a year before the Alberta election which brought in the Aberhart administration, Arthur Brenton, editor of *The New Age*, made a most telling comment on social thinking and politics in the twentieth century:

> The Douglas Movement bases its educational activities on two funda-mental propositions, the one being technical and the other political. The first is that the financial system *automatically causes a shortage of purchasing power*. The second is that something called the Money Monopoly exists, and that the people at the head of it are deliberately *preventing the public from getting to understand* that this is so. The Douglas advocate, insofar as he is able to make contact with the public, is called upon to explain the 'how?' of the technical proposition, and the 'who?' of the political one. 'Give us a *reason* – give us a *name*,' cry the multitudes, oblivious of the fact that in the first place they are without a background which would make the reason intelligible to them; and that, in the second, no direct evidence can be brought against any person at all. 'Show us a sign,' cried the multitudes of old, 'that the words you speak are true'; and they were told that they were not going to be given a sign – that if they could not feel the power of the truth in the words spoken, no sign would commu-nicate that feeling.

> It is true that the reason is intelligibly communicable, but only to those who are patient enough to undergo the discipline of systematic research. But to the Douglas advocate the task of contacting such people and persuading them, in an atmosphere of mass-incredulity, to assume the

antecedent possibility of the proposition being true (without which assumption who is going to spend time on study?) comes as near to being insuperable as any task that can be conceived. The masses, when they demand a *reason*, are demanding something which is really a *substitute for reasoning* – something which commands conviction without demanding thought. This is because they have been trained to expect instruction in that form, and because it has always been possible for them to get it in that form in respect of the policies and programmes of which political parties have strewn about for them to wrangle over. Little pieces of irreconcilable truths is all they want, and it is all that they have been allowed to have. And, mentally disarmed as they have become by this armoury of heterogeneous convictions about trivialities, they yet expect, mostly subconsciously, to understand the financial technique for economic synthesis and political reconciliation merely by inspecting an article in a newspaper or hearing a speech in a meeting-place.[32]

Despite the passage of over seven decades, Arthur Brenton's words continue to ring true.

Due to the general failure to engage in systematic thought, the same 'little pieces of irreconcilable truths' all too frequently continue to stand as substitutes for reasoning. After World War II the leading Social Credit politicians in Alberta became ardent Zionists. By 1948 they had 'purged' the Social Credit party of its non-Zionists,[33] and Douglas Social Credit faded from the West. The mantle was taken up by Louis Even and the Roman Catholic Social Crediters of Rougemont, Quebec.

NOTES
1   Additional material can be found at www.Douglassocialcredit.com
2   Hooke (1971). See also www.Douglassocialcredit.com
3   Douglas, 'Your War in Alberta', *Social Credit Supplement*, December 10, 1937.
4   Douglas (1937) p103.
5   J.D.B. See Appendix 6b: Coast to Coast.
6   J.D.B. See Appendix 6b: Coast to Coast.
7   See Appendix 6a: Douglas on Aberhart.
8   See Appendix 6c: *The Economist*.
9   Notes of the Week, *The New Age*, 8 March 1934.
10 Cited in *Social Credit*, March 13, 1936.
11 Hooke (1971) p84.

12 Hargrave (1937) page 3.

13 Hargrave (1937) page 4.

14 Hargrave (1937) page 5.

15 Hooke (1971) p135.

16 Gesell (1929)

17 Douglas (1937) pp. 125-198).

18 Reproduced in Douglas (1937) pp99-118.

19 Hooke (1971) page 121.

20 Hooke (1971)

21 Hooke (1971) page 127.

22 Byrne's Preface to Douglas (1937) (1984 edition).

23 Quoted in Mallory (1954) p73

24 Mallory (1954) p74

25 Cited in Mallory (1954) p74

26 Cited in Mallory (1954) p75

27 Mallory (1954) p75

28 *The Fig Tree*, No.9, June 1938, pages 46-62.

29 Douglas quoted in Appendix 6d How Alberta is Fighting Finance.

30 Hooke (1971) p135-6.

31 http://douglassocialcredit.com/resources/archives/aberhart_broadcast.pdf

32 *The New Age*, Vol. LIV. No. 19. Thursday March 8, 1934

33 Stingel (2000)

Appendix 6a
Majpor Douglas on Aberhart

Social Credit, September 6, 1935

The interest which has been excited by the sweeping victory of the Social Credit Party in Alberta in the provincial election which has just taken place is not, I think, unjustified. Those who are concerned with monetary science are aware that a verdict has been given against orthodox financial policy. Students of politics recognise that, **for the first time in modern history, a Government has been elected against the wishes of those financial powers which, for the most part, control all Governments**; while the general public senses instinctively that the problem of poverty amidst plenty is about to be tackled (perhaps for the first time) without fear of vested interests.

An Unparalleled Achievement

Fifty-six out of a total of sixty-three seats in the Legislature have been won by the Social Credit Party. Mr. William Aberhart, to whom this result is, beyond all question, mainly due, is a leader of great force of character and sincerity, and has the population of the Province behind him to an extent which, so far as I am aware, is without parallel. He has not himself been a candidate but, as Premier, will remain the political leader of the new Government, as he has been of the party during the period of propaganda and political organisation.

Our Objective is Identical

For reasons which are fairly obvious, strong efforts have been made to suggest that there is a radical difference between Mr. Aberhart's views and my own. So far as objectives are concerned, such a difference is non-existent. To the extent that the application of Social Credit in Alberta has reached the stage of plans, it is my own opinion (and here, of course, I speak only for myself) that Mr. Aberhart has successfully drawn a picture to the electorate by means of which he has depicted an objective subject in terms which could be understood by a rural population. I should be surprised if he or they attach any special importance to any details of this picture. I feel confident that both his own judgement and the force of circumstances will lead him to adopt methods which will enable him to implement his promises. Politics in Alberta, and indeed in the whole of Western Canada, is a deadly serious business. The condition of affairs is bad, and it is getting worse. Alberta itself is a province of immense natural resources, almost wholly unexploited, and its population is hard-working, decent and reasonable. But it is determined to have a square deal, and I believe that, under Mr. Aberhart, it will get it.

Opposition to be Expected

Since the application of Social Credit principles involves the use of financial credit for the benefit of the general population rather than the banking system, it is certain that the new Government will meet with all opposition that can be provided by International Finance. Whilst this opposition may delay the result, I do not think it will ultimately affect it.

The repercussions on both the Canadian Federal election and upon the Social Credit Movement which exists in practically every British Dominion overseas, are likely to be great, with consequent, and probably irresistible, pressure upon the policy of the British Cabinet at home. So far as Canada is concerned the problem of debt, more particularly in the Western Provinces, has now reached a stage in which either fresh methods must be used to deal with it or repudiation must become inevitable. Taxation has definitely come under the influence of the Law of Diminishing Returns. Properties are being abandoned from sheer inability to pay the tax upon them, with a result that a smaller and diminishing base for the tax structure is left to bear the load. The result of the drying up of purchasing power and the draining of the resources of the country to meet the demands of the Eastern creditors has had, among other effects, that of so reducing the traffic of the railways that they are faced with bankruptcy or worse. Every prediction of post-war Canadian Governments has been falsified, and practically no promises affecting the security and prosperity of the individual have been kept.

These is no belief in any of the old parties, and it is by no means improbable that, even in the short time available before the Federal elections of October 22, a new party, possibly headed by Mr. Stevens, the revolting Conservative Minister, may obtain the balance of power in co-operation with the Alberta Government, and transfer the Social Credit victory to Ottawa, with results not only very important in themselves, but quite probably decisive in the coming New Zealand elections, which are already certain to turn upon the question of Social Credit.

Such results may quite possibly occur even in advance of any actual concrete achievement in Alberta, in the field of practical economics, while the successful inauguration of even the early stages of a reformed financial regime, effectively abolishing the absurdity of scarcity amidst riches, will, beyond question, provide an object lesson capable of modifying world politics.

C.H. Douglas
August 30, 1935

Appendix 6b

Coast To Coast

CANADA and ELECTORAL POLICY

Social Credit, September 6, 1935

It is to be hoped that no new reader mistakes this paper for an organ of opinion. As Major Douglas wrote not long ago, it is an organ of policy; that is to say, it exists to achieve a definite objective, not to run a pleasant debating club. Its very beginning was the direct outcome of his great speech at Buxton, when he defended the proper function of democracy as being to decide *what* is to be done, but not *how* it is to be done or who is to do it.

Protection Against Fraud

This paper accepts that statement as both true and of fundamental importance, but more particularly for the fast-growing number of readers overseas, there are two points which touch on every one of us, whether we agree with this abstract definition of democracy or not. The first is that to demand results is the only safe way to protect ourselves against fraud. By fraud I mean the sort of *imposed and diluted* social credit that the financial interests will eventually offer us, which they are probably already resigned to offering us, if we make the serious tactical error of demanding *methods* rather than *results*. They can easily divide and confuse us on questions of technique, for they are experts and we, for the most part, are not. There is hardly any country with whose social credit history I am familiar where they have not already had considerable success in doing so. Whether they succeed further depends on peoples' success or failure to close their ranks and demand those results which, as we know, only social credit can give.

The Devil Drives

The second point is that *time is limited*. I wish I could feel sure that even among those working to save democracy there is a full realization of this fact. Within the next three or four years various alternatives, or a combination of them, face Great Britain and the world. War, revolution, widespread epidemics or, to avoid these, iron dictatorship compared with which the present régimes in Russia or Germany will seem almost innocuous. Fear for one's own safety is a bad incentive to action, and I mention this aspect of the matter simply because it cannot fail to be at the back of everyone's mind, and had better be taken out and looked in the eye before it is replaced by some more fruitful emotion. If anyone still doubts the possibility of dictatorship in Anglo-Saxon countries (imposed always, of course, in the name of liberty, and with a minimum of uniforms), he does not yet appreciate the truth of the motto by which modern governments live. 'Needs must when the devil drives.' They have no choice; Major Douglas has made it clear enough for anyone to understand in his Alberta report, and the treatment of the unemployed both in Canada and elsewhere in recent months is bearing him out to the letter.

Canada is World Centre

At this moment, ludicrous as it may sound to those who have not considered the matter, the centre of the world's stage is not Geneva, or Rome, or Moscow, but in Canada. **There the battle is joined which will decide the fate not only of nations, for they do not matter, but of men and women and children who do.** Albertans have challenged the Money Monopoly by demanding results, through the medium of a government pledged to the abolition of poverty. To debate at such a point whether this or that member of the Social Credit League committed himself to technical statements incompatible with those of Douglas, and still more to accuse them of not understanding the intricacies of the subject, are courses, as I suggested last week, which would show a complete lack of appreciation of the dynamic possibilities of the situation, and might, in fact, become actively dangerous. It has been said that the enemies of social credit will try to 'confuse' Douglas and Aberhart in the popular mind. But apart from the strategic point of view nothing could be better. It seems to me **equally likely, however, that they will try to split them in the popular mind, by magnifying the importance of any discussion of technical discrepancies, where they exist, and ignoring the fact that the two men are essentially at one in objective and increasingly so in strategy. There have already been signs in the London press that this course is being pursued,** and I shall be surprised and pleased if Canadian comments do not confirm it. To discredit the popular leader who raised public enthusiasm, by setting him against the technical consultant from overseas who in the nature of things cannot do so, is the course I should pursue if I were behind the

Economic Safety League, or importing professors and Washington feature-writers to do my dirty work.

Once Aberhart was removed as a dynamic force, finance probably feels, rightly or wrongly, that it could prolong technical discussion in Alberta till the cows came home and died in their stalls for lack of feed. If anyone in the province feels worried about the technical position of the Social Credit League, I will ask him to **remember that Major Douglas remains the economic advisor of the provincial government, whichever party is in power, and that Mr. Aberhart has more than once expressed his full intention of asking him back to formulate a plan of action for the province**.

The Federal Elections

The Federal elections have now been fixed for October 14, and the relation between them and the Alberta situation is a complex matter which is keeping the keenest Canadian observers awake at nights. At one time there were rumours that the Social Credit party and Mr. Stevens' Reconstruction party would join forces, but this has since been denied and it seems unlikely that any positive alliance will occur. A defensive alliance, however, should be by no means impossible, especially since Mr. Stevens' statement reported in The Observer of August 25, that in view of the overwhelming support for Mr. Aberhart in Alberta, 'it is obviously the duty of the federal authorities to give every reasonable co-operation and assistance to him to carry out the policies which have been so definitely endorsed.'

Let us assume that the Reconstruction party carries a large proportion of urban seats in Ontario, and a certain number of rural constituencies there and in British Columbia, Stevens' own province. He can probably count on the support of the U.F.A. federal members if some of them retain their seats, and in any case if, as seems likely, they are replaced by members of the Social Credit League, the two parties between them may well have a large minority in the House of Commons, the one pledged to social credit, the other at least to sympathetic and prompt investigation of the possibilities of monetary reform. Under these circumstances it would be difficult, if not impossible, for a Liberal government at Ottawa to interfere with such provincial action to secure political control of credit as Major Douglas might advise the provincial government to take. (In all this, of course, I am assuming that there will be no conflict of social credit forces anywhere in the federal field; such a development would quite clearly be disastrous.)

The Morning After

Assuming, then, that the Liberal party is returned to (doubtful) power, the question of the utility of an electoral campaign[2] on the same general principles as that in Great Britain naturally arises. I described at the beginning of this article the two factors which make a demand for results of practical urgency, whatever my be the theoretical position, and it is difficult to escape the conclusion that what might well be desirable in the provincial field is essential in the federal. It must not be forgotten that such a campaign is genuinely non-party in a sense which no other can be, and that it is beyond question the quickest way of rousing a whole people to the full realization of what their united votes can do. According to circumstances, it may act as a threat (as in Great Britain), or as a non-party vote of confidence and support.

In the unlikely, but not impossible, event of a coalition of monetary reformers being returned to power, the usefulness of such a campaign, for the reasons just given, would be in no way lessened, and this would be particularly the case since it is almost out of the question that such a coalition would be powerful enough to force through a controversial programme, without such support. It might be several years before an enthusiasm comparable with that in Alberta could be developed throughout the Dominion for social credit, whereas an electoral campaign could quite probably be carried through in a shorter time than in this country [GB], in spite of our much smaller distances. Of course, pledges through the mail or as the result of broadcast appeals might play a big part, and it is unlikely that the energy and resource of Canadians would fail to finish the job successfully if they once undertook it.

J.D.B.

Appendix 6c
A Pointer To Success
Curious Attitude Taken Up by
The Economist

Social Credit, September 6, 1935

The Economist of August 31, commenting on the Alberta election results, points out that the financing of the dividend by any form of retail turnover tax would be a 'burdensome and apparently pointless form of redistributive tax,' and that to attempt to finance it by loans 'would be merely to increase the deficit and indebtedness of the Province.' In any case it says such expedients would not be genuine 'Social Credit' for 'The essence of that doctrine is the financing of free consumers' credits by a steady and permanent creation of new money.'

Money for Alberta

There is no need to quarrel with this definition, incomplete though it is, and I find the subsequent statement of the difficulties to be overcome of great interest; it is as follows:

> But how is Mr. Aberhart, as Prime Minister of Alberta, to create new money without transgressing the limits set by Canadian banking law? He cannot found a Government bank and issue an unlimited amount of notes. For the Bank Act of June 1934, provides that from the day on which the Bank of Canada commenced business the maximum of notes issued by a chartered bank should not exceed 'the amount of the unimpaired paid-up capital of the bank on that day; and that subsequently the maximum should be progressively reduced. The only possibility before Mr. Aberhart would presumably be to found a Government bank and issue unlimited credit irrespective of cash reserves. He has already spoken of using the 'real resources' of the Province as a 'basis for credit.' Such credit would not be convertible into cash and would only be usable within Alberta if its citizens chose to accept it. If they did so accept it,

however, and it was expanded indefinitely, it would eventually dwindle in value terms both of commodities and of the Canadian dollar. In any case, there are further legal obstacles to such a scheme. The Bank Act of June, 1934, provides that a 'bank cannot issue notes or commence the business of banking until it has obtained from the Treasury Board a certificate permitting it to do so.' Mr. Aberhart cannot set up a new bank, therefore, without the Treasury's permission. But even if he obtained permission, the amount of credit which the bank could issue would be severely limited. For the Bank of Canada Act provides (clause 27):-

> Every chartered bank shall ... maintain a reserve of not less than 5 per cent. of its deposits with the Bank (of Canada) and notes of the bank held by such bank.

> Unless therefore, Mr. Aberhart can devise some form of tax certificate or I.O.U. which will be accepted as currency by the citizens of Alberta, but not regarded as such by the Dominion lawyers, it does not seem likely that any genuine Social Credit scheme will be attempted in that Province.

Victory Expected

Thus *The Economist* anticipates defeat. But does it really? As one of the innumerable loud-speakers of finance, surely this is not the line it would take if it did? **Would it not be more likely, in such circumstances, to suggest that there is nothing to stop Social Credit being given a fair trial in Alberta, and its fallacies exposed for all time?** But, in view of the quotation above, should the defeat it professes to expect occur, it cannot very well suggest that the Douglas proposals have been so tested [Emphasis added].

In the circumstances, I regard this defeatist propaganda as most encouraging. The difficulties to be overcome are great, but not necessarily insuperable, and this admission of their existence is of value as explaining in advance any delays which occur in the transition from poverty to plenty.

'Where there's a will, there's a way,' and who can doubt the will of Major Douglas, the economic adviser to the Alberta Government? His tenacity is proved by the way in which he has hung on during the past sixteen years despite attacks from every quarter.

M. Jacklin

Appendix 6d
How Alberta is Fighting Finance

'WHAT ALBERTA MAKES MAKES ALBERTA'

The British public which has been taught by its newspapers to say that 'Social Credit failed in Alberta' knows that there is something wrong about this even while it says it. What is it that is wrong about it? The following statement answers this question:-

William Aberhart, the Premier of the Province of Alberta, had been in power for five years when he sought re-election in 1940 – and won it. Major C.H. Douglas, whose demonstration of what is possible in a modern community in the way of 'Life, and Life more abundant' had inspired Aberhart to promise its attainment to the people of Alberta, said of this second victory:-

> After years of careful preparation every trick that is known to the underworld, and some that are not, has been employed, to confuse, intimidate, and bribe the electorate into 'ridding the Province of Social Credit.' They have all failed. Rivers of dollars have poured into the towns for the same purpose – and have, it is hoped, permanently added to provincial purchasing power.

> *It is, of course, perfectly well unĪderstood in Wall Street, Lombard Street, and Moscow that a world issue was at stake in Alberta – and Liberals, Conservatives, Socialists and Communists all disappeared to be replaced by 'Independents,' each with a nice little local policy for election purposes – to make it impossible for a Government not controlled by Finance ever to get back in power. Radio, Press, Pulpit – all were manipulated. The Alberta Electorate remained almost completely silent – and then voted the Social Credit Party (i.e. The Albertan Party led by Mr Aberhart) back to power with a majority, which is probably stronger than ever before.*

What story does the record have to tell? What has the Social Credit Government of Alberta done, and what has it *not* done because the Federal Government of Canada, or the Lieutenant-Governor, or the Supreme Court of Canada or the Privy Council – all bent single-mindedly upon the one policy of preventing the declared will of the electorate from prevailing – stood in its way?

The answer is given in Mr Hand's pamphlet, *The Case for Alberta,* from which the following particulars are taken. Thirty years of Liberal and United Farmers Association rule resulted in the following legacy inherited by the Aberhart Government:

Provincial Debt (Nil in 1905)	$161,000,000
Municipal Debt	$70,000,000
Mortgage Debt	$200,000,000
Private Debt	$171,000,000
Total	**$602,000,000**

Business failures (in five years)		**307**
Registered Unemployed	7,406	
Inadequate health services		
Unpaid teachers' salaries		**$250,000**

All this in a land of plenty, with elevators and stores crammed full, mines and forests standing idle; oil in abundance unused, and enough live stock, dairy, poultry and garden produce for all. This was the Aberhart Government's starting point.

THE ACCOMPLISHMENT

The Hon. Solon Law, Provincial Treasurer, in introducing the Bill for the institution of a system of Treasury Branches designed to facilitate trade within the Province, - a part of the famous 'Interim Programme' summed up the position thus:-

> After demonstrating that every action to secure for the people of the Province the economic reforms they desired could be blocked from the top, and after repeated threats from the banks to withdraw essential services from various points in the Province, the Government, in obedience to a wide demand, prepared plans to give the people facilities for deriving increased benefits themselves through co-operation.

Opposition, chiefly from combines whose headquarters lay outside the Province, has been fomented; but the system has shown what might be done without the actual creation of credit instruments – an activity which is still the monopoly of the great banking 'interests.' Here are some other results of the measures which form part of the 'Interim Programme':-

In the first year, the provincial debt fell $900,000; in the second $700,000; in the third $1,400,000 – a total of *$3,000,000 while the debts of other provinces in Canada were increasing.* Interest payments were cut by 50 per cent and $3,464,057 worth of Savings Certificates were redeemed.

Income Account Revenue rose by $2,243,594 accounted for by (a) revenue increases without tax increases and (b) tax increases on financial corporations *not paid by the public* ($353,843).

Social and other public services increased.

While Saskatchewan, from 1936-9, had $7,502,000 worth of maturities refunded and the Dominion cancelled $26,679,996 worth of Treasury Bills, there was discrimination against Alberta in the same period, and the financiers' refusal of assistance resulted in defaults totalling £11,855,200.

Education was extended and improved, the cost reduced, and teachers' unpaid salaries paid off.

Improvement in health services resulted in decrease of 12 per cent in the death rate; Alberta had in 1933 *the largest tubercle-free area in the Empire.*

The Government passed the first general wage order in Canada, extended the scope and efficiency of previous wage acts, passed a Tradesmen's Qualification Act, enforced the Industrial Standards Act and at the outbreak of war was in the vanguard of progress in regard to Labour Legislation.

New industries have been opened up and payrolls (industrial) rose from $62,000,000 in 1934 to $75,000,000 in 1938. Employment increased 20 per cent. Trade increased. Manufactures increased. Construction increased 134 per cent. Minerals increased 56 per cent. In farming, a bull exchange policy and a boar exchange policy banished debt, and a hog policy raised the quality, as measured by the 'selects' market, 36.5 per cent. Improvements were effected on farms. Butter and cheese qualities improved. Families beaten by the debt-system were re-established and most became self-supporting in four years.

Roads have been built with up-to-date efficiency, without increasing debt, whereas before 1935 the Edmonton to Calgary road was gravelled at a cost of $2,358,030. This investment was gone in 10 years, leaving $1,164,447 of debt as a continuing burden.

Alberta is producing 97 per cent of Canada's oil and 70 per cent of Canada's gas.

Alberta fire premiums in 1935-38 amounted to $12,722,831. Only $4,432,320 was paid out on fire losses. So Alberta can tell the world what happens to Insurance profits? Or won't the Federal Government let it?

Bureaucracy? The Civil Service Staff increased 2,907 to 3,324, not much; and the increase was due to Adjustment Board work and the King's Printer doing the people's work effecting a saving of forty to fifty per cent - $100,000 a year – and other causes.

In the Treasury Branch organisation, also, the Province has the germ of an exchange system run in the public interest.

This is part of what the Alberta Government has done while trying, in face of hidden opposition using the Federal Government and other administrative agencies as its tools, to carry out the will of the people of Alberta.

How has democracy been denied? An Albertan says:

DEMOCRACY DENIED

During the past three years there has been a most deliberate and unjustifiable attempt to block several measures designed to relieve the suffering and want which exists throughout the Province. Everything that could be done to deceive the people has been done. Propaganda has been used over the air, on public platforms and in the newspapers which is an iniquity and a disgrace to any civilised people.

The people elected the Government to achieve a certain objective, but every possible obstacle has been placed in its path; its legislation has been held up by the Dominion Government or by reference to the Court. Every device has been used to thwart the Will of the People of Alberta.

Almost every country in the world is in a state of war or preparing for one. Solution of the Underemployment Problem and a state of so-called prosperity is being brought about by a programme of armament building, but by no other country except Alberta is the real cause of suffering humanity being fought.

We, the people of Alberta, are at war with International Finance. It is a war that is worth while because it means freedom and security for ourselves and our children for all time. It is a war in which human life need not and will not be sacrificed. We have so far answered those who seek to discredit us with three years of honest, progressive Government and persistent effort. We have answered the destructive criticism of old party politicians with the mellowed tones of sound reasoning. We have answered the mailed fist of money dictatorship with the padded glove of peaceful fellowship, but war may have many phases, and if our battle must finally be won by still more aggressive methods, better we do it now, so that our children may enjoy the heritage it will be our privilege to hand on, in peace and security.

There is no argument that the root cause of all our ills today, as it always has been, is lack of money, leading to war, unemployment, poverty, with all their attendant evils of murder, suicides, desperation and madness. The logical spot then at which to apply the cure is at the cause of our trouble. Even old party leaders are now telling us they too, believe we are right in our demands. If they enter the fight with their hands clean we welcome them. Social Credit is not a party issue and we must never permit it to become a party football. We are prepared to welcome people of every political creed into our ranks, but they must take up the fight on our terms and according to our rules.

We, who believe implicitly in the philosophy of this great movement, and the justice of our cause, believe that not only our province, but the Dominion and other countries of the world will gradually come to realise that only be removing the cause of the poverty, so widespread over the Dominion of Canada, can they ever hope to bring order out of the chaos which exists today. It is, therefore, not surprising to find men, who have in the past been leaders in the world of orthodox financing, having realised that its downfall is imminent, taking their places in the ranks of those who have challenged its power, and are determined to sever for all time the strangling effect its hold has on the very life of every country in the world.

Credit of Alberta Regulation Act

Why passed

1   Because there was widespread poverty and distress throughout Alberta.

2   Because Alberta, one of the richest provinces in the Dominion, could produce abundance for her people.

3   Because the only reason why Alberta's people were living in poverty was the lack of purchasing power.

4   Because such purchasing power should be made available to the people by using their own credit, as would enable them to obtain, at all times, what they wanted.

5   Because this could be done by a scientific balancing between money and goods produced.

6   Because control of Credit being, in the words of Hon. McKenzie King, 'A public matter not of interest to bankers alone, but of direct concern to every citizen,' credit policy should be vested in an authority responsible to the representatives of the people.

7   Because banks, being manufacturers of credit and functioning as public utility concerns, supplying a service of primary and vital importance to the lives of the citizens of Alberta, should be licensed and subjected to supervision only in regard to policy – the results they provide, and unless

the people of Alberta can use the resources of their own Province as they desire, and determine the results which shall accrue to them, they have no property and civil rights in the full sense. (Banking administration being under Federal Jurisdiction was in no manner affected by the Act).

What happened

Disallowed by Federal Government August 17, 1937.

What it would have done

1 Would have secured the results demanded by the People – a lower cost to live, and monthly dividends.

2 Would have provided markets for Alberta manufacturers and traders.

3 Would have led to tremendous industrial development in manufacturing Alberta goods by processing Alberta produce.

4 Would have resulted in rapidly absorbing every unemployed person into useful employment and relieved the aged and infirm of the necessity of working for a living.

5 Would have led to increased business activity in which industrialists, wholesalers, retailers and banks would all have benefited.

6 Would have enabled taxation to be reduced drastically.

7 Would have made it possible to deal with the debt problems.

Bank Taxation Act

Why passed

1 Because, under the present system, the Government has one source of revenue only – Taxation.

2 Because the people of Alberta are already taxed beyond their ability to pay.

3 Because banks are the only institutions claiming the legal right to monetise the credit of The People to such an extent that they create and issue monetary credits many times in excess of the legal tender money they hold.

4 Because banks can thereby create money out of nothing.

5 Because the present method of taxation of individuals is confiscatory and unnecessary.

What happened

Assent withheld by Lieutenant Governor. Declared unconstitutional by Supreme Court of Canada. Appeal by Province from Supreme Court decision to Privy Council dismissed.

What it would have done

1   *Would have placed over Two Million Dollars new money in circulation.*

2   Would have permitted an equal amount, otherwise paid in taxes, to remain in the ordinary channels of industry, thus aiding employment and acting as a tremendous impetus to business generally, or,

3   Would have enabled the Government to embark on a six million dollar highway and market roads programme under the three way Dominion-Provincial-Municipality plan, or,

4   Would have provided a hospital and medical service in districts where those are not available, or,

5   Would have set up a fund for Crop Insurance, or,

6   Would have given decreased School Taxes.

7   Would have provided increased purchasing power for the People of Alberta.

Reduction and Settlement of Debt Act

Why passed

1   Because, under the present financial system debt cannot be paid without creating new and larger debts. The People of Alberta possess only about 20c. money except as a debt to the bankers.

2   Because private debts, largely due to accumulated interest, had increased to such an extent that they were out of all proportion to value received.

3   Because many outstanding debts had been incurred during the war (1914-18 phase) and immediate post-war years when values were high.

4   Because the original debt had already, in many cases, been paid in interest charges while the principal remained unchanged or showed little reduction.

5   Because people could no longer continue to pay interest of 8 to 10 per cent.

6   Because financial corporations refused to recognise that the inability of

people to meet their obligations was due to lack of adequate returns on what they produced.

7 Because no people or country can prosper and progress so long as they labour under a burden of those who deal in money as a commodity.

What happened

Declared *ultra vires* of the Province by the Courts.

What it would have done

1 *Would have established a basis of settlement for all outstanding debts.*

2 Would have reduced all debt incurred previous to July, 1932, by applying all interest paid from that date to the passing of the act on reduction of principal.

3 Would have settled definitely the question involved in debts which had become uncollectable.

4 Would have led to a restoration of confidence and encouraged those who, through no fault of their own, were living in poverty and struggling against odds they could not possibly overcome.

Act to Ensure Publication of Accurate News Information

Why passed

1 Because the control of news and the control of credit are both exercised by the financial interests.

2 Because 'The freedom of the press' has become license to distort news, *misrepresent facts and withhold information from the public.*

3 Because this anti-social aspect of the press, under inspired direction, is being *used to thwart the people of Alberta in their struggle against finance.*

What happened

Assent withheld by Lieutenant Governor. Declared unconstitutional by Supreme Court of Canada. In the appeal of the Province of Alberta from decision of Court of Canada, the Privy Council refused to hear argument by their counsel.

What it would have done

1 Would have ensured that all newspapers in Alberta would publish all the facts in their news reports of Government matters so far as this was

possible, and if from any cause false statements appeared, equal space would be given for authoritative correction.

2 Would have ensured that the same information which every publisher demands from correspondents to his columns, i.e. the names of contributors of articles, would be available to The People when demanded by their representatives.

Home Owners Security Act

Why passed

1 Because under stress of world conditions and a falsified financial system, over which individuals had no control, many were forced to mortgage their homes.

2 Because conditions had changed since these loans were received so that commodity and labour prices bore little relation to the continued high price of money.

3 Because there was grave danger of many Alberta Citizens losing their homes.

4 Because, in most cases, these homes represented the total life savings of many people.

5 Because it is just as much the duty of any government to protect the homes of individual members of Society against the confiscatory practices of unscrupulous lenders as it is to defend its people against the invasion of a foreign aggressor.

6 Because there can be no Sanctity of Contract which does not recognise that Human life has, at least, as much value as considerations of 'money.'

What happened

Disallowed by Mackenzie-King Government, June 15, 1938.

What it would have done

1 Would have prohibited foreclosures or sale under mortgage proceedings of any farm home.

2 Would have prohibited foreclosure or sale under mortgage proceedings of any Home in a town, city or village, unless the plaintiff first deposited $2,000 with the Court which would be paid to the owner, if dispossessed

to enable him to Purchase another home.

3   Would have induced debtor and crediter alike to seek equitable basis of settlement through medium of the Debt Adjustment Board.

4   Would have enabled home-owners to enter into new contracts commensurate with their present ability to pay.

Security Tax Act – 1938

Why passed

1   *Because the Government required additional revenue for one year to replace the loss of revenue from the Bank Taxation Act before the Privy Council.*

2   *Because the additional revenue was essential to provide the people with the benefits they needed.*

3   *Because it was equitable that equitable companies and similar institutions should make good some of the taxation they have escaped for years.*

4   *Because the Government is pledged to the people to remove the burden of Taxation from individuals, and until we gain control of our credit resources, this can be done only by transferring it to institutions which are better able to bear it.*

What happened

Disallowed by Mackenzie-King Government, June 15, 1938

What it would have done

1   *Would have realised $1,500,000 – sufficient revenue to balance the Provincial Budget.*

2   *Would have helped the Government considerably to give tax relief, to provide additional relief projects, increase School Grants, and undertake many other benefits planned for the people.*

Credit of Alberta Regulation Act (1938 Amendment)

Why passed

Because Credit of Alberta Regulation act had been disallowed by the Dominion Government.

What happened

Assent withheld by Lieutenant-Governor. Declared unconstitutional by Supreme

Court of Canada. In the appeal of the Province of Alberta from decision of Supreme Court of Canada, the Privy Council refused to hear Alberta's argument by their counsel.

What it would have done

Would have brought all the benefits of the Credit of Alberta Regulation act, which it supplanted.

Appendix 6e

Douglas on Constitutions

Your War In Alberta

Clifford Hugh Douglas, *Social Credit Supplement*, December 10, 1937

The British North America Act

The Constitution of Canada, so far as it is supposed to have one – is contained in the British North America Act, commonly called the B.N.A. Act. This is an Act of the British Parliament of 1867, which confers certain rights on the Dominion and on the Provinces, including rights regarding disallowance. The power of disallowance was a delegation to the Governor-General of a power residing in the Sovereign, who in 1867 was Queen Victoria, and her powers were much greater than they are today. In theory the reigning sovereign has the right, known as the Royal Prerogative, of refusing assent to Bills passed by Parliament, but we all know quite well what would happen if it were to be exercised today, and it certainly does not seem possible to invest a Governor-General with greater powers than his sovereign.

In the B.N.A. Act the only reference to disallowance which I can find are in Sections 55, 56, and 57, which read as follows:

'55. Where a Bill passed by the Houses of Parliament is presented to the Governor-General for the Queen's Assent, he shall declare according to his discretion, but subject to the provisions of this Act and to Her Majesty's Instructions, either that he assents thereto in the Queen's name, or that he withholds the Queen's Assent, or that he reserves the Bill for the Signification of the Queen's Pleasure.

'56. Where the Governor-General assents to a Bill in the Queen's name, he shall by the first convenient opportunity send an authentic copy of the Act to one of her Majesty's Principal Secretaries of State, and if the Queen in Council within Two Years after Receipt thereof by the Secretary of State thinks fit to disallow the Act, such Disallowance (with a Certificate of the

Secretary of State of the Day on which the Act was received by him) being signified by the Governor-General, by Speech or by Message to each of the Houses of Parliament or by Proclamation, shall annul the Act from and after the Day of such Signification.

'57. A Bill reserved for the Signification of the Queen's Pleasure shall not have any force unless and until within Two Years from the Day on which it was presented to the Governor-General for the Queen's Assent, the Governor-General signifies, by Speech or Message to each of the Houses of Parliament or by Proclamation, that it has received the Assent of the Queen in Council.

'An Entry of every such Speech or Message, or Proclamation shall be made in the Journal of each House, and a duplicate thereof duly attested shall be delivered to the proper Officer to be kept among the Records of Canada.'

That is to say that the only case when it ceases to be a personal matter for the Governor-General is when he refers it to the British Privy Council.

Section 90 of the Act gives the same right of disallowance and reserved assent to the Lieut.-Governor in respect of Provincial Laws as the Governor-General has in respect of Dominion Laws.

I went carefully into the whole question in 1935, when I was in Alberta, with the best Constitutional lawyers, and they were quite clear that the power of disallowance, to the extent that it still existed, lay with the Governor-General in person, and not with the Governor-General in Council – the latter term, of course, being another way of saying the Dominion Cabinet.

Opposition Tactics Illegal

At the time when Mr. Mackenzie King 'disallowed' the Albertan Acts the Governor-General, Lord Tweedsmuir, was in the Arctic Circle, and it is in my opinion, unquestionable that Mr. King's action was a flagrant abuse of the Royal Prerogative, and could properly have been taken only if the Governor-General had in the first place refused assent to the Bills.

Now the next step was for Alberta to re-pass the acts with modifications to make them more difficult to disallow, and this brought into play a power which had never before been used in Canada, when the Lieut.-Governor of Alberta, Mr. Bowen (who was appointed by Mr. Mackenzie King in 1935), reserved the Royal Assent.

As these Acts had just been passed for the second time, the nature of this action can be judged if we imagine the King to withhold assent from a vital

Act of Parliament passed by large majorities in the House of Commons and the House of Lords.

It is certain that the actions of Mr. Mackenzie King and of Mr. Bowen cannot both be legal.

All of this is a clear indication that as soon as anything is done which genuinely attacks the prerogative of international finance – and such was the nature of the Albertan Acts – then the titular governors simply become the puppets of international financiers.

The Mortgage Stranglehold

Before proceeding to explain to you in more detail the nature of these Acts, the present position of them, their objective, and the probable trend of developments in connection with them, I think it desirable to give you a brief picture of the situation as we see it, and as I think we see it correctly.

In the first place, there exists, specifically in Alberta, but to a greater or less extent all over the world, a condition of affairs, the understanding of which is absolutely essential to any grasp of world politics today. It can briefly be expressed by saying that a Government – no matter whether it is a so-called sovereign government, or whether its sovereignty is disputed, as in the case of Alberta – is regarded by the Plutocracy, by which I mean the money-lending interest, and not necessarily the rich men, primarily as the administration of an estate to be mortgaged up to the hilt, the mortgages to be created by the lending, to the population of the estate, of its own credit at the highest possible return of interest.

It is essential also to realise that the primary objective of this policy is not merely, and certainly not in any realistic sense, the acquirement of monetary wealth by the plutocrats through the machinery of the banks, mortgage companies, and insurance companies which are their agencies. Though in comparison with the rest of the population these men are immensely rich, their scale of personal luxury could in many cases be maintained upon an income of extremely modest proportions, and their immense reserves are used to perpetuate the system and to finance the wars which are the outcome of it.

The Threat Of Grinding Toil

With a full appreciation of the gravity of what I am saying, I am convinced that in the case of the ring of international financiers who control the system, the conscious objective is to keep the great mass of the population in fear of poverty and loss of social position; by which I do not necessarily mean in lack of physical necessities, but I do mean that it is intended that they should be kept in constant insecurity and under the threat of grinding toil, even though such toil is not demanded by anything realistic in the situation. In the main this is accomplished by immense misdirection of production effort – redundant factories, 'Public Works,' 'Fashions', etc. – anything but wanted consumers' goods.

I can imagine that anyone unfamiliar with the techniques of the debt-creating system with which we all exist, might say that this is merely a wild assertion incapable of proof. On the contrary, it is capable of the simplest possible proof, and arises from the following propositions:

(a) Modern life and work cannot be carried on without the use of money;

(b) All money comes into existence as a debt from the community to the money-creating agencies;

(c) The debtor is the servant of the lender until his debt is paid;

(d) The debts owing by the community to the money-lending agencies are increasing in geometrical ratio, and could never possibly be paid off, since the amount of money in existence at any time in the possession of the community is only a microscopic fraction of the debts held against them by the money-lending agencies.

The proposition which is put forward by the Governments, who act as spokesmen for the money-lending agencies, is that capacity to pay should be the measure of a debtor's liability, which means that everything that he does not require for a bare existence should be at the service of the lender.

There is another point which is frequently misunderstood, and which I should like to make to you, since it is vital in a consideration of the remedial steps which can be taken in connection with the situation, and that is that, although the debts owed by the community to the money-lending agencies are assuming astronomical proportions, they are quite small in comparison with the real wealth of the community measured in the same units.

Chapter 7
The Social Credit Debate

Throughout the 1920s and 1930s, Douglas was a major figure on the world stage. He had a worldwide following, and gave evidence at official government inquiries in the U.K., Japan, Canada, New Zealand and Australia. Leading politicians, economists, authorities in Marxist political economy and intellectuals of all persuasions discussed Douglas' writings in national newspapers and periodicals. Debates between Douglas and establishment figures took place at public meetings in major cities and on the radio in many of the countries through which he travelled.

The debate in context

'As the most articulate and persistent critic of the economic and financial system this century,' commented Michael Rowbotham in 1997, 'Douglas' omission from modern textbooks on the history of economics is astounding and worrying.' Rowbotham continues:

> Douglas' appeal transcended all barriers of class. He had followers who were ordinary working people and supporters amongst the business and wealthy sectors of society. This was because it was perceived that his ideas cut right through the timeworn adage that 'the poor are poor because the rich are rich' and showed that modern poverty was due to the financial system. Douglas pointed out that in a modern industrial society, there was potentially enough for everyone and that included a share of the leisure bound up in unemployment and progress. Douglas bridged the divide of jealousy between rich and poor created by scarcity-money, and he bridged the divide of conflict between the businessman and his employees. All could perceive that they had a common interest in the balanced functioning of the economy, a common, day-to-day, practical interest which was far stronger than the superficial difference of class. In this sense Douglas was far more shrewd than either Marx or Lenin, for he saw that the issue of class was an abstract diversion from an essentially practical matter.[1]

For Adam Smith, the accumulation of capital by capitalists made possible the division of labour which in turn created wealth. If each individual followed their own self-interest, the 'invisible hand' would ensure that all became better off. Government interference should therefore be kept to a minimum. For Karl Marx, all value was created by labour, so that capital was labour value stored up over time. Marx regarded capitalism as the final stage in the evolution of the economy, leading to an end to private ownership of the means of production. Both Smith and Marx equated increased production with increased wealth. Clifford Hugh Douglas, however, made the crucial distinction between *money* values and *real* values, pointing out that there was no *necessary* relationship between the two. *The Wealth of Nations* and *Das Kapital* are considered standard texts for the economically literate reader. *Economic Democracy*, together with Douglas' other works, is virtually unknown.

Social Credit economics seeks to facilitate economic activity, that is, the production, distribution and exchange of material goods necessary for the community's physical well-being, *within the economic sphere only*. In this scenario, the production of material artefacts ceases to be an end in itself, but is undertaken in a spirit of service and co-operation for the benefit of society as a whole. Furthermore, the cultural and the political spheres of the Threefold Commonwealth/Social Order cease to be dominated by the economic sphere. In terms of the Henderson Cake (See Chapter 2), social credit thought is capable of taking into consideration *the cake as a whole*, while orthodox economics accounts the monetised layers only, other considerations being tacked on as afterthoughts. Surviving literature from the period indicates that, in the 1930s, substantial numbers of the general public were able to follow the debate with a fair degree of understanding. Meanwhile, the economic orthodoxy of 'sound finance' was taught to aspiring career politicians, administrators and practical businessmen in a doctrinaire fashion.

In order to analyse the debate, it is essential to clarify the position of each side. Economic orthodoxy is concerned purely with the money economy. Society must live within its *financial* means. If political or cultural policy decisions run into problems of economic scarcity as so defined, they must be brought back into touch with economic 'reality'. It is economic *heresy* to suggest that there might be other ways of going about things. Equally, it is heresy to suggest that the political and the cultural spheres of society should *not* be organised according to the rules of 'sound finance'. It is from the failure of the average individual to recognise the nature of the power of finance over our everyday lives, that the true strength of the financial institutions lies.

Paper money

According to orthodox economists, both 'money' and 'labour' are commodities which exchange on the market. Leaving aside for the moment the question of 'labour' as a commodity which can be *sold* to somebody who has *money*, we are here concerned with money itself, *i.e.*, the means of payment for goods and services exchanged on the market. In a paper written in 1936, Douglas discussed the significance of the fact that banks 'create the means of payment out of nothing'.

> The whole of our civilisation rests upon the possession of the means of payment. It need not so rest, but it does in fact so rest. Taxation in money, fines as punishment for legal offences, and other devices, quite apart from the use of money as a medium of exchange, are all devised with a view to make the power of the creation of money the fundamental power of civilisation. This power is fraudulent, both in fact and ownership. ... The history of money is one long unbroken history of fraud, and the acquisition of this power of money-creation by the banks is the final chapter.[2]

Modern businessmen do not 'make' money: they get it from somebody else who makes it. If they do literally 'make' money, they end up in jail for counterfeiting. Historically, the right of issuing money has been vested neither in the creator of wealth, nor in the owner of wealth, but in the custodian of wealth, that is, the banker. The modern banknote was created by the goldsmith. It was the signature of the custodian of the wealth, not the owner, which allowed the receipt to pass from hand to hand. The money system which facilitated the process of industrialisation was based upon fraudulent debt. As Douglas explained:

> Our dishonest goldsmith had the bright idea of issuing several receipts for the one piece of wealth, on the assumption that those receipts would not all be presented at the same time. It was particularly easy where merely gold coins had been deposited, for if by any chance an owner of wealth did ask for his gold crowns, he would get them because they need not be the same gold crowns that had been deposited. So it was found quite safe in a general way to issue more receipts than the wealth that had been deposited.

> That, without doubt, was the first inflation, and of course it gave the goldsmith the value of all the receipts in excess of those which represented wealth actually deposited. That process, beginning undoubtedly

in fraud, grew so common that it became the convention amongst bankers, who were the descendents of the goldsmiths, to do this thing; and they have always, for the past several hundred years, been in the habit of issuing more receipts for wealth than the actual wealth that was deposited with them. At the present time it is a well-known convention, not denied by bankers themselves, that for every dollar of legal tender which they have, they issue nine dollars of credit money which they actually create themselves; just as the goldsmith, not by exactly the same process, created those false receipts representing deposited wealth which was not there. Now, no scheme of that kind so obviously fraudulent, in its beginnings at any rate, could have proceeded so long as it did, and for that matter does at the present day, if it had not served a very useful purpose. In fact the additional receipts were passed as money, facilitated trade, kept goods moving and were in every way an advantage, even to the general population. They were of the greatest advantage, of course, to the banker, but they were also of great advantage to the public, as they provided it with money.[3]

Until just before World War I, the convention held that a banknote or a cheque was cashable at any time for tangible wealth in the form of gold sovereigns. At times, banks failed when people tried to draw out the wealth that was supposed to lie behind the bank notes or cheques. Although, for at least a century, banks have not any actual, tangible wealth to back up bank-created money, orthodox economists who 'ought to know better' have served to confuse the issue. Douglas hit the nail on the head when he wrote:

The bank has never consisted of merely handing out at one end of the counter what was put in at the other. No bank has ever paid a dividend in the last hundred years on the process of merely lending that which it took in. There is no possible doubt at all about this thing. I sometimes wonder why it is that certain protagonists – certain defenders – of the present banking system go on arguing about this matter. There is no possible doubt about it. And since the war [World War I] the convention that you could get golden sovereigns in return for your cheque or banknote has not even had a plausible foundation. All you can get for a banknote is another banknote. There is no longer any obligation to hand over anything more tangible than some printed paper.

In brief, the creation of money, once performed by the producer of wealth, then by the custodian of wealth, who fraudulently issued more paper than the wealth he guarded, has passed to a set of people who neither produce, nor own, nor guard the wealth, but are merely book-keepers.

The great thing to notice about this situation is that the creation of wealth – the real creation of goods and services which go to make a standard of living, the thing which makes the difference between starvation and comfort, and makes all those things that we call civilisation – the actual making of these things is carried on by one organisation, but the making of money, by which alone these things can be transferred from the producers of wealth to those who wish to consume it, is carried on by an entirely separate organisation, having no real connection with the production of wealth at all, not even as its custodian.[4]

Douglas likened the situation to that of a railway network, in which the people who provide and operate the lines, rolling stock and stations hand over the creation and distribution of tickets to a separate organisation which neither produces nor uses the railway network. The upshot is an economic system based upon 'the most colossal lucrative fraud that has ever been perpetrated on society:

It is one of the tragedies of this fraud upon society that the control of credit and the control of information in all its forms – education, publicity, etc. – are concentric and interdependent, and it is obvious that the primary use which is made by the financial hierarchy of this control of information is to mould public opinion into channels which will buttress the usurped authority and hypnotise whole communities into asking for what they do not want. A commonplace instance is that of referring to the 'unemployment problem' when the achievement of leisure is what is really meant. I have even heard it stated that the proper object of labour-saving machinery is to increase work; but it is not necessary to emphasise that the idea in the mind of the inventor of a labour-saving device is to save labour and therefore achieve leisure.

The mechanism by which finance moulds economic thought is well exemplified in the London School of Economics. Its chairs were endowed by Sir Ernest Cassel, on whose behalf we fought the Egyptian War of 1882 with its present repercussions. So successful is this hypnotic process that, so far as I can judge, a thorough academic training in economics – so called – is almost a fatal handicap to commonsense apprehension of the subject. Only a brilliant economist like Mr. Hawtrey, with all the orthodox training, familiar with the thought of other brilliant economists, and steeped in the tradition of the Treasury – which is the Tweedledee to the Bank of England's Tweedledum – would suggest for instance, that a country like Great Britain, with a National Debt of £8,000 million, which is increasing daily, has on the average paid for, and is paying for, what it produced.

If I manage to live by increasing the mortgage on my house, it seems to me a misuse of language to say that I am paying my way. ... The core of the *technical* accusation made by us against the present financial system is *that prices contain items not represented by money anywhere, and that these unmonetised items are represented by debt which is increasing and which cannot be liquidated.* Mr. Hawtrey has not in my opinion dealt with this core of our charge, and, as is a patent fact, he cannot possibly deal with it. It is from this fact that the major evils of civilisation arise, including war. ... If we hypocritically claim that the employment system is a moral system and that man must be kept at work, rather than choose work, we are sealing the doom of this civilisation.[5]

The paper from which these extracts are taken forms part of the extensive debate between Douglas and leading figures in economic orthodoxy. Throughout this debate the assumptions of orthodoxy are based upon the core concept of the 'Circular Flow'. Douglas, on the other hand, analyses how *debt-based money* flows through the economy over *time*. The objective of the Douglas analysis is to find ways for society to turn finance and banking into a useful tool in service of humanity. The objective of orthodox economics would appear to be the perpetuation of the debt-based money system which presently holds humanity in chains.

For orthodox economists Say's Law holds. People go to work to produce goods and services, and in the process earn an income. They spend their incomes on the goods and services. It is the task of economists to explain how savings and investments, imports and exports, taxation and other anomalies can be regulated in such ways as to maintain the flow between production and consumption. For orthodoxy, incomes are given *by* the economy as a reward for sacrifices *to* the economy.

Dividends for all

Douglas argued that going to work does not make money. Money is created as debt by the banking system, which currently has a major influence on policy across all aspects of society. In a modern economy the division of labour, co-operation, the increment of association and the common cultural inheritance give rise to circa 95% of the productive process, with the labour of hand, eye and brain amounting to no more than 5% of the total. Hence there is no necessity for incomes to be dependent upon employment. As he explained in the 1937 edition of *The Monopoly of Credit*:

> Industry has run riot over the countryside. A population which has been educated in the fixed idea that the chief, if not the only objective in life is well named 'business', whose politicians and preachers exhort their audiences to fresh efforts for the capture of markets and the provision of still more business, cannot be blamed if, as opportunity offers, it still further sacrifices the amenities of the countryside to the building of more blast furnaces and chemical works. Since the control of credit is the most perfect mechanism for the control of industrial activity, its use in the hands of a representative [*i.e.*, democratically accountable] organisation would appear to be the best possible way of reducing the chaos which exists, to something like order.

The problem, Douglas observes, is that the banking system, informed by a philosophy of financial profitability, entrusts resources to capable practical individuals, engineers and businessmen, who 'cannot be restrained from making each successive plan more efficient than the last, with the result that output requires less and less labour', creating an unemployment 'problem': 'Only by a frenzied acceleration of capital sabotage, which is now being openly advocated in many quarters, can the population (which would, so far as the physical aspect of the situation is concerned, be free to enjoy the product of the plants already existing) be kept at work on the production of capital goods. ...

> If we assume that the constant efforts to reduce the amount of labour per unit of production are justified, and we recognise the unquestionable fact that the genuine consumptive capacity of the individual is limited, we must recognise that the world, whether consciously or not, is working towards the Leisure State. The production system under this conception would be required to produce those goods and services which the consumer desires of it with a minimum and probably decreasing amount of human labour. Production, and still more the activities which are commonly referred to as 'business' [*i.e.*, working for a financial incentive], would of necessity cease to be the major interest of life and would, as happened to so many biological activities, be relegated to a position of minor importance, to be replaced, no doubt, by some form of activity of which we are not yet fully cognisant.

In a physical sense then we should be living in a world in which economic processes were carried out by two agencies, one, as heretofore, the agency of individual effort and from an economic point of view of decreasing importance, and the other, as the result of the plant, organisation, and knowledge which are the cumulative result of the effort not only of the present generation, but of the pioneers and inventors of the past. This second agency can, of course, be collectively described as real (as distinct from financial) capital. Now it is quite easy to make out a perfectly simple ethical justification for the proposition that the share of the product due to the individual under such a state of affairs would be (1) a small and decreasing share due to his individual efforts, and (2) a large and increasing amount due to his rights as a shareholder or an inheritor, or if it may be preferred, a tenant for life of the communal capital. ...

Let us at this point for the sake of clarity identify the community with the nation and in doing so be careful not to confuse administration with ownership. It ought not to be difficult to see that a situation which may truly be described as revolutionary is disclosed. In place of the relation of the individual to the nation being that of a taxpayer it is easily seen to be that of a shareholder. ... Having more leisure he is less likely to suffer from either individual or national nerve-strain, and having more time to meet his neighbours can reasonably be expected to understand them more fully. Not being dependent upon a wage or salary for subsistence, he is under no necessity to suppress his individuality, with the result that his capacities are likely to take new forms of which we have so far little conception.[6]

Thus, lucidly and coherently, Douglas presents the case for a universal or 'National' Dividend for all citizens. Considered dispassionately, the passages quoted above cannot be logically faulted. This is not, however, the place to rehearse the technical and complicated relationship between money, the price system, investment, production and distribution. What is certain is that Douglas and his key opponents were thoroughly acquainted with the teachings of orthodoxy, the broad details of banking practice and the relationship between the two. The wonder is that Douglas brought this complex, technical debate right into the public arena, filling public halls and broadcasting to the nation. Douglas was saying something which *had* to be refuted if mainstream political economy was to maintain its credibility. Yet, as the records of the debate and the volume of publications demonstrate, it was something which *could not be* refuted.

Douglas argued that under finance capitalism, banks create money: they do not merely lend out money which has been saved up and deposited with them for safe-keeping. By law, banks are allowed to create money (a) to make loans, (b) to buy securities for themselves, and (c) to enable the Central Bank to buy gold.[7] Normally, a private individual will make a loan, or buy securities or purchase an investment from money saved up from current income or past assets. Banks, however, operate on an entirely different basis. A banker is 'a dealer in debts – his own and other people's',[8] as certain orthodox economists will admit. Banks create new money at the stroke of a pen (or, as presently, as a blip on a computer screen). The system has its built-in checks and balances, all of which relate to the maintenance of an artificial scarcity, presently related, ultimately, to gold. Douglas argued that the anchor value of money should be the *potential* wealth currently available for consumption. This could be done by an adaptation of the price mechanism so that the community of producers and consumers no longer had to carry the weight of bank-created debt. Since it could not be refuted, the 'heresy' had to be suppressed vigorously. And it was.

Social Credit and the Labour Party

Although Social Credit was initially publicised through the Guild Socialist weekly, *The New Age*, Douglas' earliest, most vehement and most enduring critics were from the political left. The notion of a National Dividend payable to all was anathema as much to Socialists, who sought a better deal for labour under capitalism, as to Communists who sought to dispossess capitalists of their ownership of the means of production. Both Socialists and Communists held that *labour* was the source of wealth, while finance was irrelevant. In this argument they remained faithful to the Circular Flow analysis. According to this view, as we have seen, in Chapter 3, people go to work to make the goods and services needed by the community. They are rewarded with money so that they can buy a share of the goods and services produced. For Socialists, the only problem is that the owners of 'land' and 'capital' hold powerful positions in the economy, so that they can take more than their fair share of the goods and services produced. The answer, according to the Socialists, is to buy out the owners of capital and bring production under nationalised control. When all work is done for the State, instead of for private owners, everybody will be rewarded for their *work*, and all injustice will be done away with. Only at that point will matters of finance come into consideration. This is the line taken by G.D.H. Cole, a Guild Socialist who became one of the leading writers on economics in the Labour Party during the 1920s and 1930s. His review of *Economic Democracy*, originally published in *The Guild Socialist*, appears in Appendix 7a: Reviews.

In 1921 trade unionists throughout the U.K. were studying Douglas' writings, most particularly the (Draft Mining) Scheme, which was published as an Appendix to Douglas' second book, *Credit-Power and Democracy*. The Scheme, described as 'A Practical Scheme for the Establishment of Economic and Industrial Democracy', was a carefully thought through plan to decentralise finance and administration of industry. It was introduced as follows:

> The following exemplary Scheme, drawn up for special application to the Mining Industry, is designed to enable a transition to be effected from the present state of industrial chaos to a state of economic democracy, with the minimum amount of friction and the maximum results in the general well-being. An explanatory commentary on the Scheme, clause by clause, appears below.[9]

In September 1920 the Committee on High Prices, a sub-committee of the Scottish Council of the Labour Party, met with Douglas on at least two occasions, and gave 'considerable time' to examining 'the thesis put forward by Major C.H. Douglas, as well as his proposals applying what may be called the '*New Age*' theories of Credit to the Mining Industry and to Industry generally'.[10] The Scottish Miners and trade unionists throughout the U.K. also gave considerable time to the study of the Douglas/NEW AGE proposals, so that in January 1921 a formal request was made to the Labour Party Executive to consider the 'Douglas Credit Scheme'.[11]

Forced by pressure of opinion to at least give some consideration to the possibility of incorporating Social Credit analysis with U.K. Labour Party policy, Sydney Webb hastily convened a 'Labour Party Committee of Inquiry into the Douglas/NEW AGE Scheme'. Following advice from banking interests and the academy, the Committee came to the conclusion that Social Credit analysis was unsound. Thus the young Labour Party rejected a body of economic thought which coherently combines theory with practice, because it was incompatible with orthodox economic theory as taught at the London School of Economics.

Popular support for Social Credit at that time, and subsequently during the 1930s, gave rise to the publication of two Labour Party reports on their findings,[12] and a number of publications by leading left-wing thinkers, including a critique of Social Credit by Hugh Gaitskell in *What Everybody Wants to Know About Money*, edited by G.D.H. Cole.[13] Throughout the literature of the political left, the emphasis is upon the necessity for all personal income to be dependent upon *employment*. As Douglas' observed:

If you can control economics, you can keep the business of getting a living the dominant factor of life, and so keep your control of politics – just so long, and no longer.[14]

The earliest attacks were a simple misrepresentation of Douglas' observation that the Circular Flow argument did not hold, since it failed to account time and money. As his popularity grew, it became necessary to put on a show of quoting directly and accurately from Douglas, but then rephrasing the quotation on the grounds of his supposed 'very obscure wording', creating a travesty and then attacking the false version. This happened time and again.

Social Credit and the professors

In the immediate post- First World War period, initial reviews of Douglas' first book, *Economic Democracy*, published in 1920, were very positive (See Appendix 7a: Reviews). As his popularity rose, however, and he became a leading public figure, he was attacked with increasing vehemence. By the early 1930s, sympathetic reports on Social Credit in the mainstream national press and media became increasingly rare. Local papers were able to take a more independent stance: see, *e.g.*, the *Liverpool Daily Post* report of Douglas' Liverpool Speech of 31 January 1933.[15]

Throughout the 1930s, and into the 1940s, leading economists and establishment figures engaged in debate with Douglas in a way which was unprecedented in the history of heretical economic thought. No other 'alternative' economic thinker, inside or outside the academy, has given rise to such a wealth of documentation of debate in the press and media. On one side were Douglas and his supporters who received no money for their labours. On the other side were ranged leading academics whose authority derived from the fact that they were in receipt of a salary from an academic institution. In these circumstances the fact that there was full-scale public debate between Douglas and the major spokesmen for economic orthodoxy is highly significant. Had Douglas been propounding complete nonsense, he would not have attained such public recognition that his case had to be refuted by 'the authorities'. The greatest irony of all is that the stance adopted by economic orthodoxy is indeed nonsensical in so far as it adheres to the notion of Say's Law. The only way orthodoxy could defend itself was by misrepresenting Douglas' analysis, and then attacking the misrepresentation. This was done with varying degrees of subtlety. Certain defenders of orthodoxy would seem to have been so completely befuddled by their training that they genuinely thought Douglas was mistaken. Others present a seemingly seamless defence of orthodoxy, interwoven with compassionate understanding of the temptation to fall under the spell of a false prophet.

The range of books, pamphlets and articles written with the sole purpose of attacking Douglas include papers by Ramsey,[16] an article in *The New Statesman* entitled 'The "Douglas Credit Scheme"', (1922), an article by Maurice Dobb, 'Does the World Need More Money? A Reply to Major Douglas', in *The Communist Review*, Durbin's *Social Credit Policy* (1933/1936), Hiskett's *Social Credits or Socialism* (1935), Lewis' *Douglas Fallacies: A Critique of Social Credit* (1935), Maurice Dobb's *Social Credit Discredited* (1936) and Hiskett and Franklin's *Searchlight on Social Credit* (1939).[17] The two papers by Frank Ramsey, 'The Douglas Proposals' (*Cambridge Magazine*, 1922) and 'A Mathematical Theory of Saving' (*Economic Journal*, 1928), assume away all the relevant variables discussed by Douglas, using integral calculus to refute a mis-stated version of Douglas' A + B theorem. Ralph Hawtrey, Geoffrey Crowther, Lionel Robbins, J.M. Keynes and other leading economists engaged in critical debate on the subject of Social Credit. An exhaustive record on the critiques of Douglas' work is yet to be compiled. Further references can be traced through *The Political Economy of Social Credit and Guild Socialism*, and works such as John King's *Economic Exiles*.

Douglas engaged in debate in written form, as with Hobson in the *Socialist Review*,[18] in debate on public platforms, as with Hawtrey,[19] and in radio broadcasts. The latter included a debate with Dennis Robertson (1933), and a broadcast on 'The Causes of War: is our financial system to blame?'[20] which was published in *The Listener*, December 5, 1934. The texts of the broadcasts by Douglas are available in print, and can be studied alongside those of critics of Social Credit. However, *The New and the Old Economics*,[21] written directly in response to orthodox critics, offers the clearest summary of Douglas' analysis of the relationship between finance and the economic processes of production, distribution and exchange. In its attempts to 'refute' Douglas, orthodoxy had to bring into play its most powerful players. Appendix 7b: Douglas Repudiates Economic Orthodoxy and offers insights into Douglas' views on these exchanges.

The Old and the New Economics

The debate between orthodoxy and Social Credit is summed up in Douglas' essay, first published in pamphlet form in 1932, and subsequently variously reprinted. In the aforementioned essay[21] Douglas takes issue with two lectures delivered in 1932 by orthodox economists on the subject of Social Credit. The first, delivered by Professor D.B. Copland, Dean of the Faculty of Commerce in the University of Melbourne, was published in the form of a pamphlet of 32 pages by the Melbourne University Press in association with Oxford University Press in 'Melbourne, London, Edinburgh, New York, Capetown, Bombay, Toronto etc.' [22] The second was a lecture delivered by Professor Robbins of the University of London, at the British Association. Since the latter was never printed in full, Douglas had to rely on a report published in the *Yorkshire Post*.

Douglas opens his pamphlet, *The New and the Old Economics*, with the observation:

> I will pass over Professor Copland's criticism of my literary style in the first section of his pamphlet, which may be summarised in his paragraph: 'Unfortunately, his writings have not been characterised by that clarity of expression that (sic) will enable the average man to follow him with certainty.' It is, unfortunately, inevitable that the process of pioneering is not usually associated, contemporaneously, with the laying down of high-speed roads, and for that reason I think Professor Copland will agree that books subsequent to the one, the first of the series, which he chooses to criticise on these grounds, have devoted a good deal of attention to making clear obscurities which appeared in earlier efforts. The subject is, admittedly, a difficult subject, involving many subtleties, both of thought and language, and I confess to a certain amount of satisfaction that large numbers of widely-separated readers of the books to which Professor Copland refers, have succeeded during the past fourteen years in grasping the meaning which they were intended to convey, although, unfortunately, he is apparently not amongst them. [23]

With the utmost clarity, Douglas demonstrates the flaws in Copland's thinking when he fails to distinguish between payments of current incomes to consumers, and payments which are on their way back to the bank. If current consumer incomes are to be sufficient to meet current prices, which are based upon *past* costs, a constant increase in debt is necessitated, a debt which has to be repaid in the *future*.

> The foregoing is sufficient answer to the quotation from Mr. J.M. Keynes, which begins: 'Let x be equal to the cost of production of all producers. The x will also be equal to the incomes of the public.' [24] This is the well-known logical fallacy known as the *petitio principii*, which consists in assuming the truth of the fact you have set out to prove and then proving the assumption from the logical conclusion. The cost of

production is *not* equal to the incomes of the public, and therefore the rest of the argument merely indicates what would happen if it were equal.

Douglas concludes that professional bankers and economists appear to know little about modern cost accounting and the physical facts relating to production. When it comes down to practicalities, theories based upon flawed assumptions must be subjected to rigorous questioning.

'The Douglas Fallacy'

Throughout the 1920s and 1930s Social Credit commentators identified the tactics used by career 'experts' to manufacture 'Public Opinion'. As early as 1935, William Bell, writing in *Social Credit*, observed:

> It is on this putty-like nature of Public Opinion that the Banking Monopolists bank in opposing the Social Credit programme. For over a dozen years they prevented public and press discussion of the only foolproof remedy for the chaotic state of affairs achieved through pursuing their own contradictory policies. They set their kept professional economists repeating the Pretty Polly prattle that the 'Douglas enthusiasts' are 'currency cranks,' 'poetic dreamers,' 'amateur economists,' 'insane theorists,' 'senseless inflationists' and other equally bombastic phrases.

In the mood of optimism of the time, Social Credit enthusiasts found such slogans amusing, since, for the past fifteen years, Douglas' forecasts had proved correct, whilst those of the 'money monopolists' had proved consistently false. Bell predicted that the word 'fallacy' would continue to play a large part in the on-going campaign to steer people back onto the course of 'sane finance':

> From press, platform and pulpit; from boards of banks and industrial concerns and from banqueting-tables; from gramophone, radio and cinematograph; from every possible source will flow propaganda on a public already bewildered into 'believing' opposite policies every few weeks. Moreover, those Balaam's asses masquerading in the British Lion's skin, the professional economists, pulling this way and that as their teamsters in The City bid them, will keep on solemnly repeating that there is a 'fallacy' in the Douglas Theorem and that 'nobody understands it,' implying there has been no fallacy in a single item of their own absurdly contradictory but nevertheless infallible policies that wouldn't work longer than about ten minutes.

Those patient animals are at last getting hot under the collar because Public Opinion is slowly realising that both the team and the teamsters are sadly behind the times. For the public are now reaping the crop of thistles sown by the Money Monopolists still doggedly following the tail of their asses'-plough as if unaware that the petrol-tractor of the New Economics is now on the market. Like Little Jack Horner the Bankers, having made a corner in the Community's Credit, are still sitting in their corner in the City, pulling out the plums from the industrial pie and saying at their annual meetings what good bankers they are. For themselves, yes; for the real owners of the Social Credit exploited by them, certainly no.[25]

As those words were written, there still seemed a fair chance that a sane financial system might be adopted through the operation of genuine democracy. Instead, the world moved towards World War II. Orthodox economics continued to be enshrined in the ivory towers of academia on the lines outlined in the following chapter.

NOTES

1   Rowbotham (1998) p235
2   Douglas, 'Money: A Historical Survey', *The Fig Tree*, No. 2, September 1936. pp139-147.
3   Douglas, *ibid*.
4   Douglas, *ibid*.
5   Douglas, *ibid*.
6   Douglas (1937) pp 107 – 113
7   Although nominally the 'gold standard' ended with World War I, gold continues to play a part in international banking. See also Crowther (1940) pp63-67
8   Crowther (1940) p81.
9   Douglas (1920b) p147
10   Labour Party (1920) p17
11   For further detailed references to this episode, see Hutchinson and Burkitt (1997) pp94 – 114
12   Labour Party (1922). Labour Party (1935)
13   See Hutchinson and Burkitt (2005) for details.
14   Quoted in later edition of Douglas (1932).
15   See www.douglassocialcredit.com
16   Ramsey (1922) (1928)
17   For details of these and other publications to which only passing

reference is made, see the Bibliography.

18   See 'The Douglas Theory: A Reply to Mr J.A. Hobson', *Socialist Review*, March, 1922 pp139-45.

19   Hawtrey and Douglas (1933)

20   Douglas and Robertson (1933). For the text of 'The Causes of War' see 1937 edition of Douglas, *The Monopoly of Credit*.

21   Douglas (1932)

22   Copland (1932)

23   Douglas (1932) pp5-6.

24   Copland (1932) p17

25   Cited from *Social Credit*, March 8, 1935, p56.

Appendix 7a

Reviews of *Economic Democracy* (1920)

The following reviews of Douglas' first book, *Economic Democracy*, (Cecil Palmer, 5s) were reprinted in *The New Age*, Thursday May 27th 1920 No.1446 Vol.XXVII. No.4

Economic Democracy Reviewed in *The Nation*

Of one thing we are convinced: Major Douglas knows his difficult subject from end to end. Obviously he has devoted time and thought to economics and politics – and for such an act of self-sacrifice alone, he deserves our sympathetic interest – and has not blindly followed his guides, but is sufficiently versed in the subjects and observant of industrial and political workings to form theories of his own.

We are not entirely convinced (to be more precise we should say, not yet), but his is a sinewy argument and most formidable in its defences. Even its opponents are compelled to recognise in any step towards the mildest social melioration the necessity of making changes in the economic structure. That we have reached an epoch when change on the revolutionary scale is imminent is not doubted. Revolutionaries, reactionaries, and moderates all recognise or fear it. Major Douglas wants the change to be complete. He sees the cause of social wrong in a Prussianised industrialism. The present cry is for more production; but the world's need is not artificially to stimulate material requirements – which for the individual are limited – but to subordinate material to mental and psychological necessity: 'the impulse behind unbridled industrialism is not progressive, but reactionary, because its objective is an obsolete financial control which forms one of the most effective instruments of the will-to-power, whereas the correct objectives of industry are two-fold: the removal of material limitations, and the satisfaction of the creative impulse.' The evil root of the present system he sees as authority exercised through finance, 'the constant filching of purchasing power from the individual in favour of the financier.' He is fearful of the danger – Capitalism, as we know it, getting nearer to its grave – of burying one kind of tyranny only to create another in the form of a bureaucratic collectivism. Co-operation should be the conception of the coming age, but it must be a 'co-operation of reasoned assent, not regimentation in the interests of any system, however superficially attractive.' – '*The Nation.*'

Economic Democracy Reviewed in the *English Review*

We shall return to this book, which is nothing less than a scheme for transforming the world's economic mechanism, and as such needs very technical and speculative consideration. For the moment we can merely indicate its purpose. First, the author diagnoses, and most serious economists will agree with his claim that an adjustment is necessary, owing to the want of inducement to Labour unable to better their slave conditions, and to the anti-social monopoly of credit, used not for the utility of the consumer, but for profit and power. In a word, what is wrong is the unequal distribution of credit which, with the war, has reached a point of unbearable pressure on the middle-class, which will grow worse as inflation compels artificial production and exports on further bank credits. Here Mr Douglas hits the bull's-eye. He does not think that finance will 'get away with the spoils.' He insists that, as the new Labour movement progresses from within, from the bottom up, so industry, if it is to save itself, must deflate from within, from the top downwards. In other words, purchasing power is the key, and credit must be controlled if there is to be wider distribution, and production must be controlled if there is to be a wider and higher general purchasing power. His actual scheme is highly technical. But with his diagnosis we agree. And we advise all serious thinkers to get this little book, which is as remarkable for its criticism and suggestiveness as it is for its brevity. Much will be heard of it, here and in America – '*English Review.*'

Economic Democracy Reviewed in the *Oxford Chronicle*

The appearance of Major C. H. Douglas's new book, 'Economic Democracy,' recalls his visit to the Oxford Labour Club in the early part of the term. Readers of THE NEW AGE have for some time past been familiar with his piquant style and heterodox theories, but very little attention has been paid to them. This is a vast pity, because in Major Douglas the Labour movement has a severe critic, who is yet as deeply opposed to the present system as any of our so-called Bolsheviks. If his case is demonstrable it will mean that an entirely new orientation is necessary. The substance of his book is an exposition of the way that 'Anarchism' can be applied economically even to a highly industrialised community like England. Starting out from the basic anarchist propositions – (a) that it is impossible to determine any just distribution of the product of industry on the basis of what each factor or man has contributed, and (b) that lust for power, in whatever way manifested, is the real enemy – he is as vigorously opposed to the Marxian position that all wealth is created by labour as he is to private ownership of the means of production. He claims that the potential wealth of the world is so great that the quarrel over the existing supply is beside the point. The Labour movement in its attempt to appropriate a great share of the product for the worker, and to secure control over administration, is merely tilting at windmills. The object of the struggle must be control over policy. Control over policy can only be obtained by gaining control over finance, through the means of the banks. Credit is the property of the community, and should be administered by the community. (Note this is not necessarily the State. A State banking system is only jumping out into the fire of the second evil, centralised power.) Therefore the community, instead of collecting taxes, should pay dividends, so that we get the delightful and true anarchistic proposal that the community should issue credit to the consumer as such! The individual, in short, should draw an income for merely being a citizen.

For how this is to be brought about, readers must be referred to the book itself, which is so compact that any précis of the economic theory is impossible in a shorter account. The importance of the book lies firstly in its bearing on the increasing centralisation which is obvious all around us. Financial amalgamations on the one side and triple alliances of trade unions on the other are but manifestations of a tendency to crush out the individual beneath some vast cosmic force – a force which threatens to become stereotyped for centuries in a League of Nations with a lie in its soul. The book is intensely worth study; even the unbeliever will be able to spend many a happy hour trying to detect flaws in the author's reasoning –

C. L. T. – '*Oxford Chronicle.*'

Economic Democracy Reviewed in *The Guildsman*

I agree that inflation, including bank credits, is the main cause of high prices, and that the community control of credit is essential. I agree further that National Guild Banks on the lines often suggested will do nothing to solve the problem, and that banks must be established, and credit 'rationed,' on a community basis. I agree further that the bulk of wealth produced is a 'community' creation and not creation of any individual producer or group of producers, and that accordingly no individual or group has a right to the whole product of his industry. This is true, even if the view is accepted that a man has a right to his own individual product – a view which I do not accept.

Where I fail to understand Major Douglas is not in his diagnosis, with which, on the above essential points I agree, but in his actual scheme for fixing prices, which seems to me to be not clearly argued in his book. I also entirely disagree with the view that the NEW AGE – Douglas scheme provides a possible form of peaceful transition, mainly for the two following reasons: (a) because, even if the disease is in the financial system, the power of the workers is not, and it seems to me that, before they can hope to deal with finance, they must seize industrial power; (b) because the capitalists, who control the State, will never accept any attack on their financial power until the workers can force them to do so, and the workers will not be able to do this until they have consolidated their industrial power. – G.D.H. Cole in *The Guildsman*.

Appendix 7b
Douglas Repudiates Economic Orthodoxy

The following two examples of Douglas' writing present a flavour of the debate as a whole, while at the same time indicating Douglas' full mastery not only of his own subject, but also of the work of the leading mainstream economists of the time. The pieces of text have been selected for their clarity and brevity, from the volumes of available literature. Both can be studied without difficulty by lay and professional economists alike.

1. Major Douglas on Mr. Hawtrey and Others

From Correspondence column, *Social Credit*, December 7, 1934

TO THE EDITOR OF SOCIAL CREDIT.

Dear Sir, – I have addressed the following letter to a correspondent, and it may possibly interest your readers.

Yours faithfully,
C. H. DOUGLAS

Dear _____, I am interested to hear that Mr. Hawtrey at the meeting of the Engineers Study Circle characterised the Douglas Theory as 'puerile.' This appears to be a relapse into the manner of an article he wrote about 1923 in *The Pilgrim*, which was unadulterated Billingsgate, and was accompanied by a statement of his belief that the correct objective of a satisfactory monetary system was a stable price level. I have never, myself, been able to find a satisfactory adjective for an objective which would require that the price of neckties rose when the price of bread fell, and I notice that Mr. Hawtrey, in common with other professional economists, is now not quite sure that this would be wholly desirable. (Cf. D. H. Robertson's chapter in 'The International Gold Problem,' F. A. Hayek 'Prices and Production,' and 'Monetary Theory and the Trade Cycle,' R. G. Hawtrey 'The Art of Central Banking,' Chapter V.)

Since, however, this tendency to become abusive appears to be inherent in some of the professional economists who deal with these matters, and as I agree with you that they do, as experts, command a considerable, though diminishing amount of attention from those interested in the problems of finance, it seems desirable to put upon record the four occasions on which my views have been the subject for formal debate with them in this country. They are (1) The Debate with Mr. Hawtrey at Birmingham in 1933, (2) The Wireless Debate with Mr. D. H. Robertson in 1933, (3) Chapter VIII of Mr. Cole's book written by Mr. H. T. N. Gaitskell, (4) My address to the Marshall Society of Cambridge on October 20, 1934. Mr. D. H. Robertson was present at this address, and took part in the debate which followed the address.

I have no hesitation in saying that neither in the case of the two formal debates, nor in the case of my address at Cambridge, in which I put forward certain aspects of my case in the form of questions to the Society, was any serious attempt whatever made to meet my position. Mr. Hawtrey's contribution to the debate at Birmingham consisted in an able exposition of the orthodox theory of the balanced budget. Mr. D. H. Robertson's reply to my opening statement of my case in the Wireless Debate completely disregarded this statement, made no attempt to reply to it, substituted a statement which was not mentioned in the opening statement of my case, and demolished this substituted statement on the basis of hypothetical answers to questions with which the time limits of the debate did not allow me to deal, and which were subsequently answered at length in *The New Age* in a totally different sense to that which Mr. Robertson evidently expected. At Cambridge Mr. Robertson, together with others, ignored completely the technical question which was put to him in my address, and which was also put to Mr. Hawtrey without obtaining an answer. Mr. Gaitskell's criticisms were completely answered and his argument disposed of by Mr. J. Adamson in *The New Age* of December 28, 1933.

I have no doubt whatever as to the fundamental reasons for the divergence of my views from those of the professional economists. The professional economist believes, whether he is aware of it or not, that it is possible to have a science of money which is self-existent and independent of the progress in the industrial arts. I do not. For this reason I do not think that any economist who at one and the same time believes in a suitable price level and a balanced budget in connection with the modern production system can have anything of value to offer towards a constructive solution of our difficulties.

I am sorry that I cannot address the Engineers Study Circle, but my engagement book was already full by June of this year.

Yours sincerely,
C. H. DOUGLAS

2. Major Douglas Repudiates Mr. McKenna's Claim That Banks Own the Credit They Create

Extract from *Social Credit Supplement*, October 8, 1937
Issued by The Social Credit Secretariat Limited
163A Strand, London, W.C.2

There is no such thing as Social Credit, Mr. McKenna, Chairman of the Midland Bank, is reported to have said, 'it is a myth uncomprehended by its own promoters.' A full account of his remarks was given in *Social Credit* on September 24, and now the following letter has been sent to him by Major C.H. Douglas, giving a reasoned reply to Mr. McKenna's somewhat hasty attack. This letter has been released to the Canadian Press.

Dear Mr. McKenna,

I have seen the reports of various interviews which you have given to the Press in various parts of Canada on the subject of the creation of bank deposits and the allied subject of Social Credit, in which my name has occurred. ....

... I am especially concerned with your statement, 'What a banker lends is – *his* (*i.e.*, the banker's) credit.' In order that there may be no misunderstanding on the matter, I will venture a flat contradiction. He does nothing of the kind. He lends something whose only value or credit depends first on what it will buy, and, secondly, whether anyone wants to buy what it will buy. To claim that both production and consumption are the banker's property, which is the only realistic meaning that can be attached to your statement that it is the banker's property that he lends, seems a little indiscreet. It is part of the banker's stock-in-trade to claim that money has some intrinsic value of its own, but I do not think such an idea is held by anyone who understands its nature.

I venture to suggest that it is a claim which has only to be understood to be repudiated. You are claiming a complete and wholly irresponsible dictatorship of Finance. Many of us are aware of such a dictatorship, and the state of the world is a testimony to its results. Events in Alberta suggest that the repudiation of such a claim has already reached the stage of action and it is perhaps not wholly unfortunate that the stake should be declared in unmistakeable terms by the chairman of the world's largest joint stock bank.

I should like to comment on your remarks regarding a loan made without security. Suppose, on the other hand, that you lend me £1,000 on the 'security' of £2,000 of Government Stock, and that I at once buy 100 tons of wheat with it. Before the farmer has had opportunity to spend the money you created by book-keeping methods, against the security I deposited with you, your bank, by arrangement with others and with the Bank of England, decides to buy unlimited quantities of securities thus causing immense inflation and a rapid rise in the prices of everything the farmer wishes to buy as well as of the wheat of which he has already disposed, thus robbing him of half the exchange value of his wheat. Whom would you suggest ought to be 'secured,' the farmer who grew and parted with the wheat, or the banker who authorised the issue of a piece of paper transferring the wheat to me, a piece of paper which would be rendered valueless by its refusal by a small number of producers?

Finally, I may perhaps be allowed to comment on your statement that Social Credit ('which does not exist') would lead to unlimited inflation. We are all aware that the very modest recovery in this country is due to hardly concealed inflation, one aspect of which is greatly to increase the banker's collective holding of securities (bought with 'his' credit); a second is to cause a rise in the public debt, a third to increase direct taxation, and a fourth to reduce the purchasing power of the monetary unit, thus reducing the value of savings. Every one of these phenomena is a direct gain to the banker, whose monopoly of credit is demonstrably strengthened by each one of them and is the result of a deflationary policy also initiated by bankers, which was directly responsible for the panic of 1929.

I feel sure that you will agree that you are not in a position to know the exact nature of the proposals in contemplation in Alberta, should that Province happily succeed in its struggle to free itself from usurious interests.

Without admitting it, let us suppose that all the processes just mentioned were to continue in Alberta but, let us say, for the benefit of a bank of which all Albertans were shareholders. I hasten to add that, so far as I am aware, no such bank is contemplated. Is it contended that such a state of affairs would or would not be (a) inflation, (b) Social Credit?

I propose to communicate this letter to the Press with any comment that you care to make upon it, unless in regard to the latter you prefer not to be quoted.

Yours truly,
(Signed) C.H. Douglas

NOTE: The Rt. Hon. Reginald McKenna, a Cambridge graduate who had served as First Lord of the Admiralty, Home Secretary, and Chancellor of the Exchequer in the Liberal government of Prime Minister Henry Asquith, left politics in 1917 in preparation for assuming chairmanship of the Midland Bank in 1919. An outspoken authority on economic matters all of his life, he was a noted ally of John Maynard Keynes. Under McKenna, Midland stopped its practice of expansion through acquisition, but only because treasury regulations in the 1920s made mergers virtually impossible. The purchase of North of Scotland Bank in 1924 would be Midland's last acquisition for more than 40 years. Despite these difficulties and the political and economic instability of the inter-war years, Midland still prospered and expanded through its branch network. By 1939, it had more than 2,100 branch offices. By 1934, it had become the largest deposit bank in the world, with more than £457 million in assets.

Chapter 8
The Discrediting of Social Credit

After 1944 very little was heard of Social Credit or Major Douglas outside Canada. The world's press was silent on the subject. The world's universities mentioned Social Credit in passing, but only as an example of a dangerous heresy to be avoided by right-minded followers of economic orthodoxy. And Douglas' books disappeared from library shelves, becoming unobtainable save through specialist booksellers. Although Social Credit periodicals continued to be produced throughout the twentieth century, they ceased to be available through newsagents, becoming instead 'in house' publications for the specialist connoisseur. In his standard text on money, *An Outline of Money*, Geoffrey Crowther dismissed Social Credit as an irrelevance. Meanwhile, 1944 saw the launch of the Rockefeller-funded Canadian Social Science Research Council's series of academic studies entitled 'Social Credit in Alberta: Its Background and Development'. The ten studies, many of which were reprinted several times in the final decades of the twentieth century, set about establishing that Social Credit was nothing more than an incident in Western Canada's historical tendency towards insurrection. This chapter explores the 'official' version of the story as presented by the post Second World War establishment, from the publication of the Appendix of *An Outline of Money* in 1940 to the 2003 publication of a paper entitled 'Social Credit: The Eco-socialism of Fools' in the academic journal *Capitalism, Nature, Socialism*.

Crowther's Appendix

Baron Geoffrey Crowther (1907 – 1972), described as 'economist, journalist, educationalist and businessman, Editor of *The Economist* (1938-56)', was a major establishment figure during the middle decades of the twentieth century. His *An Outline of Money* remained the standard text on money for generations of economics undergraduates. In May 1934 the national daily newspaper, the *News Chronicle*, printed a series of four articles by Crowther on Social Credit. These appeared in the form of an Appendix to the earliest editions of *An Outline of Money*. In all, the book, published in 1940, carried the Appendix through ten reprints until 1947. Subsequently, the Appendix on

Social Credit and a chapter on 'Forward Exchange' were omitted from the text on the grounds that they were merely of historical interest in the post-war period. Nevertheless, reference to Douglas was maintained in the Chapter on 'Savings and Capital', in a section headed 'Fallacies'. Crowther's entire text demonstrates his acute knowledge of how the debt-based money system works, although, naturally, it is dressed and presented in terms of orthodoxy. His refutation of Douglas therefore makes interesting reading.

Crowther starts by observing that anyone remotely interested in 'either politics or economics' could not fail to have noticed the 'full-fledged' Social Credit movement. The voice of authority continues:

> Why it should have a particular appeal to the general public I do not know. Social Credit deals with the extremely difficult and technical subject of monetary theory, which one would not expect to have a wide popular appeal. Moreover, the writings of its adherents are marked by obscurity rather than clarity, by ambiguity rather than precision. The magnitude of its claims would be, one would think, a deterrent to many people; one is naturally suspicious of a theory which promises 'the abolition of poverty, the reduction of the likelihood of war to zero, rapidly diminishing crime, the beginning of economic freedom for the individual, and the introduction of the leisure State' and all by means of simple bookkeeping.

No sources are given for his cited quotations, and no reference is made even to the titles of Douglas' books. In the body of the text Crowther appears to cite Douglas' evidence to the Macmillan Committee (published in 1931), but his statement bears no relationship to anything attributed to Douglas in that document. According to Crowther, Social Crediters may believe they suffer from 'a corrupt conspiracy of silence', but probably it is 'nothing more than the incredulous caution with which the working journalist treats all vendors of gold bricks or discoverers of El Dorado'. Since there was no doubt about the vigour and popularity of the movement, 'nothing but good' could result from 'the fullest possible discussion' of the Douglas' theory.

Evidently Crowther had studied Douglas' writings, since he dismisses Douglas as an engineer with 'his own individual views' which extend well beyond economics, into 'philosophy, politics, history, and a great many other subjects'. Naturally, Crowther finds himself in disagreement with Douglas on the subject of the existence of international financial houses:

> I do not, for instance, believe that behind the visible government of the country there is an invisible government of bankers who deliberately

maintain the poverty of the community to serve their own ends. I find it hard to believe that every movement for reducing the inequality of wealth – including, apparently, Socialism – is financed by 'Lombard Street, Wall Street, and Frankfort.' Nor am I quite so easily convinced as is Major Douglas that every one who disagrees with him – including, be it noted, every economist in every university in the country – is 'necessarily in the direct or indirect employ of banks or insurance companies.

According to Crowther, most of Douglas' views on the wider aims of policy are perfectly acceptable to 'most Liberals'. Douglas recognises, for example, 'the utter absurdity of trying to regain prosperity by restricting the production of everything – the fashionable doctrine of the moment'. Like any Free Trader, Douglas attacks the 'doctrine of Sabotage', noting that prosperity can only come by producing more, not less, goods. 'Further, Major Douglas wants to combine increasing wealth with increasing freedom – he has no patience with those who wish to regiment mankind into a pattern of uniformity.' He has, observes Crowther, no time for the class war or for the exaltation of Nationalism. 'On all these points, then, Major Douglas is quite definitely "on the side of the angels".' His vision is of a community of free, wealthy individuals. Thus his aim is 'to emancipate the human race from its bondage to the necessity of earning a living and to set it free to pursue its higher calling.'

Sadly, however, although his heart is basically in the right place, Douglas is, according to Crowther, mistaken in applying his engineer's logic to the much more obscure problems of the economy. It is obvious that 'much more is wrong with the world than mere faulty organisation'. Crowther passes on to 'an explanation of the Douglas theory'. The crux of Crowther's argument is that Social Credit theory is premised upon a hypothetical deficiency in purchasing power. To illustrate his point, Crowther presents a classic account of the Circular Flow, declaring that all incomes derive from the production of goods and services. Even the so-called 'leisured class,' allow their land and their capital to be used in the productive process, so that they earn an income.

In the last analysis, says Crowther, every income is provided by industry and is therefore one of the costs of industry. However, 'every income is also spent on the products of an industry or on the services of professional men, Civil Servants, cooks, housemaids, and so forth'. It follows that incomes can be looked at in two ways. In the first place, they are the costs of making things or providing services (wages, salaries, rent, dividends, interest, etc.). In the second place, they are the only source of demand for those things and services.

The economic process can therefore be represented as a circular flow of incomes. Business firms pay out sums of money which are the costs of making things; these sums of money are the incomes of those who help to make the things, and by being spent come back to the firms who paid them out.

Hence Douglas is mistaken in imagining that consumers' incomes are 'too small to purchase at remunerative prices the goods produced by industry'. Part of the trouble is, according to Crowther, that advocates of Social Credit stress the making of loans by banks. However, a bank loan is not actual currency, it is merely 'credit'. Most people are as ready (within reason) to take a cheque as a pound note, so they miss this vital distinction. Although the banks cannot create currency they can (within limits) create credit. 'Consequently, when a bank makes a loan something is created which passes for money, and, conversely, when a loan is repaid some money is abolished.'

Crowther then cites Douglas as claiming that part of the income received from the sale of a product may be used to repay a bank loan. When the bank loan was originally made, it was in the form of new money created as debt. That money having been spent long ago, the repayment of the loan has the effect of abolishing money by removing that amount of money from circulation.

> This may happen, but if it did the bank's loans would be reduced by the amount of money which had been 'abolished'. If the bank cancels one loan and immediately makes another of the same amount, it has handed on to the second borrower the money it has received from the first. And this, we know by experience, is what happens in fact. The loans of British Banks, for instance (in this connection a bank's 'investments' serve the same purpose as its 'advances'), sometimes diminish, but their general tendency is one of steady increase year by year. They are now nearly £50,000,000 larger than five years ago. In fact, therefore, no deficiency of purchasing power necessarily arises out of the use of bank credit.

This is very clever sophistry. Over seven pages the reader is lead from misapprehension to misapprehension. In what looks like a seamless whole, the reader is presented with misleading alternatives to what Douglas actually wrote, alongside disingenuous versions of orthodoxy. Crowther comes to the conclusion 'that Major Douglas is sometimes right (but even then not for the reasons he gives) and sometimes wrong'. In reality, the money spent by consumers is indeed sometimes less than enough, and sometimes more than enough, to buy the goods offered. Sometimes there is a deficiency of purchasing power, while at other times there is an excess. However, even when there is a deficiency, 'it is not due to the reasons which Major Douglas gives, but merely to the fact that the community – whether consumers or business firms – is spending less than it receives as income and consequently allowing its money to pile up in idleness.'

It follows, according to Crowther, that a simplistic addition to the purchasing power of consumers, 'would do more harm than good' as it would result in run-away inflation. Reluctantly, Crowther concludes that the only way out of economic depression, when it happens, is to persuade people to spend the whole of their incomes on consumer goods or on capital investment. It is 'not to create more money'. There are, Crowther dryly observes, several ways of persuading people to spend their present incomes, for example by presenting the public with more investment opportunities, so that they spend their money 'on increasing the capital resources of the country'. It would be a mistake to give the public additional incomes, because all they would do would be to spend 'both the addition and also the previously unused proportion of their incomes', resulting in an excess of purchasing power. Crowther insisted that he was not suggesting that the only thing to do in a depression was 'to tighten the belt, to economise, to 'cut the coat according to the cloth,' to sit and wait for better times, or any of the other conservative maxims'. Such a philosophy is 'profoundly repugnant'. There are ways of curing the depression, but they need to be 'much more flexible and scientific than the over-simple panaceas of Social Credit'.

As history demonstrates, a 'flexible and scientific' way of curing depression is war, which, as Crowther explains in the main body of his text, 'brings an enormous increase in Investment, making it very greatly exceed the volume of Saving.

> The excess – which shows itself, of course, as an excess of Government expenditure over receipts from taxes and savings – is financed by the creation of money, ... (*FN: The fact that money is being created for the sole purpose of financing the Government may be concealed. Thus in 1914-18 the British public were encouraged to borrow from the banks in order to invest in War Loan, depositing the Loan as security for the advances. The Government thus avoided borrowing directly from the banks (which everybody would have recognised as inflation). But the money it borrowed was nevertheless newly created for the purpose.*) ... and this additional supply of money competes with the existing supply to force up prices and restrict consumption.[1]

Thus Crowther confirms Douglas' analysis of the role of finance and banking in determining actual economic outcomes,[2] whilst at the same time implying that somewhere along the line, Douglas is mistaken when in fact the problem lies in orthodox analysis itself.

Crowther comes to the conclusion that there is much of value in Douglas' theories, 'but I have been unable to find in them any teachings of value which is not to be found in the writings of scores of other economists, including some of those Professors and Lecturers whom Major Douglas gratuitously dubs the paid servants of the banks'. However, Douglas' remedies would 'in most cases do more harm than good'. Crowther comes to this conclusion reluctantly, because it 'is always distasteful to disagree with enthusiastic idealism, especially when the objectives of the movement are so admirable. But the real pity is not that it is necessary to disagree, but that so much disinterested idealism should be enlisted in so unsound a cause.'[3] Thus the would-be career economist is steered firmly away from the Social Credit heresy. After a little original uncertainty, when Douglas' first book was reviewed by the mainstream (See Appendix 6a: Reviews), the 'professors' stood shoulder to shoulder in seeking to discredit Douglas and discourage open, frank and honest debate of the issues raised by Social Credit.

Although space does not allow for a detailed critique of Crowther's *An Outline of Money* from a Douglas Social Credit perspective, such an exercise would prove an invaluable tool for reduction of finance and banking to the status of useful social tools. Banks constantly create and retire money, to policy ends which they determine. In the twentieth century the general public were successfully conditioned into believing that money is something stable and scarce, like gold, in fixed amounts which cannot be altered by human agency. Hence it was the task of Crowther *et al* to refute Douglas' claim that the money system could be adapted to the needs of the social order. It is, therefore, necessary to read a text like *An Outline of Money* very carefully. What it actually says is, exactly as Douglas observed, that, under capitalism, money is created for three purposes: (1) to enable banks to make loans; (2) to enable banks to buy themselves securities; (3) to enable the Central Bank to buy gold. In respect of purpose (3), Crowther indicates that even when a country is not formally on the 'gold standard', its central bank cannot by law 'exceed a prescribed multiple of its holdings of gold'.[4] See Appendix 7a: The Struggle for Money, for an explanation of how the Bank of England, when it was originally founded, centuries before it became a Central Bank, made money to buy gold. In short, under the current financial system, banks operate according to very different rules from those which apply to an ordinary household or business. It has been the task of professional economists, wittingly or unwittingly, to confuse the issue.

Social Science Research Council of Canada

Until the publication of *The Political Economy of Social Credit and Guild Socialism*[5] there was no full record of the history of the Social Credit movement to be found on the shelves of university libraries across the world. By the 1990s the titles of Douglas' books were not listed in any literature, neither were the books themselves generally available for study. Nevertheless, a literature search would reveal a number of works which appear to offer concrete information about Social Credit. Prominent amongst these are a series of ten full scale research studies, sponsored by the Social Science Research Council of Canada, under the title 'Social Credit in Alberta: Its Background and Development', published by the University of Toronto Press. The full series of publications ran as follows:

Social Credit in Alberta

1. Morton, W.L., (1950) *The Progressive Party in Canada*, (reprinted 1967, 1971)
2. Masters, D.C., (1950) *The Winnipeg General Strike* (Paperback edition 1973)
3. Burnet, Jean (1951) *Next-Year Country: A study of rural social organisation in Alberta*, Toronto, Buffalo, London: University of Toronto Press (1978 reprint)
4. Macpherson, C.B., (1953) *Democracy in Alberta: Social Credit and the Party System*, (Second Edition 1962, reprinted 1968, 1970, 1974, 1977)
5. Mallory, J.R., (1954) *Social Credit and the Federal Power in Canada*. (Reprinted with additional preface 1976)
6. Mann, W.E. (1955) *Sect, Cult and Church in Alberta*. (Reprinted 1962. 1972)
7. Fowke, V.C. (1957) *The National Policy and the Wheat Economy*. (Reprinted in paperback 1973, 1978)
8. Thomas, L.G. (1959) *The Liberal Party in Alberta: A History of Politics in the Province of Alberta, 1905-1921*.
9. Clark, S.D. (1959) *Movements of Political Protest in Canada, 1640-1840* (Reprinted 1968. 1978)
10. Irving, J.A. (1959) *The Social Credit Movement in Alberta* (Reprinted 1960, 1968, and 1974 'in the USA'.)

The series of studies, edited by S.D. Clark, formed a massive research project which ran for fifteen years. As Clark explains in his Foreword to the first study, published in 1950:

In 1944 the Canadian Social Science Research Council, through a special grant made by the Rockefeller Foundation, undertook to sponsor a series of studies having as their primary object the investigation of the Social Credit movement in Alberta. A director was appointed by the Council and the co-operation of a number of scholars in the fields of history, economics, political science and sociology was enlisted.[6]

As a whole, the series of studies portrays Social Credit as of little interest, save as a movement of political protest peculiar to the social, economic and political character of Western Canada. Macpherson's study has become the standard 'official' text on Social Credit, not only in Alberta but on a world scale. Having quoted selected passages from Douglas' books, Macpherson dismisses social credit economics as fundamentally flawed:

Belief in the cultural heritage and in the role of the financiers became the two pillars of the social credit faith. So strong were they that the mone- tary theory was scarcely needed, and as its fallacies were exposed it could be pushed into the background. There, its very intricacy became an asset, for the mere knowledge of its existence gave the adherents of social credit a sustaining feeling that all the mysteries of economics had been probed, even if they could not fully understand them.

This curious relation between the technical analysis and the broader case facilitated a peculiar relation between leader and followers which came to characterize the social credit movement both in England and later in Alberta. The A plus B theorem and the rest of the technical analysis of money and credit played a large part in the recruitment of the original English movement. But as the movement expanded, the monetary theory became a matter of widespread public debate and came under increasingly severe critical fire. Douglas, convinced that he had got the fundamental truth, could not admit the fallacies in the technical theory. Nor could he repair them. He was therefore compelled after a time to take the position that the technical theory was not a matter for discus- sion. Soon the whole social credit movement was committed to this position. The leader and his small group of experts became the acknowl- edged and sole custodians of the mysteries; the function of the followers was to have faith in the cultural heritage, in the power of the people to overthrow the financiers, and in the wisdom and expert ability of their own leaders.[7]

Thus Douglas is portrayed as seeking to mystify his followers quite deliberately. The inference is that orthodox economists can be depended upon to blow away the mystique on the subject of the relationship between finance and economic activity.

The research series as a whole portrays Social Credit in Alberta as a political insurrection against the duly authorised 'powers-that-be'. In Appendix 8a: Rockefeller Studies, the book cover details of all but one of the series are reproduced. Several of the books make no mention whatsoever of Social Credit economics, politics, philosophy or history. At the other extreme, Irving's study presents Social Credit as fundamentally sinister. Clark's foreword labels Irving's study as a major contribution to the social psychology of collective behaviour. The people of Alberta, according to Clark, reacted to Aberhart's 'great powers of oratory':

> For someone who believed that political action was the outcome of a rational process of discussion and deliberation, the observation of political developments in Alberta in the years 1932-5 would have been a disillusioning experience. The people truly appeared to have taken leave of their senses, and nothing but disaster, it seemed, could result from the election to office of persons who had so little understanding of the economic and political world as Mr. Aberhart and his Social Credit colleagues.

> Yet to the social scientist who has learnt not to be shocked by the conduct of his fellow humans, whether on an isolated island of the South Seas or in a fashionable residential district of a big city, there are no actions of people which do not make sense if viewed within the social context in which they occur. ... The debt-ridden farmer, unable to sell what little he was able to produce, could scarcely be expected to behave like a bank president, church bishop, or even a professor of economics.[8]

For Irving, the Social Credit movement provided a small-scale example of the potential of philosophies such as 'socialism, communism, fascism or Nazism' to seek to transform society through attaining political power. In his preface he states:

> This book is based mainly upon interviews with people in Alberta, but private papers, private collections of newspaper and other files, mimeographed materials, leaflets, pamphlets, government brochures,

newspaper articles, and books have also been used. In nearly every instance, people have not wished their names identified with interviews, private papers or private collections. Every effort has therefore been made to protect the identity of informants and owners of private papers and files.[9]

Irving's words must be among the most curious ever written on the subject. The intention is clear: it creates the impression that Social Credit is something that one does not talk about. It would, however, have been useful to know on what grounds people providing information on Social Credit for a book published in 1959 on the subject of a democratic election in 1935, would wish to remain anonymous. What had they to fear, and from whom could any threat possibly emanate?

From the texts of the studies it is clear that the researchers had access to the full range of published literature on Social Credit from the earliest days of its inception in the Guild Socialist movement. The use made of this material indicates clearly that the purpose of the research studies was to portray Douglas Social Credit as an aberration which appealed to ignorant farming communities merely because of the desperate economic circumstances of the times. The reader who may be unfamiliar with the original Social Credit texts is led to believe that no useful purpose would be served by seeking them out. In his chapter on 'The Quasi-party System' Macpherson, for example, portrays Douglas as a false prophet of utopianism:

> There is in the social credit theory much of Fourier, with his rejection of the work fetish, his belief that the cause of poverty was the abundance of goods, his fascination with the laws of gravity, and his catalogue of waste. There is something of Saint-Simon, with his faith in 'les industriels' who actually operate the productive and distributive system, his belief that 'government' would be replaced by 'administration,' and his assurance that diffusion of credit would save the world. Even more striking is the similarity to the ideas of Proudhon, the archetype of petit-bourgeois radicalism. Like Douglas, Proudhon explained the source of profit as the 'increment of association,' and the emergence of profit as a result of a miscalculation. Like Douglas he explained poverty as due to the depredation of industry by finance, which made it impossible for those who produced everything to buy back their own products; and found the solution in a scheme of free credit for producers, along with price-fixing. Like Douglas, he found that the handing over of the nation's credit to the national bank had elevated finance to the position

of an occult power enslaving the whole country. Like Douglas, he held that the destruction of this power by credit reform would remove oppression and misery without altering the labour-capital relationship; competition and private property would remain.

The perceptive reader is left wondering how Douglas could logically string such divergent ideas into a coherent whole. If he rejected the 'work-fetish', for example, how could he at the same time leave the 'labour-capital relationship' intact? Macpherson ploughs on regardless:

> Like Douglas, he denounced majority rule and popular sovereignty, holding that progress was always accomplished not by the people but by an *élite*. Like Douglas, he hated bureaucracy and the omnipotent state for their repression of individual liberty. His theoretical anarchism, being a rejection not of all coercive power but only of absolute state power, is essentially similar to the social credit position. Like Douglas, Proudhon was scornful of political parties, and saw a Jewish conspiracy dominating the press and the government.[10]

Thus half-truth and innuendo are skilfully interwoven so that the reader is led firmly away from bothering to seek out and study Social Credit texts in the originals. In the same passage Macpherson states that, since Proudhon's 'false individualism' led him to support the dictatorship of a leader like Louis Bonaparte, who could prevail on the masses to give him power, Douglas sought personal power in the same way. Hence from 'Proudhon to Hitler, doctrines which have singled out finance as the source of social evil have led to a plebiscitary state'. Words are very carefully chosen and juxtaposed. A footnote suggests that Douglas may have come across Proudhon's ideas through Gesell, implying at once that (a) Douglas was not initially well-read and (b) that Douglas derived his own ideas from studying Gesell, a minor maverick monetary reformer whose work posed no challenge whatsoever to economic orthodoxy.

Throughout the series of studies, little if any reference is made to the existence in Alberta of the vast mineral resources which were already being exploited by corporations based elsewhere. The studies focus on the economics and politics of farming communities whose needs contrast with those of urban settlements, both inside Alberta and in the East of Canada. With post-war exploitation of Alberta's oil fields and other natural resources, the Province moved into prosperity, and the 'Alberta Experiment' was deemed 'unnecessary'.

'Social discredit' and 'anti-Semitism'

After World War II, Social Credit disappeared from the mass media outside Canada. Nevertheless, publications continued to appear on the subject throughout the twentieth century and into the present century. The themes of these publications fell into one or all of three categories: (a) Social Credit was economic heresy; (b) Social Credit was anti-democratic; and (c) Social Credit was anti-Semitic. The research for many of these documents was largely funded from corporate sources, and all make very interesting reading. In 1972 John Finlay[11] presented Social Credit as part of the English political 'underground' of the inter-war years. In 1993 Edward Bell revealed that Social Credit in Alberta had some working class support.[12] A glossy tome published, in 1998, presents pictures and text under the title *Aberhart and the Alberta Insurrection 1935 – 1940*,[13] giving the impression that some subversive political event had taken place. But the accusation of anti-Semitism has created a highly effective barrier to rational discussion of Douglas' work, or the course of events in Alberta following the 1935 election of a Social Credit government.

Finlay, one of the more sympathetic commentators on the Social Credit phenomenon, devotes a couple of pages to the question of Douglas' attitude towards Jewish people. Douglas does make reference to the presence of Jewish individuals in key roles in international finance. Citing Douglas on the subject at some length, Finlay is of the opinion that 'the nature of this anti-Jewish outlook must be probed, for it is doubtful whether it can be called anti-Semitism in the normal sense'.[14] For Douglas, Jewishness is a philosophical description rather than a racial term. According to Finlay:

> This point was made very clearly when he once divided systems into two, the characteristics of the first being 'Deductive, Totalitarian, Machiavellian, Idealistic, Jewish, Love of Power, Planned Economy,' and of the second and balancing group, Inductive, Democratic, Baconian, Realistic, Christian, Love of Freedom, Organic Growth.' Anti-Semitism of the Douglas kind, if it can be called anti-Semitism at all, may be fantastic, may be dangerous even, in that it may be twisted into a dreadful form, but it is not in itself vicious nor evil. It is merely an extreme form of religio-philosophic propaganda, to be classed with Coulton's anti-Catholic tirades.[15]

The passage cited by Finlay occurs in *The Fig Tree* of June 1938. Finlay further comments that Douglas was, above all, concerned with individual freedom, and in no way suggested that any group should be discriminated against. That was not in the nature of Douglas' way of thinking.

The end of the century saw the publication of two further studies of Social Credit in Alberta, funded by the Social Sciences and Research Council of Canada. In *Major Douglas and Alberta Social Credit*, Bob Hesketh comes to a considered conclusion, having read all Douglas' work:

> My research has convinced me that Douglas's conspiracy-based under-standing of the world, rather than his monetary and political theories, holds the secret for comprehending his ideas. He believed a Jewish financial conspiracy was orchestrating world events ranging from the First World War to the Great Depression. The primary source of his ideas was *The Protocols of the Learned Elders of Zion*. He created social credit specifically to undo the power of the conspiracy as revealed in the *Protocols*. His monetary and political theories were tactics for defeating Finance.[16]

According to Hesketh, Douglas was basically a socialist who sought to wipe out capitalism by taking the ownership of the means of production from the financiers and capitalists and somehow transferring it to the population as a whole. Moreover, Douglas was so authoritarian that 'he could – and did – reject the implementation of social-credit measures'. In spite of the wealth of written resources to hand, Hesketh thus presents Douglas as merely a sinister figure whose work had neither substance nor meaning.

A further study, published in 2000, confirms the direct involvement of Jewish organisations in Albertan political affairs. In *Social Discredit: Anti-Semitism, Social Credit and the Jewish Response,* Janine Stingel demonstrates how the Canadian Jewish Congress worked to persuade *democratically elected* members of the Albertan legislature to drop Douglas Social Credit in favour of a conventional conservatism which was Social Credit in name only. Stingel includes 22 'Social Credit Career Sketches' and 19 'Canadian Jewish Congress Career Sketches'. The biographies make very interesting reading, not least because the places of birth, the linguistic, cultural and religious affiliations are so varied, yet the two groups of men – and they are all men – are divided on the basis of their Jewishness or non-Jewishness. The general tenor of the book can be gleaned from the cover blurb reproduced in Appendix 8b: Hesketh and Stingel, and from just one example taken from the Career Sketches. Solon Low was a senior member of Aberhart's administration who later (1945-58) served as Social Credit MP for Peace River in the Ottawa Parliament. Stingel observes:

> A member of the Mormon Church, Low expressed extremely anti-Semitic statements throughout his career. When Manning conducted his purge of the anti-Semitic Douglasites in 1947-8, Low technically

followed Manning's directive but continued to espouse anti-Semitism. In the 1950s, however, Low visited Israel and became an ardent proponent of Zionism.[17]

The book documents the strategies used by the Canadian Jewish Congress to root out Social Credit from Alberta, from the date when Ernest Manning took over the premiership in 1943, indicating that the death of Aberhart proved to be a watershed. By April 1946 Premier Manning had joined the Canadian Palestinian Committee for the furtherance of Zionist aims.[18] With the assistance of the Zionists in Alberta, Premier Manning purged the Province of all true Social Credit policies.[19]

Game, set and match to mainstream orthodoxy?

Wherever and whenever serious discussion of Douglas Social Credit occurs, the debate is silenced by a claim that Social Credit is nothing but 'anti-Semitism', and hence obviously a 'no-go' area for any career academic or politician. The Stingel and Hesketh books provided ammunition for an article which claimed that the 'ecosocialist' anti-globalisation movement was in danger of being co-opted into fascism and anti-Semitism through studying Douglas's writings. Published in 2003 in the U.K.-based journal *Capitalism, Nature, Socialism* under the title 'Social Credit: The Ecosocialism of Fools', the article contains the following assertion:

> In contrast, [to those who consider Douglas' work worthy of 'critical attention'] this essay argues that far from being a link to an historical ecosocialism, Douglas's philosophy functioned as a tragic episode in its disintegration. Social credit has ominous parallels and shares elements with traditions of anti-semitic populism. The danger that social credit, along with other right wing political economies [sic], presents within the anti-globalization movement is examined. The case of social credit indicates why ecosocialism has the potential to degrade into ecofascism and how such degradation can be fought as part of a vitally important hegemonic battle within the anti-globalization movement.[20]

The above passage takes some translating. It appears to suggest that the entire paper will explain how the failure of previous attempts to establish a 'green' or 'eco' – socialism can be attributed to Douglas. By adopting Douglas' philosophy, it would seem, a whole generation of would-be sound 'eco-socialists' found themselves frog-marched into 'eco-fascism'. If a recurrence of the 'tragedy' is to be avoided, the 'anti-globalisation movement' must now prepare for battle between the angelic Wall-ites and demonic Social Crediters. The article, which runs to 22 pages, names the names of all who have made even the slightest positive reference to Douglas, Social Credit, or any publication on the subject. The editor of a Green Economics journal comes under suspicion because his *parents* studied Douglas' works. Leading authorities such as David Korten and Herman Daly are included in the negative references because they endorsed Michael Rowbotham's book on the subject.[21] Readers are invited to make their own assessment of the Wall paper by reading it for themselves as it appeared in *Capitalism, Nature, Socialism*.[22]

If it is true that all mention of Clifford Hugh Douglas, Social Credit, international finance and the existence of some Jewish names in the arena of world affairs is to be interpreted as 'anti-Semitism', there can be *no alternative* to mainstream political, economic and cultural orthodoxy. In that case, the present impasse of poverty amidst plenty, war, social injustice, environmental destruction, periodic depressions and general sense of purposelessness must continue unabated. The next chapter reviews the potential for positive alternative thinking. This, however, cannot exist in a vacuum. Social Credit, building, as it does, upon the work of thinkers like Douglas, Marx, Veblen and Guild Socialism, is a body of thought which provides a coherent alternative to economic orthodoxy. All the rest – Henry George, Silvio Gesell and all the other minnows in the economic underworld – have failed to generate a substantial literature capable of posing a coherent challenge to the existing socio-economic order. Hence at best they merely illuminate the road back to orthodoxy.

NOTES

1   Crowther (1940) pp180
2   Douglas' explanation of the financing of World War I (1924, Part 2, Chapter V) is identical with that of Crowther.
3   Except where noted, quotes from Crowther (1940) are taken from pages 432-445.
4   Crowther (1940) page 63.
5   Hutchinson and Burkitt (1997)
6   Morton (1950) pvii.
7   Macpherson (1953) pp118-9.
8   Irving (1959) pvii
9   Irving (1959) px
10   Macpherson (1953) pp264-5.
11   Finlay (1972)

12   Bell (1993)
13   United Western Communications (1998)
14   Finlay (1972) pp103-4
15   Finlay (1972) pp104-5
16   Hesketh (1997) pp5-6
17   Stingel (2000) pp200-1
18   'From Week to Week', *The Social Crediter*, April 20, 1946.
19   See Hooke (1971)
20   Wall (2003)
21   Rowbotham (1998)
22   Wall (2003)

Appendix 8a
The Rockefeller Studies

SOCIAL CREDIT IN ALBERTA
Its Background and Development

The series of studies sponsored by the Canadian Social Science Research Council, directed and edited by S.D. Clark, was originally published between 1950 and 1959. The paperback reprints carried the following information on the book covers:

1. The Progressive Party in Canada
By W.L. Morton

> 'a wonderfully alive political history from 1896 through the twenties ... strongly recommended for both the political neophyte and his more experienced cohort!' *Saskatoon Star-Phoenix.*
> *Winner of the Governor-General's Award for Academic Non-Fiction, 1950.*

A striking and significant phenomenon of the Canadian political scene immediately following World War I was the rise and fall of a third party. Professor Morton describes and analyses the background and political history of this movement, and gives a graphic description of western economy and politics generally which will assist all readers towards a better understanding of the Canadian west and its problems.

The Progressive party represented essentially an agrarian revolt against what western Canada considered to be Canadian economic policy and Canadian political practice. As seen through western eyes, our economic policy at the time seemed a metropolitan economy, designed by control of tariffs, railways, and credit to draw wealth from the hinterland and country-side into the industrial and commercial centre of Canada. Political practice appeared in much the same light. The classic national parties took on the guise of instruments used by the vested interests of metropolitan Canada to implement this national policy. Distrust and dissatisfaction mounted over the first twenty years of the century and the impetus for independent political action on the part of the farmers increased proportionately.

While the grievances were shelved during World War I, party lines were weakened by the coming to power of the Union Government, and allegiance in the west was easily turned away from the unsatisfying traditional parties after the Union Government was defeated. By 1919-20, organised farmer groups were definitely committed to a programme of political action.

Born and educated in Manitoba, WILLIAM LEWIS MORTON graduated from the University of Manitoba in 1932. The following year he went to Oxford as a Rhodes scholar and took his M.A. there in 1937. Professor Morton is the author of, among many other works, Manitoba: A History and The Canadian Identity. He is currently Professor of History at Trent University.

Printed 1971

2. The Winnipeg General Strike

By D.C. Masters

'This job very much needed doing, and Dr. Masters has done it in a scholarly and judicial yet forthright manner. The hysteria engendered by the Winnipeg general strike of 1919, heightened by the singularly unenlightened form which government intervention took, continues to trail clouds of distortion and bitterness. By careful analysis of facts, circumstances, and the personalities of the strike leaders, Dr. masters has cleared away the haze and given us a historical record of the utmost value.' *Canadian Forum*

Printed 1973

3. Next-Year Country
A STUDY OF RURAL SOCIAL ORGANIZATION IN ALBERTA

By Jean Burnet

In this study of the problems of social organization in a rural community of Alberta, a drought-afflicted wheat-growing area centring round the town of Hanna is described as it appeared to the sociologist in 1946.

Dr. Burnet examines geographical and economic conditions in Hanna, and shows how farming practices, ways of living, and modes of tenure brought into the area from more humid regions proved ill adapted to the dry belt and delayed economic adjustment. In turn, the difficulties in the realm of economics had adverse social and cultural consequences in both the households and the community as a whole.

The Hanna area was chosen for study, though not altogether typical, because it revealed more clearly than other areas not so severely hit by the drought of the 1930s the kind of disturbances within the Alberta social structure which made possible the rise of the Social Credit movement.

'Dr. Burnet's book is destined for a place in the small but indispensible shelf of studies which have made genuine contributions to the sociology of Canadian communities.' *Queen's Quarterly*

'Dr. Burnet's factual story is as fascinating as a novel. Brilliantly organized, and written with striking clarity, the work never loses touch with human values. ... This searching analysis admirably fulfils its purpose in revealing the *kinds* of disturbances present in the rural social organisation of Alberta, but its findings are of much more general application.' *Canadian Geographical Journal*

JEAN BURNET is a member of the Department of Sociology at Glendon College in York University.

Printed 1978

4. Democracy in Alberta:
SOCIAL CREDIT AND THE PARTY SYSTEM

By C.B. Macpherson

'This is a brilliantly conceived and executed study of the western Canadian province's rejection of the usual type of British party government. It will no doubt incite Canadians to re-examine the foundations of their party system or systems. ... The central portion of the books is devoted to an admirably lucid exposition of the Douglas doctrines in their English setting and their application in Alberta by Aberhart and Manning. It is, however, the eighth and last chapter, 'The Quasi-party System,' that gives the volume wider interest and in fact makes it of significance for all students of parliamentary and democratic government.' *Parliamentary Affairs*

'C'est, croyons-nous, la meilleure synthèse qui ait été faite jusqu'ici des événements et des idées se rattachant à un des plus importants phénomènes de la vie politique canadienne. Jusqu'à présent, c'était avec trop de passion, soit pour l'attaquer et le défender, qu'on avait écrit sur le Crédit Social. Le professeur Macpherson nous donne, lui, une étude scientifique et objective.' *Culture*

C.B. MACPHERSON, D.SC.(Econ.), D.LITT, LL.D., F.R.S.C.., F.R.HIST.S., Professor in the department of Political Economy, University of Toronto, is widely known on both sides of the Atlantic for his work in political theory. *Democracy in Alberta*, in which he first put forward a new general theory of party systems, was recognized at once as a striking contribution to the understanding of modern party systems. He is also the author of *The Political Theory of Possessive Individualism: Hobbes to Locke, The Real World of Democracy,* and *Democratic theory: Essays in Retrieval.* He was the Chairman of the University of Toronto committee which reported on *Undergraduate Instruction in Arts and Science* (1967) published by the University of Toronto Press.

Printed 1977

5. Social Credit and the Federal Power in Canada

By J.R. Mallory

During the twenty or so years after William Aberhart became premier of Alberta and head of the world's first Social Credit government, there occurred a profound change in the nature of the Canadian federation, affecting the constitutional balance between the provinces and Ottawa. Aberhart and his Social Credit government, almost in spite of themselves, played a major role in the resurgence of federal power.

This is essentially a book about federal-provincial relations, for to Professor Mallory the events in Alberta following the election of 1935 have their deepest significance in the light they throw on the development of the Canadian constitution and the role of the Supreme Court in response to the challenges of the twentieth-century environment.

'Mr. Mallory's volume is a most useful and judicious combination of a searching examination of the federal power of disallowance with a detailed analysis of the relations of the Social Credit Government of Alberta with the federal Government. It will be consulted by those who wish to understand the victory and continued vigour of Social Credit in Alberta; it will also be added to the brief list of indispensable reference books on Canadian politics.'

W.L. Morton *The Canadian Historical Review*

'Professor Mallory has blended law, history and politics into a book of extraordinary interest. Much of this result is due to the literary quality and complete readability of the book.'

Donald M. Fleming *The Canadian Bar Review*

J.R. MALLORY is Professor of Political Science at McGill University.

Printed 1976

6. Sect, Cult and Church in Alberta

By William E. Mann

'As a cogent interpretation in sociological terms of what happened in Alberta, the volume is an excellent study in social history.' *American Journal of Sociology*

'a clear and firm appraisal of the criss-cross religious culture which engendered the Aberhart movement ... a fascinating study of the incredible proliferation of sects and cults in a frontier community.' *Queen's Quarterly*

This study, which has been in steady demand since its publication in 1955, is a sociological and historical report of the growth of sects and cults in Alberta from 1887 to 1947 based on interviews, observations, and other primary material. The author, a student of sociology when he began his research and later an Anglican minister and professor of social science, presents an impartial and thorough report of the history, nature and composition, liturgy and doctrine, programmes and organization, leadership, and techniques of evangelization of the non-conforming religious groups in Alberta.

Printed 1972

7. The National Policy and the Wheat Economy

By V.C. Fowke

First published in 1957, this study traces the development of the national policy as it affected the growth of the Canadian trade and discusses the grain marketing problems of Western Canada in the decades that followed, with detailed attention to legislation and moves by various growers' groups in an attempt to meet these problems. This important study in political economy is organised into four main parts. In Part One the author traces the development of the national policy and its impact on the growth of the wheat empire in the years before 1900. In Part Two, he discusses the grain marketing problems of western Canada during the 1900-1920 period. Part Three is a masterful exposé of the history of the open market system and of the history and policies of the Canadian Wheat Pools, and Part Four examines the economic philosophy behind the development of the national policy.

'The author is without rival in his historical grasp of Canadian agricultural policy.' W.L. Morton *Canadian Historical Review*

'In this important study of the dynamic role of prairie wheat in the first and formative phase of Canadian national development, Professor Fowke has drawn on the work of a whole generation of scholars and on his own intimate knowledge of the Canadian west.' *The Economist*

Vernon C. Fowke (1907-1966) was for many years Professor of Economics at the University of Saskatchewan.

Printed 1978

8. The Liberal Party in Alberta:
A History of Politics in the Province of Alberta 1905-1921

By L.G Thomas

Author's Preface:

Among her sisters in the Canadian federation, Alberta has achieved a reputation for political eccentricity. For nearly forty years her governments have been of a political shade unfashionable in most of the rest of Canada. This study examines the earlier years of Aberta's political history, when at least the outward appearance of her governments was more in accord with the accepted Canadian conventions. It is particularly concerned with the fortunes of what was, in those formative years between 1905 and 1921, the dominant Liberal party. Alberta was among the first of the provinces to reject the conventional parties of Canadian federal politics; she rejected them more decisively than some of the others. Her behaviour, this study suggests, was at least in part the result of her experience, under three premiers, of the rule of one of the older parties.

L.G. THOMAS
Printed 1959

9. Movements of Political Protest in Canada 1640-1840

By S.D. Clark

In this volume, Professor Clark shows that for two hundred years Canadian society was subject to the same kind of disturbing and disruptive forces that revealed themselves in the United States in the Revolutionary period. In Canada, as in the United States, there was a frontier element which, economically, socially, and culturally, did not feel itself part of the established political order, and which periodically reacted against that order. In Canada, however, the spirit of the frontier regularly met defeat, and the author analyses the causes of this defeat in a thorough and illuminating manner, dealing in sequence with each area of conflict. The study is divided into four parts: The First American War of Independence, 1660-1760; The War of the United Colonies, 1865-1785; The Struggle for the West, 1785-1815; The Canadian Rebellions, 1815-1840.

The author, an economist and sociologist, diverges sharply from the traditional historical interpretation of events in Canada from 1640 to 1840, which has been to emphasize the differences between the two countries rather than the similarities. His realistic and penetrating study may prompt many to re-examine and re-assess the bases of their interpretations.

S.D.CLARK graduated from the University of Saskatchewan in 1930 with honours in history and politica science. After taking his M.A. at Saskatchewan, he spent a year at the University of Toronto on an open fellowship studying history, and then a year at the London School of Economics in economic history, political science, and sociology. Returning to Canada, Dr. Clark instructed and lectured at McGill University, the University of Toronto, and the University of Manitoba. He took his Ph.D at Toronto. Since 1938, he has been on the staff of the University of Toronto, where he is now Professor and Chairman of the Department of Sociology.

Dr. Clark is the author of numerous articles in the field of Sociology; he contributed to *Canada and Her Great Neighbour,* and he is the author of *Church and Sect in Canada, The Developing Canadian Community, The Suburban Society* and editor of *Urbanism and the Changing Canadian Society.* He is a fellow of the Royal Society of Canada, and was President of the Canadian Political Science Association in 1958-59.

Printed 1968

10. The Social Credit Movement in Alberta

By John A. Irving

'On the night of August 22, 1935, as Canadians listened to their radios, they heard, with amazement and incredulity, that the first Social Credit government in the world had been elected that day in the province of Alberta ... Before the tabulation of votes was completed, telephone calls from New York and London, headlines in newspapers, spot news in broadcasts, had confirmed the slogan of Social Crediters, 'The Eyes of the World are on Alberta.' The morning after the election a number of people lined up at the city hall in Calgary to collect the first instalment of the Social Credit dividend of $25 monthly, which, they confidently believed, would be immediately forthcoming from their new government.'

This quotation from Professor Irving's book indicates how the apparent suddenness of the Social Credit rise to power and the magnitude of the victory aroused world-wide comment. Why had the doctrines of Social Credit, promoted unsuccessfully in the British Commonwealth and the United States for nearly twenty years, achieved political acceptance in Alberta? Why had the people of Alberta elected to public office persons so little experienced in the economic and political world as William Aberhart and his Social Credit colleagues? Professor Irving answers these questions and analyses systematically and comprehensively the rise of the movement as a phenomenon of mass psychology. His study, based mainly on interviews, supplemented with references to private papers, newspapers, and government sources, provides a truly fascinating record.

' ... a valuable contribution to the literature of Canadian social science.' *Queen's Quarterly*

'Carefully documented and interestingly written, this book is of value not only to the student of Social Credit but to the researcher on the political process and techniques of mass persuasion.' *Western Political Quarterly*

Until his death in 1965 John A. Irving was Professor of Ethics and Social Philosophy at Victoria College, University of Toronto.

Printed 1974

Appendix 8b

Cover Details of Two Books

1. MAJOR DOUGLAS AND ALBERTA SOCIAL CREDIT

By Bob Hesketh (1997)

The Social Credit movement had a broad and significant impact on the social and political history of Alberta. A number of authors have examined this phenomenon, usually focusing on the economic and social conditions that influenced Social Credit's rise to power. *Major Douglas and Alberta Social Credit*, however, is the first work dedicated expressly to the intellectual history of the Social Credit government of the 1930s and 1940s.

Bob Hesketh challenges us to revise previous thinking about Social Credit by placing new emphasis on the influence of Major C.H. Douglas's conspiracy-based ideology on the Aberhart and Manning governments. The author is the first to contend that Douglas's beliefs were strongly influenced by the infamous anti-Semitic book *The Protocols of the Learned Elders of Zion*. Douglas believed that a Jewish financial conspiracy with the single goal of enslaving mankind was orchestrating world events. Hesketh analyses the shared ground between Douglas's conspiratorial thinking and the fundamentalism of Aberhart and Manning. He suggests that both premiers understood and applied Douglas's teachings to a wide variety of government policies, from the famous monetary bills to numerous lesser-known economic-diversification initiatives.

This book develops important new interpretations of Social Credit's behaviour as a movement, party, and government, providing an unprecedented focus on ideology. It will be an essential reference for historians and political scientists concerned with the history of Social Credit in Alberta.

BOB HESKETH is sessional lecturer at the University of Alberta.

2. SOCIAL DISCREDIT

Anti-Semitism, Social Credit and the Jewish Response

By Janine Stingel (2000)

Social Discredit offers a new perspective on both the Social Credit movement and the Canadian Jewish Congress, substantively revising Social Credit historiography and providing a valuable addition to Canadian Jewish studies.

Janine Stingel shows that both Social Credit and the Canadian Jewish Congress changed considerably in the post-war period, as Social Credit finally abandoned its anti-Semitic trappings and Congress gradually adopted an aggressive and pugnacious public relations philosophy that made it champion of human rights in Canada.

In *Social Discredit* Janine Stingel exposes a crucial, yet previously neglected, part of Social Credit history – the virulent, anti-Jewish campaign it undertook before, during, and after World War II. While most Canadians acknowledged the perils of race hatred in the wake of the Holocaust, Social Credit intensified its anti-Semitic campaign. By examining Social Credit's anti-Semitic propaganda and the reaction of the Canadian Jewish Congress, Stingel details their mutual antagonism and explores why Congress was unable to stop Social Credit's blatant defamation.

'A path-breaking study.' J.L. Granatstein.

'This is a masterful, insightful study of a Canadian community under attack. Using new sources Stingel presents both a stinging indictment of the obsessive anti-Semitism underlying the Social Credit movement and a fascinating look inside the Jewish community as it defends itself against this frightening assault on its existence in Canada.'

Irving Abella, past president of the Canadian Jewish Congress and Shiff Professor of Canadian Jewish History at York University.

'Others have touched obliquely on some aspects of this history but no one has made it the subject of a detailed and scholarly analysis until now. Dr. Stingel has added immeasurably to our knowledge of Social Credit and the history of Canadian Jewry in the inter-war, war, and post-war eras.'

David Bercuson, Director, Strategic Studies, University of Calgary

Chapter 9
Finance and the
Threefold Social Order

In the article cited in this chapter, Philippe Mairet reflects on the observation that Douglas' analysis of the relationship between finance and the 'real' world of people and nature complements Rudolf Steiner's ideas on the Threefold Commonwealth. Here it is essential to note that neither Douglas nor Steiner proposed a Utopian scheme or blueprint for the 'good society'. Both recognised that the essential pre-requisite for social change is a change of heart of the people. A change in the laws can be little more than illusion so long as people continue to expect to gain *financially*, whether as individuals or as organisations, from participating in the economy: my/our work will continue to create my/our money, which I/we can spend as I/we like. For the rules of the game to change in any meaningful sense, it would be necessary for people to change their assumptions about their reasons for participating in the game in the first place.

Real and financial value in the social context

Douglas' core theme was that human society consists of a 'real' economy of people and things, and their inter-relationships on the one hand, and a 'financial' economy on the other. As it evolved over the twentieth century, the financial economy came to regulate the real economy in a purely arbitrary fashion. Douglas used a number of examples to illustrate this point. For instance, he pictured a farmer planting a field of potatoes. It is possible for a farmer to take a field of land which is his property in law, to take his own labour, seed potatoes which already belong to him, tools in his possession, and, using skills handed down from generation to generation, to tend the field until harvest time. At this point in time the farmer has a very 'real' sack of potatoes. If he now takes the sack of potatoes to a neighbour and sells it for £5, he cannot in any sense whatsoever say that he has 'made' £5. That £5 pre-existed independently of the farmer, having been created by the financial system which operates in complete independence from the physical facts of life. If there is no other money in the system, no further financial transactions can take place until the farmer spends his £5. If there *is* more money in the system, the neighbour may opt not to consume the potatoes himself, but to sell them on, in which case the farmer has contributed a part of the 'real' wealth upon which the financial system depends for its existence. The farmer has not, however, 'made' any money at all. 'His' money is, and remains, a part of a complex money system which exists only in the context of human society as a whole.

Moreover, the farmer cannot even be said to have created the sack of potatoes by his own labour. Without the natural resources of the land, without the legal right to the use of the land, without the ownership rights over the seed potatoes and the tools, without the skills and knowledge which went into the making of the tools, without the handed-on farming skills, without the upbringing provided by his family and the community in childhood and adolescence, and without the supply of food, shelter and accommodation provided by society as a whole to sustain him throughout the year, the farmer would have been in no position to claim his £5 money reward for the sale of his potatoes. If the farmer consumes the sack of potatoes himself, it has high material value to him (and his family), and such wastes as are incurred are naturally returned to the land. However, not only do the potatoes have no financial value, the process of potato production contributes nothing to society as a whole which, as we have noted, is essential to the farmer's ability to produce the crop in the first place.

If the farmer's neighbour happens to be a butcher, the farmer might use the £5 from the sale of the potatoes to buy £5s worth of meat. This type of 'butcher-baker' exchange is indeed happening all the time. These barter-style transactions, which are complete in themselves, are not helpful in explaining the relationship between the 'real' economy and the financial economy. If, however, the farmer sells his potatoes to a food manufacturing industry, we enter a whole new ball game. Let us suppose the potatoes are turned into potato crisps. The farmer markets his potatoes, which are transported to the factory, a purpose-built building which houses machinery to slice the potatoes, fry them, and put them into bags and boxes. The boxes are loaded onto lorries, transported to wholesalers and on to retailers, where the bags are bought by customers at several hundred percent of the financial value paid to the farmer for his potatoes. Leaving aside questions of the 'externalities', *i.e.*, the extra costs of waste disposal, the pollution caused by transport, the health problems of obesity from snack-type foods, the process can be seen to make *financial* sense.

We are here presented with a conundrum. The £5 received by the farmer for his sack of potatoes opens up a vast array of consumer choices to the farmer, which his sack of potatoes did not. Although finance did not play any role whatsoever in the actual process of production it cannot, in the present state of human society, be dispensed with. Money is at present the life-blood of human society. For people to function as teachers and doctors, as arms manufacturers and politicians, as artists and engineers, as farmers and shop-keepers, parents and carers, money is an essential pre-requisite. In the present state of humanity, finance cannot be dispensed with. All day, every day, every individual's life is impacted upon by their relationship to money. However, that relationship is both arbitrary and poorly understood. Apart from custom, there is no necessary reasoning to endorse the ways in which money flows through society.

The crucial question which needs to be explored is how finance presently dominates human associations across the entire realm of the institutions of society. Other considerations do, indeed, exist. But they only come into play as secondary considerations. The dictum of the orthodox economist – 'If a thing is worth doing, it is worth being paid to do it!' – currently applies throughout the whole of society. It is expected that every household should have at least one member engaged in an activity which is financially prof-itable, and hence brings in an income to the household. Any 'work' or activity endorsed by the *financial* system is deemed socially acceptable. If the activity degrades the natural environment or erodes the social fabric of society, it is nevertheless considered worthwhile if it is financially profitable. If we now look at the economic process from the corporate perspective, we can see that all the households, institutions and communities in the world are essential to the financial economy in so far as they *get* and *spend* money.

The individual and society

The division of labour, facilitated by the money system, has radically altered the relationship of the individual to society. People are now reared through the educational and media systems to be prepared to work for money first, and to put all other considerations second. Working for money is by its very nature an egotistical act, motivated by pure self-interest. *My* money so earned gives *me* the right to buy exactly what *I* want, to the limit of my allotted income, and to provide materially for *my* children. The practice of working for money has become so commonplace that the suggestion that work and income need not necessarily be inextricably interlinked, rarely gives rise to a coherent intellec-tual exchange. The individual's primary duty is to work *for money*.

With the money obtained *from* the system an almost unlimited number of purchase choices now become available to the consumer. All these opportunities are, however, dependent upon the original financing of each separate enterprise. Although finance is not necessary to produce goods and services, finance is essential to make goods or services available on the market. Throughout each stage of production of the inputs of the various resources, of machinery, labour, semi-manufactures, transport and so on, finance flows to and fro, with implications which range far beyond the individual transactions. In these circumstances it becomes impossible to trace any single manufactured product back from household to source in any meaningful sense.

From the soil/source/cradle to my home

In 1994 Helga Moss, a Norwegian mother in her thirties, gave some consideration to her own role in the global economy:

> I do not grow any food, or weave or sew clothes; I have not built my house or made the furniture in it. Everything I use has been made by other people. It is like a global household. But of course, normally, you do not reflect on that. If you have the money you buy things in stores. When they are no longer useful they become waste and will be disposed of by a public service. If I look around my flat I see hundreds of items whose history I know nothing about; in this respect I am a 'normal' Western urban individual.[1]

Moss estimates that she buys roughly ten items per day. She is well aware that many items she buys ought to be boycotted on grounds of unacceptable social justice or environmental costs. Equally, she is conscious that 'buying is a political act'. Nevertheless, time pressures are such that she persuades herself that the task of becoming a 'conscious, informed consumer' is too vast to be tackled. In order to be fully informed, for each purchase she would need to know the history from the very beginnings of the commodity to the point where it reaches her home.

Taking the example of a radio, Moss drew up a model to trace the product back to its source, *via* the retailer, the wholesaler, the factory that produced the radio, the subcontractors who made the component parts, the machine factories which contributed to each process along the way, including the extraction of the natural resources. Altogether, an unknowable number of factories provide the multitude of components and materials which eventually make up the radio, each having an environmental impact at each stage. To complete the model it is necessary to take the workers into account, both in respect of their working conditions, and also through their part in the web of consumption and production relations. Moss concludes that buying 'is an act in which my money carries the power and my moral judgement has to be suspended'.[2] The model as described by Moss illustrates several key points about the post-industrial economy:

1. It follows from the very nature of the productive system, as described in her models, that the consumer is 'delinked' both from the natural world from which all resources are derived, and from the vast majority of the people who produce the commodities essential for everyday life.

2. Although the people and the ecosystems contributing to the production of any commodity are invisible, nevertheless, every single member of humanity remains utterly dependent upon 'a web of seemingly infinite concrete relations to the varying ecosystems and working people of the world'. In these circumstances, economic orthodoxy, with its belief in the rational but *independent* actor on the market, becomes untenable.

3. It follows that, with the best will in the world, it is impossible for people to be ethical consumers. By the very nature of our participation in the modern economy we constantly violate the very value system we seek to teach our children. Were we to practice what we preach, to exercise care, sharing solidarity, and responsible action, and to live in harmony with the natural world, we and our families would starve to death.

Viewing the 'global household', it becomes clear that workers in the Third World contribute to each and every household in the 'developed' West, destroying themselves and their environment in the process. As Moss explains:

Increasingly, peoples of the Third World, particularly women, have become the industrial workers of the world. They contribute to my household with their labour power and their natural resources; and to such an extent that their environment is being destroyed (through such activities as cash cropping, for example). For these efforts, however, they receive precious little in return. The goods a woman in the South produces for the world market I can buy very cheaply because the Southern woman is paid very little for her work; her wage is so small that it cannot sustain her or her children.[3]

Helga Moss's text is included in a compendium of studies which introduces the work of leading women thinkers of the late twentieth century, and the women's movements with which they are associated. During the past two decades a wealth of writings by women have been published demonstrating the impact of the Northern economic system upon the lives of women, children and men. The money economy can 'demand' not only ecological services and cheap labour, but also child prostitution and the sale of human body parts for transplant surgery. Where families are faced literally with starvation, such options become tenable.

In the affluent parts of the world, where time is spent primarily earning, spending and consuming, births, deaths and sicknesses have become unwelcome intrusions into 'real' life. In this situation millions of individuals face the dilemmas described by Helga Moss. In order to rear their families they seemingly have no choice but to earn money in order to buy the products of the corporate world. Those products are all, somewhere along the line, impacting upon the lives of others and their local environments in ways which intolerably defy moral codes and common sense. However, in order to keep one's own household going, it is necessary *to support the system by working for it*, accepting sets of rules which are not of one's own making. There is no time even to begin to think 'outside the box'.

The taming of money

In a lecture delivered in 1922, and reprinted in *World Economy*, Rudolf Steiner observed that in the economic process money undergoes 'metamorphoses':

> it acquires different qualities as it becomes loaned money or gift-money. But we mask this fact if we simply let money be money, and use the number inscribed on it as the unit of measurement and so forth. We mask it and the reality takes its revenge – a revenge which reveals itself in fluctuations of price, with which (though they are actual enough in the economic process) our reasoning faculty cannot keep pace. We ought to be able to follow them. If I may say so, we ought not to let money merely flow into circulation and give it freedom to do what it likes. For we thereby do something very peculiar in the economic life. If we require animals for some kind of labour, the first thing we do is to tame them. Think how long a riding-horse has to be tamed before it can be used. Think what would happen if we did not tame our animals, but used them wild, taking no pains to tame them. But we let money circulate quite wildly in the economic process. If and when it chooses to do so – so to speak – we let it acquire the value it has as loaned money or as gift-money. And we do not foresee when somebody who is an indus-

trialist possesses a money, from whatever source, which has been wrongly transformed from loaned money into gift money and pays his workmen with it, the result is quite different from what it would have been if he had paid them, say, out of pure purchase-money.[4]

Steiner suggests money can take three different forms, purchase-money, as used in 'butcher-baker' type transactions, loan-money which is used to set up a business enterprise, and gift-money which may facilitate some artistic venture. He also observed that: 'In its essential concepts, our economic science still fumbles about with the economics of barter',[5] i.e. of the Circular Flow. It was Douglas' task to blow away the mystique of money and demonstrate that finance is merely the way society keeps its books.

The Threefold Commonwealth

As the chapters of this book have shown, outside the mainstream world in which the present generation of academics has been reared, there exists a wealth of alternative ideas which offer a starting point for thinking 'outside the box'. The economic philosophy of Clifford Hugh Douglas and its political repercussions have been explored in some detail in previous chapters. Even less well-known, in mainstream circles, is the work of Rudolf Steiner.

During the 1920s Steiner lectured in a variety of venues in the U.K. on a range of issues, including education. His book, The Threefold Commonwealth, excited considerable interest throughout the English-speaking world. First translated from German as The Threefold State: The True Aspect of the Social Question, and published by Allen and Unwin in 1920, it was subsequently translated as The Threefold Commonwealth and published in 1922 by the Anthroposophical Publishing Company, and Macmillan. Evidently Steiner's work was widely discussed among the intelligentsia of the time. During 1925, in a series of three articles in The New Age, Philippe Mairet, who was a key figure in the Social Credit movement, and who subsequently edited The Douglas Manual, set out the basic themes of Steiner's thinking on threefolding in society. What follows is based upon Mairet's articles.[6] Unless stated otherwise, all the quotations in the following sections are from the same source.

Mairet introduces Steiner as 'a Theosophist', meaning 'a thinker of a kind not likely to appeal to the typical student of economics'. Nevertheless, Steiner's book The Threefold Commonwealth had been read by leading diplomats attending the Peace Conference following the First World War. Essentially, the book explains how the institutions of the State fall into three categories, cultural, political and economic. Whether the fact is recognised or not, by their very nature, all forms of human association necessarily have threefold characteristics. Problems arise because cultural, political and economic questions are thought of as belonging under the single umbrella of the Unity of State. The failure to recognise the threefold nature of human institutions results in the failure to shape society according to the needs and wishes of the people who live and work within them. It is the mode of thought which is remote from life: the modern life of the spirit is at fault.

It is, nevertheless, something of a paradox that social systems are made by human beings, yet at the same time, the social institutions within which we live shape our perceptions of how we work with others.

Mairet summarises the differences between the three spheres, starting with the Spiritual Life:

Freedom

'The training of the emotional and intellectual life is the *Spiritual Life*. Everyone is involved in it; but it has its own organisation, which cannot be democratic. The places of power in the spiritual life are attained by one thing only – by spiritual power. The writers whom people cannot help reading, the speakers whom they crowd to hear, and (much more) the thinkers from whom these speakers and writers derive their inspiration – these are the real pontiffs, in this and every age. But their power in the spiritual life is not greater than the power of any individuals who show, by beauty and dignity of manner, mood or movement, the supremacy and the freedom of the spirit within them. The spiritual life needs for its health nourishment from the highest regions of thought and emotion. In our age State education and the exaggerated economic problem have given it garbage to feed upon, and its condition is desperate. As it is the life of the freeing of the innermost and highest in man, it is pre-eminently the life of FREEDOM.'

Equality

'The designing of communal laws and institutions, the sphere of politics, is the *Life of Rights*. Since institutions must be worked by all, and cannot much surpass current ideas about them, this life must be democratically based. Its places of leadership must go by election. Though it settles questions ultimately by the vote of the majority, it discusses them in relation to criteria of *Right*. This life is satisfactory just so far as it is felt that the majority are voting in accordance with what discussion has proved to be right. Now it is evident that the criteria of *Right* flow into the political life from the spiritual. That is their living relation. And as the political life interprets rights as they apply to all men equally without distinction, it is essentially the life of EQUALITY.'

Fraternity

'Inherent in the economic idea is a money or credit system subservient to the free exchange of all the goods and services we have the will and capacity to produce. When the economic life is organised according to its own nature, its credit-power will not be monopolised by an excrescent plutocracy. It will adopt a credit-system designed directly to facilitate the production and distribution of the required goods and services. It will still be possible for ability to acquire power in the economic sphere, but such power will not of itself, extend beyond it. The political life, the expression of human equality, will, to a great extent, condition the life of economics. And, though the economic life cannot rest upon equality, being based upon specialisations of skill, it has a natural subservience to the life of Rights, and exists for the good of all its members, to give them a richer life and larger leisure. Its highest and truest ideal is FRATERNITY.'[7]

To date, change in education, in the political life and in the economic sphere has resulted in very little positive progress. Mairet cites reactions to 'the New Economic Principles' advocated by Douglas, noting how difficult it was to keep its opponents to the point of *economics*:

Business men – of the supposed 'hard' or 'sound' varieties – were as incapable as idealists of believing that an economic problem should be related to purely economic principles. When we said it was impossible to sell goods to a public who did not have enough money to buy them, they became vaguely disturbed about the immorality of giving goods for nothing. When we pointed out the defects of accountancy, they would wander dreamily into generalisations about the need for a 'change of heart.' When driven into a corner they said with asperity that it was absurd to put down the failure of a whole civilisation to a mere error in book-keeping; but *economically considered*, that is exactly where to ascribe it. It is the *bureau* that rules in modern economic life, and it is just there, in the office, that its error is written most clearly. But we found businessmen were shakiest of all on pure business, and financiers the haziest in mind as to the nature of credit. As soon as it comes to a discussion of the economic life considered as a whole, we realise that the modern world, with its enormous development of industry, is very far from developing a true economic life, self-controlled and conscious of its own nature. Instead, it is throwing up a Plutocracy. Our age is essentially plutocratic. The powers of landlords, politicians, and teachers are all being superseded. A highly developed but quite chaotic life of production is rapidly overwhelming politics and choking the sources of opinion. The nature of Plutocracy is such that those who achieve power in finance acquire direct influence in politics and printing (which last touches the spiritual life). Having captured the State, plutocracy strengthens the idea of the Unity-State, for its aim is to reduce all the three spheres of life to a coalition of confusion in which it may be itself supreme. And plutocracy is inconsistent with the existence of a free economic life. For while it arises out of the life of production, it only seeks to use that life as an instrument of power.

Far from being organised on lines of fraternity, the economic sphere of society is organised on grounds of *financial* viability. If any form of production does not 'pay' it is, by definition, not 'economic'. The way forward is, however, to be found as much in the spheres of freedom and equality as it is in fraternity.

Secular materialism

Mairet's objective in writing the series of articles cited was to demonstrate the harmony between Rudolf Steiner's writing and the 'New Age Economics' of Douglas. Mairet observed that the economic forces which dominate the political sphere have brought the life of the spirit under the influence of economic forces. Throughout childhood, thought is moulded predominantly by employment requirements. The individual comes to sense that their spiritual life is not under their own control. Instead, the system draws the individual into its servitude. The taking over of education by the State may have been necessary in order to introduce universal schooling. However, the entire system of teaching lies at the very roots of the spiritual life. Hence for the health of the Commonwealth, it is essential that teaching should have absolute autonomy. The whole business of teaching, the academic life and the organisation of knowledge should be managed by teachers alone. There should be no interference by the forces at work in the State or in industry in the management of teaching. The modern paralysis of will is due to the absence of clearness of thought on the problems facing society. To this end, it is necessary that the spiritual, the political, and the economic faculties of the Commonwealth are allowed independent development.

Mairet wrote in 1925, during the great period of industrial unrest in the build-up to the Miners' Strike of 1926. According to secular materialism at the time, the unregulated growth of industrialisation had given rise to exploitation of the workers. Nevertheless, observed Mairet, 'when one observes the working-class revolt closely, one sees that the great motor nerve of its being is a particular system of thoughts:

> It is a *trend of thought* which has become the centre of the spiritual life of the workers as a class; a trend of thought which they have inherited from the ruling classes, to whom it meant not much, but to the workers it has become a dynamical impulse and a faith. The materialist philosophy of the last century, which was but an interesting ideology to the ruling classes, became, when applied to the problem of the workers, the very faith, the religion, the way of salvation.

> Labour thinkers … would be the first to disbelieve that there is any force in ideas and thoughts of themselves that could contribute a resolving force to the grim deadlock between the classes of society. To say that there is anything which could help them in a purely spiritual movement would be regarded as mere ideology, if not worse. Inevitably so, because from the point of view of the materialist philosophy all that there is in the spiritual life is only ideology, a mere reflected glitter of material facts. Yet it is clear to anyone who knows something of the minds of intelligent insurgents among the workers that the dynamic of their own movement is in thoughts – thoughts which have become their spiritual life, which nevertheless they are obliged to feel as only ideology. The way of salvation allowed to the proletarian by his new way of thought is *class-consciousness* – that is the highest conception he can really believe in. But as it is a *human* consciousness to which he truly aspires, this gives him but a miserable religion. There is real unhappiness in the proletarian life.

Mairet's extended exploration of Steiner's criticism of modern economic thought demonstrates how a way of *thinking* lies at the roots of social disharmony. Only when the way of thought is changed will the disharmony be resolved. That may happen as a result of external catastrophe or by the vigour of a spiritual movement within society as a whole. Present ways of thought based upon materialistic ideas of class conflict can do nothing but throw up futile Utopian blueprints for top-down control over every aspect of society.

> The idea that all spiritual life is more or less unreal ideology could never have come into being in a community where the life of the spirit was free and independent. It results from – or at least goes with – its bondage to State and industry. At present, despotic severance of education from the State might be of little immediate value, for the spiritual life has lost its

power of self-synthesis. The various spiritual and educational bodies have now no cohesion, and what is required is no less than a voluntary co-operation between all learned and learning institutions whatsoever, with a basis for conference and common expression. It is no light matter to reconstitute an autonomous spiritual life. Yet, without it, the Community cannot evince its threefold nature, and without this three-foldness clearly expressed in actual organisation, modern democracy cannot understand its own nature.

For Mairet, the autonomous re-creation of the spiritual life, by itself and for itself, is the essential pre-requisite of the existence of any future democracy. And that can only happen if and when the economic and the political facul-ties are equally autonomous.

Mairet and 'The New Age' economics

It was a characteristic of the twentieth century that ideologies abounded in which the cultural, political and economic organisation of society were perceived as being merged into one identity. Socialism, Capitalism, Communism, Liberalism and various religious cults seemed to suggest a unity, a common belief system, to be imposed on all members of society. Hence people did not readily recognise the urgent necessity for a clear sepa-ration between the political and the economic spheres. A little thought reveals that politics and economics have entirely different origins historically.

In pre-industrial times such economic associations as existed held their power from the political. The political, in its turn, held its rights from the spir-itual powers, at least this was so in theory. The order is now reversed: economic power is supreme. The development of steam power and modern productive technologies has changed human society entirely, by the formation of multi-national companies and the financial powers that have grown up with them.

These bodies, with their secret councils and purely economic interests, were quite unforeseen by the ages from which we have inherited our instruments of law, politics and culture. They are strong enough to use law and politics and culture in their own interests. ... As citizens of the world we find this to be the fact. But it remains unforgivable that so many thinkers and theorists have accepted it as the everlasting truth about human society, which it certainly is not. Our very idealism, which is Socialist, and our Socialism, which is all more or less Marxian, is based upon the assumption that economic power is the supreme power, and that a just and equitable system of economy is all that is needed to give birth to a new life and culture. Distribute the loaves and fishes and all else will be added unto you! And yet, when we try to represent this new and just economic system, we must perforce fall back upon a political, and not an economic idea. We have nothing to suggest but the organisation of industry *upon political lines*. All Socialist schemes for the common, or the National or the proletarian 'ownership of the means of production' boil down to the same thing – the political management of production. And political management kills production, as surely as the entrance of industrialists and financiers into political life is killing politics. Few people any longer really believe in Parliaments, because they are run by rings of economic interests. And the most determined Socialists can now hardly keep their faith in the idea of running factories by democratic committees.

Mairet's observations, printed in a national weekly in 1925, are quoted at some length because they demonstrate that very little has changed since they were written, except, perhaps, that people are even less well informed as to the true state of affairs than they were nine decades ago. Academics still espouse Marxism as a political, economic and cultural ideal. Secret councils meeting behind close doors are regarded as a figment of the conspiracy theorists' imaginations, while all aspects of society are run on pseudo-democratic, *i.e.*, bureaucratic lines. Above all, the biggest danger which Mairet identified in 1925, the control of Parliament by economic interests, continues unabated to the present day.

Mairet continues (a full decade before the Alberta Election):

Now, quite apart from the backstairs, the fact is that finance is too openly and visibly organising itself into the life of politics. Much might be said about this, but it would not be to our present purpose. Certainly, it is true that the human Commonwealth is threefold already, in fact. Human society is eternally threefold in fact. The mischief is that we have begun to *think* of it as a unity, and if this thought is long continued, as it already has been, there will be an actual coalescence into chaos. The idea that human society could be expressed by the Unity State is a social insanity. The appearance of this idea ought to alarm us for the health of the State, just as much as a man's having the idea that he was a tea-pot would concern us for his reason. The further 'separation' that we would propose, therefore, is a *separation in thought*. For the real value of a work like Steiner's *Threefold Commonwealth* is that it is founded upon thinking in accordance with the realities of life instead of upon operations with abstractions.

Steiner's work was not considered acceptable in Labour circles because it is fundamentally opposed to the notion that human labour is a *commodity*, such that all had the right and duty to work for money, to sell their labour. The socialist view of economic 'democracy' was totally unacceptable to Steiner, who, like Marx and Douglas, distinguished between honourable service and wage slavery.

It is in the understanding of what is meant by the 'economic' sphere and the 'political' sphere, and the distinction between the two, that the greatest difficulty lies. Steiner provides only very outline thoughts on the nature of finance, both as a circulating medium and as a means of financing production throughout its various stages. Mairet suggested that 'The New Age' economics, by which he meant Social Credit economics as developed by Douglas, could fill that gap. However, he failed to explain how a right to an income, through which alone the products of the economic sphere can be accessed, can be determined without the political encroaching on the economic sphere. Without the means of subsistence as an inalienable right, all talk of spiritual freedom, political equality and economic fraternity for each and every individual becomes so much empty rhetoric. Mairet merely noted that Steiner regarded the 'financial organisation' as the 'arterial system of economic life' as if it has no bearing on the cultural and political spheres. If the State is not to disintegrate into chaos, it is necessary to recognise three distinct forms of association, each of which must operate independently in order to create an enduring social unity capable of offering the individual the freedom to develop as an independent yet social being, with a part to play in each of the three spheres of the social order.

The Macmillan Committee on Finance and Industry 1929-31

On May 1st 1930, Douglas was invited to give evidence before the Macmillan Committee on Finance and Industry. In his Statement of Evidence, published as an Appendix to *The Monopoly of Credit*[8], he observed that virtually all effective demand is dependent on the availability of finance, which derives, directly or indirectly, from bank loans. The value of those bank loans is in turn dependent upon the willingness of the industrial community to supply goods and services in exchange for the loans:

> While it is conceivable that an industrial system might operate without money, it is inconceivable that a money system could operate without an industrial system.[9]

However, under present circumstances the general community which alone produces and consumes the products of industry, is beholden to the financial system for access to its own production. Douglas saw clearly that the so-called economies of scale and advantages of centralised control, whether by the state or large corporations, were largely illusory. In the course of his submitted evidence Douglas cited Steiner's *The Threefold Commonwealth*:

> Modern socialism is absolutely justified in demanding that the present-day methods under which production is carried on for individual profit, should be replaced by others, under which production is carried on for the sake of the common consumption. But it is just the person who most thoroughly recognises the justice of this demand who will find himself unable to concur in the conclusion which modern socialism deduces: That, therefore, the means of production must be transferred from private to communal ownership. Rather he will be forced to a conclusion that is quite different, namely: That whatever is privately produced by means of individual energies and talents must find its way to the community through the right channels.[10]

Financial credit should reflect real credit, being a measure of the capacity to produce and deliver goods and services as, when and where required. This implies the existence of an orderly, stable community in charge of its financial system. A financial system which separates the ownership of credit from the community is unsustainable.

The way forward

To this day the banking and financial system continues to operate like a wild horse, determining policies across the whole of society on a world scale, yet out of rational control. It follows that money received in return for services of any kind, however intrinsically worthwhile, nevertheless implicates the recipient – in so far as they spend the money – in a system which is fundamentally corrupt. The answer is not to abolish money, but to seek to bring it under the control of the appropriate sphere. And that is not the economic sphere, but the sphere of politics and rights. The necessity for finance to be within the orbit of the political sphere was recognised by Douglas. The Alberta Experiment was no less than an attempt to use Douglas' insights in the realm of practical politics. And the very force of reaction from the 'powers-that-be' demonstrates the accuracy of this observation.

Unlike the vast majority of economists, orthodox and heterodox alike, Douglas had a thorough grasp of exactly how finance operates in the economy, and hence within society as a whole. Had Douglas been propounding sheer nonsense, the Alberta Experiment could have been left to flounder of its own accord. There would have been no point in continuing to silence debate on the fact that the banking and financial systems determine the ways in which people work together in all manner of institutions and associations throughout society. All Douglas did was to show how a process of simple book-keeping could reverse the situation in a very short space of time. Instead of feeding money into the system as *debt*, as is currently the case, he suggested that money could feed in as *credit*. Consumers' credit on the one hand, paid as a National Dividend, would enable people to be more selective in their choices of occupation. Producers' credits, on the other hand, would enable producers to meet customer demand without the necessity of meeting debt charges.

Social Credit economics as developed by Douglas is essential to demonstrate how finance could be brought under control by being turned from tyrannical master to useful tool. Systematic study of Douglas' work in the context of the present-day world economy, together with the writings of other major thinkers, is no light undertaking. Nevertheless, it is an essential prerequisite if social three-folding ideas, as presented by Rudolf Steiner and developed subsequently by others who had studied his works, are to have any practical impact upon the present cultural, political and economic institutions of society. So long as the masses are reared and educated to regard employment for a money income as their primary aim in life, finance will continue to dominate the schools, universities, mass media, politics, farming, industry and the arts and sciences across the world.

NOTES

1   See Harcourt (1994)
2   Harcourt (1994) p242
3   Harcourt (1994) 243
4   Steiner (1936) pp155-6
5   Steiner (1936) p108
6   Mairet (1925)
7   Mairet's original article has been slightly edited.
8   Douglas (1931) pp123-151
9   Douglas (1931) p145.
10   Douglas (1931) p148

Conclusion

Human society has changed out of all recognition since the news of the outcome of the Battle of Waterloo was conveyed to London by couriers travelling on horseback and in sailing ships. At that time it was the exception rather than the rule for individuals to use money on a daily basis. The vast majority of people were born into rural societies, where the practice of obtaining a livelihood from the land dated back unchanged over at least six millennia. During the century following Waterloo, Western civilisation went through a period of seemingly steady growth in terms of material, intellectual and principled progress. Machine production and transportation vastly increased the volume of material goods available to urban-based societies across the world. Material progress was accompanied by a general expansion of learning in the sciences, politics, theology, literature, the arts and the social sciences. And the century was permeated with an all-pervading sense that there *ought to be* a right way of conducting social affairs, even if reform was slow and piecemeal in its development. The era came to an abrupt end in 1914. Historians have termed the twentieth century the century of 'barbarism', of 'massacres and wars', 'the most violent century in human history'.[1]

A century of transition

It was a century of massive social revolution. Children living at the end of the century were born into a single global culture dominated by mass communications and transnational corporations. Rampant materialism had given rise to the disintegration of old patterns of social relationships, breaking the link between generations such that the continuity between past and present had become obscured. The mass of people no longer expected to live out their lives within the confines of a customary social setting, amongst known and named individuals, against a backdrop of familiar landmarks of field and forest. Born into a money economy, individuals came to expect they would spend their lives in the service of 'mother market', who can supply all their demands if, as producers and consumers, they do not challenge her caprice. As a result, groups and activists who question the system have become 'too timid or too indentured to speak of the nation's real problems: the raw power that the global corporations wield over our jobs, our quality of life, our mass media, our elections, our legislature, our schools, our courts, and indeed our minds.'[2] Hence the continuing violence against the natural world and its civilian populations is sanctioned by default. It is seemingly nobody's responsibility to do more than mop up the immediate and obvious casualties of famine and war.

During the twentieth century finance flowed through the political, economic and cultural institutions of society, quietly but effectively determining policy decisions. Throughout the century the mass of people went to work and to war as employees of an economic system which they did not understand, undertaking the tasks allotted to them by their paymasters primarily because they were *paid* to do so. It is now evident that powerful financial interests lay behind the rise of Bolshevism in Russia, the rise of Nazism in Germany, and the New Deal packages in the U.S.A.[3] As the chapters of this book have shown, beneath the massive institutional structures of high finance, ordinary individuals fought to comprehend the truth and blow away illusion. Clifford Hugh Douglas, Alfred Richard Orage, William Aberhart and the thousands of other supporters of the worldwide Social Credit movement were in nobody's pay. The Social Credit movement relied entirely upon voluntary work and voluntary donations. Its supporters had nothing to lose by telling the truth.

Institutional structures [4]

A major problem faced by individuals and groups working towards change is that human society is based upon a series of interlocking institutional structures operating in ways which seem difficult to define. According to mainstream theory, economic agents operate like a collection of Robinson Crusoes on a desert island, pursuing their own self-interest as social isolates. In practice, all forms of human activity are undertaken when people come *together* to form a set of ground rules within an institutional framework. Once set up, institutions mould new members to conform with the existing normative framework. Working groups as widely diverse as a family, a school or the World Bank all fit into the definition of 'institution'. Inevitably, the bigger the institution, the slower it is to change. In the course of her extensive research into debt, poverty and the world's financial systems, Susan George has observed:

> Economic policies are not neutral. Contrary to received opinion, they can even kill. To be sure, those who made them would be outraged at the suggestion that their intent is to deprive people of their livelihoods

or to murder, yet the outcome is often the same. The managers of the quiet institutions whose decisions shape millions of destinies are not trained to entertain the notion that their activities might have anything to do with such embarrassing categories as life and death. They are competent, well-paid technicians and go about their work at a comfortable remove from those whose lives they will ultimately touch. Their world is an insulated one, somewhat like that of the encapsulated bomber pilot ... for whom the shattered bodies 50,000 feet below are simply not there. He too is simply doing his job. ...

The pilot does not feel responsible for the international tensions and diplomatic failures that have led to his mission. He is an instrument. Nor does the national or international civil servant feel responsible for the years of misbegotten policies in North and South, the risky loans, the slump in commodity prices, the general economic morass. His job is to administer the correct medicine, the poor lose their jobs and their children and their hope, if they riot and are shot down for protesting against sudden and unendurable increases in the cost of survival, this is not the international civil servant's concern.[5]

The root of the problem lies in the nature of the evolution of the institutions of global corporatism. Capitalist institutions have evolved through predatory types of activity indicative of prowess and achievement in hunting and warfare. Large scale banking and business ventures are best served by the 'predatory temperament' which lends itself to individual acquisition and accumulation. Hence under corporate capitalism types of employment fall into a hierarchical gradation of respectability, from the most to the least predatory.

Those which have to do immediately with ownership on a large scale are the most reputable of economic employments proper. Next to these in good repute come those employments that are immediately subservient to ownership and financiering, - such as banking and the law. Banking employments also carry a suggestion of large ownership, and this fact is doubtless accountable for a share of the prestige that attaches to the business. The profession of the law does not imply large ownership; but since no taint of usefulness, for other than the competitive purpose, attaches to the lawyer's trade, it grades high in the conventional scheme. The lawyer is exclusively occupied with the details of predatory fraud, either in achieving it or in checkmating chicane, and success in the profession is therefore accepted as marking a large endowment of the barbarian astuteness which has always commanded men's respect and fear. Mercantile pursuits are only half-way reputable. They grade high or low somewhat in proportion as they serve the higher or lower needs; so that the business of retailing the vulgar necessities of life descends to the level of the hand-icrafts and factory labour. Manual labour, or even the work of directing mechanical processes, is of course on a precarious footing as regards respectability. [6]

Already, as Veblen wrote those words in the last year of the nineteenth century, the development of the industrial arts was such that predation was becoming wasteful and counterproductive to the welfare of communities. According to Veblen, the production of more and more goods in order to satisfy the desires for 'emulative consumption' of the latest model, together with maintenance of 'the tradition of war and rapine' was serving no useful purpose. On the contrary, in a mature industrial society, the 'collective interest is best served by 'honesty, diligence, peacefulness, goodwill, an absence of self-seeking' and a belief in the value of necessary work. In reality, in the total, complete and utter absence of those latter traits, the economy would collapse overnight.

Nevertheless, in the 21st century the tradition continues that personnel are trained to inherit top positions in institutional structures founded on principles of predation rather than co-operation. The vast majority of people have, seem-ingly, little option but to seek to obtain an income through employment in an institution which is prepared to take them onto the payroll. Under current conditions, whether that institution is turning out weapons of mass destruc-tion, fast foods, medical services, cute soft toys or certified students prepared for the 'job market' matters very little. The institution is run on military lines, using financial rewards and penalties, so that obedience to the dictates of the 'line manager' takes priority over the personal judgement of the employee. Such employment is accurately termed wage (or salary) slavery.

As people identify with roles within the institutional set-up, they find proposals for change, such as that of a Universal Basic Income or National Dividend, too much of an intellectual challenge. But since the longest journey starts with the first step, the envisioning of change must be the starting point: how would a National Dividend affect my life and my attitude to any paid work I might undertake? This is an exercise that could be undertaken by every single individual member of society. In whichever social sphere one's line of employment might fall – the cultural, political/legal or co-opera-tive/economic, one can start to imagine what it might mean not to work *primarily* as an employee under instructions from an employer.

The 'New Economics' of Guild Socialism

Douglas and Orage formulated a theoretically sound and practically feasible 'New Economics'. It arose from Guild Socialist theorising about good work designed to meet the needs social, spiritual and artistic of the community as a whole, combined with the practical observations of Douglas, the skilled engineer. The Draft Mining Scheme, drawn up by Douglas and Orage, is an ingenious combination of guild organisation with Douglas finance. It envisages a decentralised guild-style organisation of production, with worker control of credit by means of local producers' banks. [7] Writing in 1936, Philip Mairet, a leading proponent of Social Credit, observed that for many 'generous minds' the demise of the National Guilds movement in the early 1920s was a 'bitter disappointment':

> It is doubtful if any social movement in England since that time has enlisted so many people of intelligence, social conscience, and a genuine capacity for self-denying effort; unless it be the Social Credit movement which was born at its demise.[8]

At the time he wrote those words (1936) Mairet was fully justified in believing that the Social Credit movement would continue to be a major force in world politics for decades to come. At that date, as the chapters of this book have demonstrated, the volume of literature on the subject of Social Credit, both for and against, was massive. By 1936, every week *The New Age*, *The New English Weekly* and *Social Credit* carried substantial articles on the arts, sciences, economics, education, local, national and international politics and current affairs generally. Similarly, in Australia, New Zealand, Canada and the U.S.A., periodicals carried news and views that were not to be found in the mainstream presses. All carried details of prints and re-prints of Douglas' books and major speeches. Leading figures in politics, banking, economics and public life generally took up the debate, attempting to refute the Social Credit analysis of the role of finance within the social order. In archives and libraries across the Western world, and elsewhere, copies of all the publications cited in this work can be consulted to substantiate the claims made here. By 1938, however, a full year before the outbreak of the Second World War, a number of factors seem to have combined to make it increasingly difficult for the truth about events in Alberta to circulate.

The meaning of the silencing of Social Credit in Alberta

By electing a Social Credit Government with an overwhelming majority in 1935, the people of Alberta won the legal right to political and economic self-determination. This was achieved democratically, through the ballot box. Although the regime challenged international corporate interests, no military force was used against the people of Alberta, as was invariably the case with 'politically unacceptable' regimes in the post-war decades. As these pages have shown, the ability of the elected representatives of the people of Alberta to implement the policies demanded by their well-informed electorate was frustrated at every turn by the supra- national powers of finance. Moreover, paid employees of the press, media and academy allowed themselves to be used so that the full story of Social Credit in Alberta could never be heard by the watching contemporary world, still less by succeeding generations.

In 2005 John Pilger edited a book of extracts from articles, broadcasts and books celebrating the very best of investigative journalism, taking as a starting point the year 1945. In the course of this substantial book, truths are revealed behind critical events of the previous fifty years, including Hiroshima, the Lockerbie cover-up, the secret war against Arthur Scargill and the miners, and the epic injustices committed against the peoples of Vietnam, Cambodia, East Timor and Palestine. Pilger cites the Soviet dissident Yevgeni Yevtushenko: 'When truth is replaced by silence ... the silence is a lie'. Pilger continues:

> There is a surreal silence today, full of the noise of 'sound-bites' and 'grabs' of those with power justifying their deception and violence. This is presented as news, though it is really a parody in which journalists, variously embedded, gesture cryptically at the obvious but rarely make sense of it, lest they shatter the 'one-way moral screen' described by Richard Falk [Professor of International Relations at Princeton University] between 'us' and the consequences of political actions taken in our name. Never has there been such a volume of repetitive 'news' or such an exclusiveness in those controlling it.[9]

The claim against the Social Credit Government in Alberta was that it sought to act 'unconstitutionally', *i.e.,* to flout the authority of the Dominion Government as constituted by the British Crown. In 1994, Wilfred Burchett, reporting on the events behind the Miner's Strike of 1984-5 observed:

> Britain's secret state remains a dangerous political and bureaucratic cesspit, uniquely undisturbed by any meaningful form of political accountability.[10]

Social Credit literature offers a rich resource of published texts on the corruption of the press, the media, academia, and the constitution of the 'mother of parliaments', to which the chapters of this book have offered no more than a brief introduction. Within that literature, the future course of events, if finance was to continue to be allowed free reign over the political, economic and cultural spheres of the social order, was predicted with an astonishing degree of accuracy.

Should he who pays the piper call the tune?

Under corporate capitalism of the early 21st century the institutions of finance operate as paymaster, and hence as controller, over institutions in all three spheres of the social order. It follows that professionals in education, health, arts and sciences are increasingly treated like factory hands, expected to perform their duties merely in order to receive a wage or salary, acting under instructions from the paymaster above. As Margaret Atkins explains, the 'paymaster' assumes that the 'piper' pipes only in order to earn a wage, and that he will pipe to instructions.

> The purpose of piping is 'the tune', which is seen as a product rather oddly separable from the playing of it. Indeed, the paymaster thinks of the piper as a producer of tunes; his actions are characterised simply by their 'products'. The piper, in his view, should discover what he must do by receiving his orders; he should obey the paymaster rather than any other person, or any musical impulse or understanding of his own. His obedience is secured by the promise of money that he needs: his motivation to act is external to his action. He is free (assuming he is not destitute) to accept or reject the contract, but he is not free to contribute his own views of what the contract should be. The paymaster will consider him a responsible person to the extent that he fulfils his instructions.[11]

The piper is thus required to be accountable to the paymaster *because* he is being paid. Where payment is not involved, the piper is free to play whatever tune he likes, according to his personal talents, judgement and ability. In that case, however, the 'piper' has to find the means of support from some other source than his music. The custom of 'paying the piper' dates back at least to the Renaissance, when patrons came forward to fund works like the painting of the ceiling of the Sistine Chapel. However, the notion that a Michelangelo should tailor his work according to the instructions of a board of paymasters is a peculiar product of the twentieth century. Under corporate capitalism professionals in every walk of life throughout all three spheres of society – the cultural and political as well as the economic - have been reduced to the status of employees whose incomes are dependent upon the following of the instructions of an anonymous band of corporate paymasters.

Scholarship versus taxonomic studies

The Introduction to this book noted several key questions raised by Mark Anielski in *The Economics of Happiness*. Directly or indirectly, these chapters have indicated routes towards finding answers to those questions. Throughout the institutions of Higher Learning, however, scholarship has been very largely replaced by the learning of the performance of taxonomic tasks in preparation for paid employment. Degree courses in golf course management or building regulations can be afforded a place in the curriculum, whilst the study of literature must struggle to justify its existence because there is virtually no market amongst employers for workers with degrees in literature.

The role of finance in the institutions of society is rarely questioned by campaigners for peace, justice and environmental sustainability. The works of significant thinkers, writers and activists are debated, new strategies and methods of communication are tried and tested, while experimental not-for-profit co-operatives and exchange schemes come and go. But if the key role of finance in the institutions of society, is taken as read, such experiments are merely the playthings of the well-to-do.

Over recent decades many reformers and activists have registered for degrees in economics in the hopes of thereby better understanding economic questions. Few stayed the course, and those who did remained as mystified as ever. Shorn of its institutional setting, the study of orthodox economics amounts to little more than a catalogue of taxonomic hypotheses. In order to understand how the economy actually works, it is essential to take account of the distribution of legal rights to land, to finance, to capital buildings and to the acquisition of intellectual skills.

In his address to the Canada Club in London in 1923, three years before the Miners' Strike of 1926, Douglas used practical examples to illuminate exactly how finance works within the economy. He pointed out that, as the First World War ended, Great Britain was 'absolutely chock full of the newest and best plant that it ever had:

> The farms had been intensively cultivated. There had been no unemployment and there was no real desire for unemployment in the sense that people were still quite willing to work. Yet within a short time after the Armistice things began to go from bad to worse.

> First of all, as we all know, we had a feverish boom, and then we had a spectacular rise of prices, and then, for no reason that you could see on the face of it – although, of course, plenty of reasons were put forward – we had an equally spectacular slump. People began to be discharged.

There arose this thing we call the unemployment problem, and all these wonderful plants began to be broken up by the owners of them going into bankruptcy, and it began to be obvious, and it is obvious now, that given a little time it would be true that we were a poor, poor country. But it was not true in 1919 in Great Britain, and I do not suppose it was true anywhere else. ...

I know of my own technical knowledge and by the sight of my own eyes that there is practically no production problem in the world today at all; that there is no single thing which you can demand, and which, if you will put your money on the table, you cannot get. There is nothing very seriously wrong with the administrative system. The problem is not a problem of administration; therefore what is commonly called Socialism, which is an administrative panacea, is no remedy at all.

The only way in which administration comes into the problem is by a consideration of the undoubted fact that administration does not control policy, but finance controls policy. *It is the man who pays the piper who calls the tune.* Therefore, if you take that into consideration, you realise that indirectly you may have a sort of administration problem, because you get the control of the appointment of administration in the hands of the financial system.[12]

Over the intervening decades since those words were written, every effort has been made to eliminate from the academy, and from the public consciousness, all knowledge of the twentieth century story of a body of people, both men and women, who systematically studied a coherent analysis of the role of finance in the modern world, and evolved practical routes for securing active public support for measures designed to turn money from master into the servant of humanity.

A positive coherent vision for the future

Any movement for change must put forward solutions and a positive alternative coherent vision for the future. This poses the most difficult question of all. Criticism of the existing system is a relatively straightforward matter. Piecemeal sticking plaster solutions to the worst and most obvious evils can also be conceptualised and implemented, with relative ease. But 'a coherent vision for the future'? That is asking a lot. Fortunately, however, we do not need to go back to the drawing board and re-invent the wheel. As the chapters of this book have demonstrated, a lot of the preparatory work has been done already.

During the 1930s, the term 'wage slavery' was widely applied in the campaign for a National Dividend based upon Douglas' analysis of the financial system. The term was used to indicate the power of finance over all forms of useful employments. It appealed to all sections of society for whom personal advancement in terms of power, prestige and money was less important than forms of social, spiritual or environmental concerns. In the weekly and other periodicals of the period, including *The New Age*, *The New English Weekly*, *Social Credit*, *The Social Crediter*, and those circulating across Canada, the U.S.A., Australia, New Zealand and elsewhere, articles and letters can be found from people in all walks of life. Farmers, clergy, teachers, political activists, industrial workers, women across the spectrum of interest groups, the unemployed, and academics in all fields except economics, wrote on a variety of related subjects. All were familiar with the writings of Douglas and other social crediters. Despite the passage of time, a great deal of the material published in those periodicals remains relevant to the present day, and can be reprinted with very little alteration. People in the 1930s were already thinking 'outside the box'. Hence it was necessary, if the predatory system was to survive, to eradicate knowledge of the events in Alberta and the work of the Social Credit movements as a whole.

The problem is that people continue to be trained to work in institutions based upon the principles of predation and control so that, having become part of the institutional set-up, they find proposals for change, such as that of a National Dividend, too much of an intellectual challenge. However, the longest journey starts with the first step. In this instance, the first step is to envision change: how would a National Dividend affect my life and my attitude to any paid work I might undertake? This is an exercise that could be undertaken by every single individual member of society. In whichever social sphere one's line of employment might fall – the cultural, political/legal or co-operative/economic, one can start to imagine what it might mean not to work *primarily* as an employee.

Institutional change on the scale necessary to affect the power of global corporatism must necessarily be slow. Nevertheless, the visioning of change is a powerful and necessary first step. Once it is undertaken on a personal level, it becomes possible to seek out and work together with others to find ways out of the institutional straightjacket. In this task, the institutions of education and higher learning have a crucial role to play. At the turn of the present century, Johannes Hemleben included the following quote in his biography of Rudolf Steiner:

One of the intellectual curiosities of the 20th century is that the academic world has seen fit to consider that Steiner's works have no foundation and are of no significance. But whoever takes it upon himself to study his voluminous works with an open mind will find himself in the presence of one of the greatest thinkers of all time, whose mastery of modern sciences is as wonderful as his knowledge of the sciences of antiquity. Steiner is no more a mystic than Albert Einstein: he was first and foremost a scientist, but 'a scientist who has the daring to penetrate the mysteries of life'.[13]

It is perhaps not such an 'intellectual curiosity' that the work of Steiner, Douglas and others presenting alternatives to orthodoxy have been studiously ignored in the course of the 20th century. An academic world run according to the pecuniary rules of 'sound finance' could scarcely have been expected to accommodate an open minded approach to study across the spectrum of the arts and sciences. Whether the challenge will be met or not, only the future will tell. If not, all that will remain of humanity will be miles of empty tarmac and millions of lost golf balls.

NOTES

1   Cited in Hobsbawm (1994), p2
2   Peter Montague quoted in Rowell (1996) p373
3   See Sutton (1974) (1975) (1976)
4   See the works of Thorstein Veblen as listed in the Bibliography.
5   George (1988) pp6-7
6   Veblen (1899) pp227-232
7   Douglas (1920b)
8   Mairet (1936) p76
9   Pilger (2005) pxxvii
10   Milne (2005) p326
11   Atkins (2003)
12   Douglas (1923) Emphasis added.
13   Russel W. Davenport *The Dignity of Man*, cited in Johannes Hemleben (2000) *Rudolf Steiner: An Illustrated Biography*, Sophia Books, London, p197

Bibliography

Aberhart, William (1935) *Social Credit Manual: Social Credit as applied to the Province of Alberta,* Calgary.

Adams, Capt. W. (1925) *Real Wealth & Financial Poverty*, London: Cecil Palmer.

Anielski, Mark (2007) *The Economics of Happiness*, Gabriola Island, Canada: New Society Publishers.

Atkins, Margaret (2003) '*Should* He Who Pays the Piper Call the Tune?', Council of University Classical Departments Bulletin 32. Available at: http://www.rhul.ac.uk/Classics/CUCD/atkins.html

Baker, Canon A.E. (1946) *William Temple and his Message*, Harmondsworth: Penguin Books.

Bell, Edward (1993) *Social Classes and Social Credit*, Montreal & London: McGill-Queen's University Press.

Boardman, Terry M. (1998) *Mapping the Millennium: Behind the Plans of the New World Order*, London: Temple Lodge.

Caldecott, Moyra (1992) *Women in Celtic Myth: Tales of Extraordinary Women from the Ancient Celtic Tradition,* Vermont: Destiny Books.

Carson, Rachel (1962) *Silent Spring*, London: Hamish Hamilton.

Cato, Molly Scott (2009) *Green Economics: An Introduction to Theory, Policy and Practice*, London: Earthscan.

Clark, S.D. (1959) *Movements of Political Protest in Canada, 1640-1840,* Toronto: University of Toronto Press.

Colbourne, Maurice (1933) *The Meaning of Social Credit*, London and Canada: Social Credit Board (reprinted several times).

Copland, D.B. (1932) *Facts and Fallacies of Douglas Credit with a Note on Australian Credit Policy, Melbourne*: Melbourne University Press.

Corti, Count (1928) *The Rise of the House of Rothschild*, London: Victor Gollancz.

Corti, Count (1928) *The Reign of the House of Rothschild,* London: Victor Gollancz.

Crowther, Geoffrey (1940) *An Outline of Money*, London: Thomas Nelson & Sons Ltd.

Curry, Patrick (1998) *Defending Middle-Earth: Tolkien, Myth and Modernity,* London: HarperCollins.

Davidson, W.M. (1935) *The Aberhart Plan: A survey and analysis of Social Credit Scheme as placed before the electors of Alberta*, Calgary: Economic Safety League.

Davies, Glyn (1994) *A History of Money: From Ancient Times to the Present Day,* Cardiff: University of Wales Press.

Dobb, Maurice (1936) *Social Credit Discredited*, London: Martin Lawrence.

Douglas, Clifford Hugh (1920a) *Economic Democracy*, London: Cecil Palmer (1974 edition).

Douglas, Clifford Hugh (1920b) *Credit-Power and Democracy*, London: Cecil Palmer.

Douglas, Clifford Hugh (1922a) 'The Douglas Theory: A Reply to Mr. J.A. Hobson', *Socialist Review*, March, pp139-45.

Douglas, Clifford Hugh (1922b) *These Present Discontents* and *The Labour Party and Social Credit*, London: Cecil Palmer.

Douglas, Clifford Hugh (1923) 'Social Credit History', reprinted in *The New Economics,* November 23, 1934.

Douglas, Clifford Hugh (1924) *Social Credit*, London: Eyre & Spottiswoode (1933 edn).

Douglas, Clifford Hugh (1925) 'Socialism and Banking: A Reply', *The Nineteenth Century*, March, pp384-387.

Douglas, Clifford Hugh (1931) *The Monopoly of Credit*, London: Eyre & Spottiswoode (second enlarged edition 1937).

Douglas, Clifford Hugh (1932) *The Old and the New Economics*, Sydney: Tidal Publications (1973 reprint). See www.douglassocialcredit.com

Douglas, Clifford Hugh (1934) 'The Causes of War: Is Our Financial System to Blame?' *The Listener*, 5 December.

Douglas, Clifford Hugh (1935) *Money and the Price System*, (Oslo Speech) London: Stanley Nott (Institute of Economic Democracy, 1978 reprint).

Douglas, Clifford Hugh (1937) *The Alberta Experiment*, London: Eyre and Spottiswoode (Veritas, Australia, reprint 1984).

Douglas, Clifford Hugh and Dennis Robertson (1933) 'The Douglas Credit Scheme', *The Listener*, Vol.9, pp1005-6, 1039-40.

Durbin, E.F.M. (1933) *Socialist Credit Policy*, London: Gollancz (second edition 1936).

Even, Louis (1996) *In This Age of Plenty: A new conception of economics: Social Credit*. Rougemont: Pilgrims of St. Michael (first published 1946).

Feiner, Susan (1999) 'A portrait of *Homo economicus* as a Young Man' *in* Martha Woodmansee and Mark Osteen, *The New Economic Criticism: Studies at the intersection of literature and economics*, London and New York: Routledge.

Ferguson, Niall, (1998) *The House of Rothschild: Money's Prophets 1798-1848*, Viking Penguin.

Finlay, John L. (1972) *Social Credit: The English Origins*, Montreal and London: McGill-Queens University Press.

Fukuyama, Francis (1992) *The End of History and the Last Man*, New York: Free Press.

Gaitskell, H.T.N. (1933) Four Monetary Heretics, in G.D.H. Cole (ed.) *What Everybody Wants to Know About Money*. London: Victor Gollancz.

George, Susan (1988) *A Fate Worse Than Debt*, London: Penguin.

Gesell, Silvio (1929) *The Natural Economic Order*, London: Peter Owen (1958 revised edition).

Gilbert, Martin (1999) *A History of the Twentieth Century (Vols. I, II, and III)*, London: HarperCollins.

Guerrien, (Bernard) (2002a) 'Is There Anything Worth Keeping in Standard Microeconomics?', post-autistic economics review, issue no. 12, March. http://www.autisme-economie.org/article115.html

Guerrien, Bernard (2002b) 'Once Again on Microeconomics', post-autistic economics review, issue no. 16, September 16, article 1. http://www.btinternet.com/~pae_news/review/issue16.html

Harcourt, Wendy (ed.) *Feminist Perspectives on Sustainable Development*, London. Zed: Books.

Hargrave, John (1937) *Alberta: Official Report: A documented record of Mr. John Hargrave's visit to the Province of Alberta, Canada, December 8, 1936 to January 25, 1937*, London: The Social Credit Party.

Hawtrey, R.G. (1937) Chapter on 'Social Credit: The Financial Misfit' in *Capital and Employment,* London: Longmans Green.

Hawtrey, R.G. and Douglas, C.H. (1933) 'Report of Birmingham Debate', *The New Age*, April 6, pp267-279.

Hemleben, Johannes (2000) *Rudolf Steiner: An Illustrated Biography*, London: Sophia Books.

Henderson, Hazel (1988) *The Politics of the Solar Age: Alternatives to Economics*, Indiana: Knowledge Systems, Inc.

Henderson, Hazel (1996) *Building a Win-Win World: Life Beyond Global Economic Warfare*, San Francisco: Berrett-Koehler Publishers.

Hesketh, Bob (1997) *Major Douglas and Alberta Social Credit*, Toronto: University of Toronto Press.

Hiskett, W.R. (1935) *Social Credits or Socialism: An Analysis of the Douglas Credit Scheme*, London: Gollancz.

Hiskett, W.R. and Franklin, J.A. (1939) *Searchlight on Social Credit*, London: P.S. King.

Hobsbawm, Eric (1994) *Age of Extremes: The Short Twentieth Century (1914 – 1991)*, London: Michael Joseph.

Hobson, J.A. (1922a) 'The Douglas Theory', *Socialist Review*, Feb, pp70-77.

Hobson, J.A. (1922b) 'A Rejoinder to Major Douglas', *Socialist Review*, April, pp194 – 199.

Hooke, Alf (1971) *30+5: I Know, I Was There*, Edmonton: Institute of Applied Art.

http://douglassocialcredit.com/resources/resources/Alf%20Hooke%20Chapter%201.pdf

House of Commons, Canada (1923) *Proceedings of the Select Standing Committee on Banking and Commerce, Appendix No.2*, Ottawa: Government Printers.

Hughes, John W. (2002) *Major Douglas: The Policy of a Philosophy*, Glasgow, Scotland: Wedderspoon Associates.

Hunt, E.K. (2003) *Property and Prophets: The Evolution of Economic Institutions and Ideologies*, New York and London: M.E. Sharpe.

Hutchinson, Frances and Brian Burkitt (1997) *The Political Economy of Social Credit and Guild Socialism*, Charlbury. Jon Carpenter (2005 reprint).

Hutchinson, Frances (1998) *What Everybody Really Wants to Know About Money*, Charlbury: Jon Carpenter.

Hutchinson, Frances, Mary Mellor and Wendy Olsen (2002) *The Politics of Money: Towards Sustainability and Economic Democracy*, London: Pluto Press.

Irving, John A. (1959) *The Social Credit Movement in Alberta*, Toronto and Buffalo: University of Toronto Press (1974).

Jackson, Trudy http://www.online.wea.org.uk/file.php/45/Getting_Involved/Brief_History_of_WEA.doc 6 September 2009

Keynes, John Maynard (1936) *The General Theory of Employment, Interest and Money,* London: Macmillan.

King, John (1988) *Economic Exiles*, London.:Macmillan.

Korten, David C. (1995) *When Corporations Rule the World*, San Francisco: Berrett-Koehler and Kumarian Press.

Korten, David C. (2000) *The Post-Corporate World: Life After Capitalism*, San Francisco: Berrett-Koehler and Kumarian Press.

Labour Party (Scottish Council) (1920) *Report of Sixth Annual Conference*, Glasgow.

Labour Party (1922) *Labour and Social Credit: A Report on the Proposals of Major Douglas and the 'New Age'*, London: The Labour Party.

Labour Party (1935) Socialism and 'Social Credit', London: The Labour

Party.

Lewis, John (1935) *Douglas Fallacies: A Critique of Social Credit*, London: Chapman & Hall.

Livingstone, Richard (1941) *The Future in Education*, Cambridge University Press.

Mabey, Richard (1997) *Flora Britannica*, London: Chatto & Windus.

Macpherson, C.B. (1953) *Democracy in Alberta: Social Credit and the Party System*, Toronto: University of Toronto Press (1977 edition).

Mairet, Philippe (1925) 'A New Proposal for Guild Organisation' *The New Age*, Part *I*, July 23, 1925 pp139-40: *Part II*, August 27, 1925, pp199-200: *Part III*, September 3, 1925, pp210-211.

Mairet, Philip [sic] (editor) (1934) *The Douglas Manual*, London: Stanley Nott.

Mairet, Philip (1936) *A.R. Orage: A Memoir*, London: J.M. Dent &Sons.

Mallory, J.R. (1954) *Social Credit and the Federal Power in Canada*, Toronto: University of Toronto Press.

Mansbridge, Albert (1920) *An Adventure in Working-class Education: Being the Story of the Workers' Educational Association 1903-1915*, London: Longmans, Green & Co.

Midland Bank Company History (noted 25.03.09) http://www.fundinguniverse.com/company-histories/Midland-Bank-plc-Company-History.html

Milne, Seamus (2005) 'The Secret War Against the Miners' *in* John Pilger (ed) *Tell Me No Lies,* London: Vintage.

More, Thomas (1516) *Utopia*, London: Penguin Books (2003 edition).

Morton, W.L. (1950) *The Progressive Party in Canada*, Toronto: University of Toronto Press.

New Statesman, The (1922) 'The 'Douglas Credit Scheme'', *The New Statesman*, February 18, pp552-554.

O'Duffy, Eimar (1932) *Life and Money: Being a Critical Examination of the Principles and Practice of Orthodox Economics with A Practical Scheme to End the Muddle it has made of our Civilisation*, London and New York: Putnam.

O'Duffy, Eimar (1933) *Asses in Clover*, Charlbury: Jon Carpenter (2003 edition).

Oppenheimer, Franz (1908) *The State* (1922, first English language edition, available at http://www.franz-oppenheimer.de/state0.html).

Oppenheimer, Franz (1903) 'A First Program for Zionist colonization', *in:* I. H. Bilski (ed.) *Means and Ways towards a Realm of Justice. A Collection of Articles dedicated to the Memory of Professor Franz Oppenheimer (1864-1943)*,

Tel Aviv 1958, pp71-82.See http://www.franz-
oppenheimer.de/fo03a.html

Oppenheimer, Franz 'A Critique of Political Economy: A Post Mortem on
Cambridge Economics', first published in *The American Journal of
Economics and Sociology*, Vol.2, No.3, 1942/1943, S.369-376; Vol.2, No.4,
1943, S.533-541; Vol.3, No.1, 1944, S.115-124).

Orage, A.R. (1926) 'An Editor's Progress', *The Commonweal*, February 10,
pp376-379; February 17, pp402-404; February 24, pp434-435. Reprinted
in *The New Age Supplement*, November 22, 1934.

Pilger, John (2005) *Tell Me No Lies: Investigative Journalism and its Triumphs*,
London: Vintage.

Preparata, Guido Giacomo (2005) *Conjuring Hitler: How Britain and America
made the Third Reich*, London: Pluto Press.

Ramsey, Frank P. (1922) 'The Douglas Proposals', *Cambridge Magazine*,
Vol.11, pp74-6.

Ramsey, Frank P. (1928) 'A Mathematical Theory of Saving', *Economic
Journal*, Vol.38, pp543-59.

Rowbotham, Michael (1998) *The Grip of Death: A Study of Modern Money,
Debt Slavery and Destructive Economics*, Concord, MA and Charlbury: Jon
Carpenter Publishing.

Rowell, Andrew (1996) *Green Backlash: Global Subversion of the Environment
Movement,* London and New York: Routledge.

Schumacher, E.F. (1973) *Small is Beautiful: A Study of Economics as if People
Mattered*, London: Abacus.

Sheffield Educational Settlement Papers (2009)
http://www.shef.ac.uk/library/special/shefed.html

Smith, Adam (1776) *An Inquiry into the Nature and Causes of The Wealth of
Nations*, London.

Smith, H. Norman (1934) 'Social Credit and the Labour Party', *Social
Credit*, September 28, p82.

Steiner, Rudolf (1916 Lectures, published 1988 in English) *The Karma of
Untruthfulness: Secret Societies, the Media, and Preparations for the Great War*,
Vol.1, Forest Row, U.K. Rudolf Steiner Press (2005 edition).

Steiner, Rudolf (1919) *The Social Future*, New York: Anthroposophic Press
(1972 edition).

Steiner, Rudolf (1920) *The Threefold Commonwealth*, London: George Allen
and Unwin. (Now available as *Towards Social Renewal: rethinking the basis
of society*, Rudolf Steiner Press, 1999).

Steiner, Rudolf (1922) *Spiritual Life, Civil Rights, Industrial Economy*, London:

Anthroposophical Publishing Co.

Steiner, Rudolf (1936, First English Edition) *World Economy*, London: Rudolf Steiner Press (1977 edition).

Stingel, Janine (2000) *Social Discredit: Anti-Semitism, Social Credit and the Jewish Response*, Montreal: McGill-Queens University Press.

Sutton, Anthony (1974) *Wall Street and the Bolshevik Revolution*, New York: Buccaneer Books.

Sutton, Anthony (1975) *Wall Street and FDR,* N.Y.: Buccaneer Books.

Sutton, Anthony (1976) *Wall Street and the Rise of Hitler*, Suffolk: Bloomfield Books.

Temple, William (1927) *Essays in Christian Politics and Citizenship and Kindred Subject*, London: Longmans.

United Western Communications (1998) *Alberta in the 20th Century: Vol. VII, Aberhart and the Alberta Insurrection 1935 – 1940*, Edmonton: United Western Communications.

Veblen, Thorstein (1899) *The Theory of the Leisure Class*, New York: Prometheus Books (1998 edition).

Veblen, Thorstein (1904) *The Theory of Business Enterprise,* N.Y. and London: Mentor (1932 edn).

Veblen, Thorstein (1923) *Absentee Ownership: Business Enterprise in Recent Times: The Case of America,* New Brunswick: Transactions (1997 edn.).

Veblen, Thorstein (1948) *The Portable Veblen*, New York: The Viking Press (extracts).

Veblen, Thorstein (1990) *The Place of Science in Modern Civilization*, New Brunswick and London: Transactions.

Wall, Derek (2003) 'Social Credit: The Ecosocialism of Fools', *Capitalism, Nature, Socialism*, 14.3, September 2003, pp99-122.

Index